I had to assume the gun was loaded. Did he have three rounds in the chamber, or five? Thoughts raced through my head. Double '00' buckshot shells contain eight .32 caliber lead pellets, the kind used in police work. On the other hand, the gun could be chambered with slugs. A single, two-ounce piece of lead at close range would be capable of destroying my entire chest cavity.

"You killed my cousin and now I'm going to kill you and two more policemen," Nelson announced with a frightening calmness. That was one of his strings of illogic. He knew that Nuccio had killed Ronald and I was not Nuccio—and yet he didn't, not now. His rage had made all policemen a target. As he spoke, he took up a shooting position, angled his head, closed one eye again, and looked at my face down the long black barrel.

If I show fear, he'll kill me. If I look tough, he'll kill me.

D0967662

Copyright ©2018 byDebra DiMaggio
ISBN 978-1-949914-74-0
Cover art design by Mat Devine, Devine + Conquer Artists
and interior graphic art design by Debra DiMaggio and Lily Shannon.
All rights reserved. No part of this book may be used or reproduced in any manner
whatsoever without written permission except in the case of
brief quotations embodied in critical articles and reviews
For information address Crossroad Press at 141 Brayden Dr., Hertford, NC 27944
A Panta Rei Production - Panta Rei is an imprint of Crossroad Press.
www.crossroadpress.com

First Edition

SARGE!

CASES OF A CHICAGO POLICE DETECTIVE SERGEANT

IN THE 1960S, '70S, AND '80S

BY JOHN A. DIMAGGIO

IN MEMORY OF

JIMMY "THE KID" NOLAN

AND

JOHN PHILBIN

May the road rise up to meet you,
May the wind be always at your back,
May the sun shine warm upon your face,
And the rains fall soft upon your fields,
And until we meet again
May God hold you in the palm of His hand.

(IRISH BLESSING)

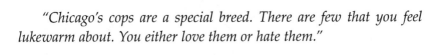

"Chicago's cops are a special breed. There are few that you feel lukewarm about. You either love them or hate them."

—*Journalist Peter Nolan*

INTRODUCTION

This memoir was written by our father, John A. DiMaggio, in the 1990s.

Growing up, we of course knew he was a cop, but it wasn't until much later that we fully appreciated the *kind* of cop he was. As kids, we thought he was just a strict dad because he had two daughters and a son, and we were indeed a handful. As it was, he was most likely terrified every time we left the house, let alone the neighborhood. Chicago was and still can be a "rough town." One thing is for sure—the youngest and middle children's antics did much to hone our father's detective skills!

Upon Dad's retirement in 1991, he sat down to write this fascinating account of the four decades he worked in the Chicago Police Department. The manuscript languished among his personal effects until after his death in 2008, after which we decided to resurrect it, spruce it up, and submit it for publication. It turns out that he was an excellent word craftsman and storyteller; in fact, he was no stranger to writing—for many years he wrote the "Ask Sarge" column for the Mystery Writers of America Midwest Chapter newsletter.

What makes the book so interesting is not only the many captivating stories of burglary, robbery, murder, and riots contained in the manuscript, but also the you-are-there time travel element. For example, Dad takes the reader back to the turbulent 1960s, when the police department was making a painful transition from "old school" to modernization. It was a different time and, in many ways, a very different place.

Our father retired to Las Vegas with our mother after becoming one of the most decorated officers on the force. Some of the awards and honors he received are listed elsewhere. To us, though, he was Dad. No awards or honors made much difference as to how we thought of him. To us he was the bravest and most loving father any kid could have.

We know our father would like to thank many individuals who helped him in his career and assisted with the writing of this manuscript, so we would like to mention them. If there is anyone we've left out, please forgive the oversight.

Great appreciation goes to Wayne Klatt, who worked with Dad on the manuscript in the 90s, and to Raymond Benson for editing and polishing it.

Our father would most certainly want to acknowledge the men who were his partners and colleagues. These were names we heard a lot in our household, and some of these fellows were like family: (alphabetically) Kurt Bartall, Frank Cale, Frank Cappitelli, Mike Carone, Mike Chasen, John Coughlin, Bob Cody, Mike Conforti, Tom Cronin, Ralph DeBartolo, Larry Evans, Dennis Farina, John Farrell, Jules Gallett, Frank Hanley, Ron Kelly, Jack Kennedy, Jim Maurer, Al Neri, Nick Nickeus, Jimmy Nolan, John Philbin, Steve Pizzello, Richard Riccio, Frank Riggio, Paul Roppel, Sherwin Ruer, Rich Stevens, Jerry Stubig, and O.W. Wilson.

Lastly, the biggest thank you of all goes to his wife and our mother, Rosemary, who assuredly spent many sleepless nights wondering if Dad would come home.

He always did.

Diane DiMaggio
Debra DiMaggio
John DiMaggio
June 2017

RETIRED DETECTIVE SERGEANT JOHN A. DIMAGGIO WAS ONE OF THE MOST DECORATED OFFICERS IN THE CHICAGO POLICE DEPARTMENT.

HIS AWARDS INCLUDE:

Superintendent's Award of Valor (Two)

Mayor Richard J. Daley's Praiseworthy Acknowledgment Plaque for Exceptional Act of Bravery Involving Risk of Life

Presidential Citation of Appreciation

Vice Presidential Citation of Appreciation

Governor of Illinois Award of Recognition

llinois Police Association Award of Valor

Unit Meritorious Award

IX Department Commendations

Numerous Honorable Mentions and Written Citations

A POLICE CHAPLAIN'S NOTE TO THE READER

The police officer has one of the last few exciting jobs still left in America. The fabric of the average officer's day has the ridiculous interwoven with the sublime, and he or she becomes familiar with a day that is saturated with heroism, humor, and horror. No wonder we want a peek into that world!

We Americans have an odd relationship with those who police us. We want them to be closely monitored and exquisitely sensitive when they enter our personal world, but when our personal world is attacked by the powers of hell, we want those police to be fearless, tough, and unlimited in their willingness to take action. In life's dilemmas, we keep learning that you just can't have it both ways.

I have been a priest for twenty-five years, and a Chicago police chaplain for sixteen of them. I have been a parish priest for the first ten of those twenty-five years, and I met some wonderful people. That said, I never met such high quality, bona fide heroes—and comedians—as I have since I started working with the police. There is no other group like them. The rest of the country might not know that, but the police know it, and that's enough for them.

John DiMaggio was one of them. His reputation among the Chicago police officers who worked with him is still lively and intact.

"If I did something wrong, he's the last copper I'd want looking for me. He'd get me!" That's what the ultimate police compliment sounds like when they talk among themselves.

The day-to-day work of a big city police officer is spent working for peace, justice, and order in the midst of life's messiness. Sounds pretty noble and idealistic, doesn't it? It is. And the warp and woof of the big city police officer's day makes him or her an acquaintance of Satan—but also a friend of God.

No wonder we can't get a long enough peek into their world. John DiMaggio goes a little farther and gives us a peek into their hearts.

Good for us!

—Fr. Thomas R. Nangle, Director, Chaplains Unit, Chicago Police Department

PREFACE

Maybe it's true that only a cop can understand a cop, but I would like to show you the world we live in, using incidents that occurred during my thirty-three years as a Chicago policeman. These stories unfolded as I served as a patrolman, a chauffeur/bodyguard for the police superintendent, in the Intelligence Unit, as a detective, and then as a detective sergeant in robbery, homicide, and specialized units.

I originally intended to write about just a slasher case that haunted me for years after the attacker's arrest, but friends suggested that I would be passing up too many interesting people and events.

I was apprehensive at first because some of the stories are strikingly unconventional, bizarre, and maybe shocking. Many might seem unbelievable, but I have kept a file of reports and newspaper articles to document them.

Overcoming my reluctance, I began writing about some of the officers I had known. One was killed by a "mad bomber," and another was struck down in the prime of life by a medical condition. I also wrote about good cops and bad cops, departmental politics, some things we did that were not standard procedure, and a few events that are still painful to recall.

You have to understand that the milieu of burglars, robbers, psychos, and killers is unpredictable and unnatural, and there is always a strain on police because they have to remain in the natural world while fitting into the shadow world. Nevertheless, most of us were hard working officers who cared more about the public than the people ever realized. We were shot at by rioters and we've been called "pigs" by others, and one man tried to run me down with a car—yet we helped keep a city together in a troubled time.

So here it is, how the police really work—in good times and bad—as seen through one pair of eyes. Everything is told just as it happened, except for fictionalized names that are marked with an asterisk on first mention. Many of these stories I have never told anyone before, not even my friends and family.

And there are many other stories to tell...

—John A. DiMaggio

1

THE ACTION SHIFT

"The possibility exists that after the operation, you will be in a wheelchair for the rest of your life," the orthopedic surgeon told me after evaluating my injuries from when a robber knocked me down a flight of stairs in a North Side police station. The surgeon was speaking in the presence of a doctor who would serve as a witness if something went wrong.

"The possibility also exists that after the operation, you will not have any control of your bladder," Dr. Louis Kolb droned on. "The possibility exists that..."

I felt as if I were being read my rights. How was I going to tell my wife that I had decided to go ahead with a spinal fusion? She thought that traction would be a cure-all and that I would be heading home in a few days. I was gambling with my life, but it was *my* life. No one could make the decision for me. So I told Dr. Kolb just to get it over with.

The surgery was performed at Chicago's Illinois Masonic Hospital in late 1971, and I underwent the most difficult seven months of my life. I was thirty-eight years old. The operation, out of necessity, destroyed some of my muscles and I had to learn to walk all over again. I'll save that story for later, but let me say now that pain pills alone provided the ability to be able to joke with my wife and the officers who came to see me.

"Hey, John, you done enough," one of my police friends said as I was recovering from the surgery. Chicago accent. "You done enough." Not "You've done enough." That's the way we talk in Chicago.

"Take the disability. You'll be livin' easy."

I would receive seventy-five percent of my pay, tax free, with all the medical benefits extended to me and my family until I reached the age of sixty-three. After that, I would receive a seventy-five percent pension.

But I had been a cop for fourteen years, and it had become a way of life.

Since I would have to exercise daily, I was determined to do it by climbing the stairs to the third floor Robbery Squad room. Nevertheless, I wasn't going to get a clean slate from Dr. Kolb by telling him the truth, the whole truth, and nothing but. Not that I lied. It's just that when we sat down to talk about what my duties might be, I said the work normally performed by a detective sergeant was answering phone calls, going over case reports, and filing papers.

"Will there be any lifting involved?"

"Just lifting papers, doc," I answered. "It's really an easy job—a lot of sitting."

Maybe Dr. Kolb believed me, and maybe he just saw that this was somebody who wasn't going to stay down.

"John, I'm going to leave it up to your good judgment," he said. My heart took a leap. "I'll write up a report recommending that you be returned to full duty. But promise me you won't do anything that would be detrimental to your back operation."

So I promised, and it wasn't a total lie. I could not see anything down the line that would be dangerous, but knowing the streets of Chicago—who could tell?

In May 1972, I returned to full duty in the Robbery Unit at what was then called Area Six. Our office at Damen and Grace was in a dilapidated three-story building holding on until a wrecker's ball could flatten the place. The first floor housed the traffic division and had a roll call room in the rear. A creaking staircase led to small rooms on the second floor for the youth division, task force, and general assignment unit. On the third floor, the Burglary Unit was at the front and there was an adjoining space for auto theft detectives. The rear was shared by detectives from the Robbery and the Homicide/Sex Units.

Unlike modern police stations, the Area Six headquarters

reeked with a nitty-gritty atmosphere. The vinyl floor was worn down to its raw materials, the walls had needed paint for years, and the ceiling cracks gave us something to look at when we were tired of the alley view from our windows. In the winter, the third floor was not much warmer than outside, and in the summer it was twice as hot.

I loved the place.

You would think from the movies that we detectives work alone, handle one case at a time, and dangle over cliffs when we are not getting into shootouts. Well, not always. Most police work really is routine, but the camaraderie and the excitement of building a case from scratch makes up for everything.

We at Area Six thought we were the elite because we handled the most diverse part of the city. We had everything from the violent Cabrini-Green housing project to the Gold Coast district along Lake Michigan, and from the cardinal's mansion to the Rush Street nightclubs. The most spectacular robberies, the most profitable burglaries, and many of the strangest murders in the city came to us. Fictional detectives might be hardened from seeing it all, but we were constantly amazed at the twists and turns of human behavior. After work, the officers would meet in restaurants, bars, bowling alleys—anywhere—and tell Area Six stories into the wee hours of the morning.

We threw ourselves into our work. Any officer with ambition wanted to be assigned to our Area, and that meant detectives working there always thought twice about sloughing off because they knew someone was eager for their place. The ones who stayed on could fit right in with any problem that came along. They were intuitive and ingenious, courageous, and sometimes reckless.

When I returned to duty, the area commander put me on the day shift to help me recover, but I assured him that I was feeling great and the back brace I was required to wear for a few more months was bothersome but tolerable. I asked him to return me to the action shift, from four p.m. to midnight, and with a grin and a shake of his head, he granted my request.

"Be careful, try and stay in the office, and take care of that back," he said.

On August 14, less than three months after I returned to duty, the Robbery Unit commander went home and I was in charge. Then we received a call at six p.m. from communications about a "hostage situation" on West Giddings Street at the north end of the city.

"The Twentieth District watch commander is requesting your assistance with heavy equipment," the dispatcher said.

"Got it," I replied, and I gave my name and star number, 1091. "Tell them we're on our way."

I threw the weapons cabinet key to Detective Leonard Muscolino. "You, Bill Daly, and I will handle the assignment," I told him. "Bill Alexander will take over the desk. Take two shotguns, extra ammunition, and the big-beam flashlights, and I'll meet you downstairs."

I signed out a supervisor's car and went to the station parking lot. I checked the gas level and pulled around to the side entrance. Then I climbed out and opened the trunk. Lenny and Bill came out at a trot. Lenny was carrying the shotguns and extra ammunition, and Bill was lugging two extra-large flashlights and the bulky case with the tear gas gun, projectiles, and gas masks.

"We got everything?" I asked.

"Yeah, everything," Lenny answered.

"No, we don't. We might need the walkie-talkies."

Lenny volunteered to get them and went back upstairs for three sets.

Leonard Muscolino was six-foot-two and weighed 230 pounds, someone you wouldn't want on your tail in a chase. The funny thing was that he had such a great personality that even the criminals he arrested liked him. Lenny had the experience and talents needed for a hostage situation, but Bill was still learning the ropes. I thought I'd take him along to get him used to the completely unpredictable work of dealing with someone on the brink.

Many people who threaten someone and hole up with weapons are in a sort of depression turned inside out. Rather than feel helpless, they need a rush of adrenaline to keep from falling apart. That's dangerous enough, but these people sometimes want to kill a cop just so they can get killed, too. It's a situation where all your instincts tell you to rush right in, but your brain says you've got to keep these people talking until you can anticipate their next move.

Nowadays, every major city has special hostage negotiation teams that go by a variety of names and initials. Back then, in the early seventies, we were just learning that hostage situations require psychology rather than sheer manpower or firepower. Several officers had lost their lives in order to teach us that lesson.

We reached the scene at 6:30 p.m. and had to get out of our squad car a block away because of all the police vehicles parked helter skelter down the street and in front of the building. The 20th District watch commander was shouting through a bullhorn in the middle of it all. Twenty to thirty uniformed officers were scattered all over, and everyone looked eager to charge at the enemy.

"Come out with your hands up!" the watch commander shouted. "We have the house surrounded!" Who knew how long he had been repeating those words?

I went up to him, identified myself, and told him I had brought the heavy equipment as requested. He informed me that all this had started as a suicide attempt in the first floor apartment. A young man named Robert Nelson had slashed his wrists after his father quarreled with him about his drinking. When two officers rushed in, after being called by the father, they found the son lying in bed with a shotgun.

"He told my men that he was going to blow their brains out, so they backed out and called for assistance," the commander said.

"Who are the hostages?"

"Just a couple friends of his. Kids, just kids."

"Is the father out?"

"He's out, he's standing over there. He's all right, but the son's ranting and raving."

As the captain spoke, I gazed at the building and saw through the window a heavy young man pacing back and forth with a shotgun. The shades were drawn halfway, so I couldn't see his face.

"Captain," I said, "I'm going to position myself in the building to the east, the one with the hallway. That should afford us some protection. We'll have the heavy equipment at that location should the need arise. I would advise you to take cover and order all the policemen to do the same."

"Sergeant, I am the captain, and I am in charge and will give all the orders until I am relieved by a higher ranking officer. Is that clear?" Not waiting for an answer, he shouted his final order at me. "Stand by until I require your assistance!"

I don't know how many hostage situations the captain had been in, but as the designated heavy weapons officer at Area Six, I had been at several, two of them involving shootouts, and I was also in charge of a heavy weapons squad during the West Side riots. The captain was correct in affirming the chain of command, but I went about carrying out my own plans without defying his orders.

I briefed my two men, and then asked Bill to cover the rear of the building and keep in touch through the walkie-talkie. I had Lenny load the shotguns and tell the officers at the front, two at a time, about the seriousness of the situation. People in hostage situations have mousetrap minds, and anything can set them off.

The captain kept bellowing through the bullhorn in the street as I hung my suit coat on the knob of the hallway door and positioned myself not six feet from the shattered windows of the living room. I could see how scared those hostages were as they stood by the front window, but I had ample protection if there was any gunfire. From *his* gunfire, at least. If thirty officers decided to shoot back without taking aim, I might be in a spot. But I was hoping to take this guy down without any gunplay.

I stood in helpless anticipation for an hour and a half against the hallway door as the sunlight faded in the humid August evening. The street lights came on and the bright moon rose, but nothing else had changed. Nelson's father was still in the street, surrounded by officers and neighbors, and the watch commander kept repeating, "Come out with your hands up!"

My body jerked in surprise when Nelson used the butt of his shotgun to smash the front windows, sending the captain and the patrol officers ducking for cover. I knew there probably wouldn't be a better time to take action. Nelson's twitchy movements had just given me a better view of the room. Lenny was two feet from me with a shotgun, and I was a foot away from the loaded tear gas gun—but I wanted to use the weapons only as a last resort.

I mentioned to Lenny that I wished we had a ladder to put against the building in case we needed it. Then we would have a clear shot into the room while Nelson was standing several feet from his cowering friends. Minutes later, Lenny tapped me on the shoulder and showed me two boxes that could raise one of us to a good level. We were planning a worst case scenario.

The two of us could hear Nelson ordering his hostages to kneel. Then he put the shotgun muzzle close to the head of one friend and then the other.

"I'm going to blow your fuckin' heads off, and the cops', too!" the young man yelled.

Any motion or sound from us would make him pull the trigger. The hostages would be killed, thirty officers would start blasting, and Lenny and I would be in the middle. Sometimes doing nothing is an action in itself.

Nelson kept talking, not all of it making sense, and at one point he clearly said, "Cops killed my friend, and that fuckin' Nuccio killed my cousin!"

Oh my God, I thought. Four years before, Officer Richard Nuccio had fatally shot a teenager named Ronald Nelson after the young man threw a knife at him in an alley near Wrigley Field, the Chicago Cubs' ballpark. Nuccio, while running after Nelson, fired after the blade missed him. The act might have seemed justifiable to anybody else, but not for a police officer. Nuccio was convicted of manslaughter and sent to prison for eight years.

Robert Nelson, however, was probably just using the death of his cousin as an excuse for going out in a blaze of glory and gunfire.

The bullhorn boomed again. "Nelson, we have your mother out here and she wants to talk to you. We're sending her in."

That, I thought, could be the worst thing to do in a situation like this if her son felt any hostility toward her.

A woman in her early fifties appeared out of nowhere and stood at the front door. She was separated from her husband, and Nelson had not seen her for a while. I watched as she entered the living room and joined the two hostages near the picture window. Even if Nelson didn't kill her, she might be in the way of all the officers aiming their weapons.

Nelson pointed the shotgun at her abdomen and hollered, "You were never a mother to me, you always treated me like shit! You were never around any time I needed you!"

I whispered to Lenny, "Get those boxes ready."

There was a gentle tug on my shirt sleeve as I stood flat against the hallway door. I turned and saw Assistant Deputy Superintendent Raymond Clark, the department's point man for trouble spots.

"How's it going?" he asked in a half-voice.

"Not too well. He almost took those people out. That's Nelson's mother in there. She's supposed to talk him out of it, but so far she hasn't said a word. They evacuated his sister and her three children from the second floor. They're clearing out this building and the one on the other side. The coverage at the front and rear is adequate, but too many policemen are in vulnerable positions."

"Okay, John, what do you recommend?"

I respected Clark enough to be honest. "Boss, I've been a little aggravated since I got here. There are too many officers exposed to danger. We still don't know if Nelson's just seeking attention, but we do know he's got a grudge against police."

Then Nelson's mother said something—what, we couldn't hear—and her son shouted, "Fuck you, get out of my house!"

The woman turned toward the street and yelled through the broken window at the small army of officers, "I can't reason with him!"

It took twenty minutes, but Nelson let his mother go. Clark went and had a short talk with the captain, and then came around again. "What about tear gas?" he asked.

"Not a good idea," I replied. "Nelson's ventilated the place by breaking the windows. We'd probably get more gas than he would. Another thing, boss, we've got CN gas, and it's always a potential fire hazard. If it ignites something, the fire trucks wouldn't be able to get close because of all the squad cars blocking the street."

"Any suggestions?"

"He came close to shooting those hostages, but he smashed the windows instead. I don't think he wants to, they're supposed to be his friends. He's all confused. I'd like to get him out without deadly force, but he has to calm down first. Maybe someone can call the apartment and talk to him by phone. He'd take that as less a threat than the bullhorn. Maybe we should also consider clearing the squad cars from the street and calling the fire department to stand by."

As I spoke, I kept watching the window. Nelson suddenly turned to face me as he bent down and peered through shattered panes. With the shotgun butt ready at his hip, his eyes locked onto mine through the darkness.

"Who are you? Are you a boss?" he demanded to know.

Now, what should I say? That I was a heavy weapons expert and could blow him away before he reached that trigger? That the man standing next to me was the assistant deputy superintendent? The truth was always wide enough to use selectively.

"No, I'm not a boss," I answered. "I'm just a police detective," intentionally not mentioning that I was a detective sergeant.

"Well, what are you looking at?" he asked harshly.

"I'm looking at you." I hadn't planned on talking to Nelson, but I couldn't stop now. "I would really like to come inside and speak to you."

Did I say that? I wasn't scared, but I had no idea what I might be letting myself in for. Imagine what the watch commander would have thought had he learned I was trying to go in on my own. *Oh well*—I thought the same thing when he permitted Nelson's mother to enter the place.

"Yeah, you can come in," Nelson said with a strange grin on his face, "but you'll have to come in without your gun."

"Okay." I unsnapped my holster and slowly slid out the .38 caliber snub-nosed revolver while watching his bulbous baby face, trying to see whether trust or murder hid behind those eyes. I handed my gun to Clark, who seemed reluctant to accept it. He wanted to stop me, but he knew that any exchange of words between us might spring Nelson into some type of action. "Are you going to be all right?" Clark whispered. All I could do was nod, not really knowing how to answer.

After crossing the lawn and going up the concrete steps, I entered the small lobby of the apartment building and faced a door with a large glass window. Rather than seeing if it was locked, I wanted Nelson to believe that I was entirely in his hands. After all, I tried to convince myself, there was an essential difference between the watch commander and myself.

I didn't consider Nelson an enemy.

The guy would be one trigger-pull away from ending my life, but strangely enough I felt sorry for him. The needless shooting of his cousin was not what had set him off, but right now he thought it did. Nelson was thinking he was being a man of vengeance, and I had to show him that not all policemen behaved like the officer who had killed his cousin. The killing was what some psychiatrists would call a "risk factor," a circumstance that nudges people closer to the edge.

Having majored in psychology in college, I thought I might have an edge in dealing with someone whose mind was in its own universe. *Keep watching his face and listening to what he says,* I told myself, not so much to what he might tell me, but rather for any strings of illogic that might be clues to his real thoughts.

Nelson was so tense now that if I were going to calm him down, it would have to be with a little levity. My knuckles thumped on the door glass with that famous "shave-and-a-haircut" rhythm—*rap-a-tap tap-tap … tap-tap.*

"Open the door and search him," Nelson commanded to one of the hostages. His voice carried through the hallway. "If he's got a gun on him, I'm going to blow his motherfuckin' head off."

The lobby door swung open. I didn't move, but I scanned the corridor to start working out my strategy. Ten feet away, the large young man with glasses and a thin mustache peered down the barrel sight with one eye closed.

"Search him!" Both hostages fumbled at my pockets. "Pull up his pants legs. Pull up his shirt. All right, go back and stand by the front windows." He needed them there to make sure police didn't start firing.

Was I totally concentrating? No. I was thinking that I should have said goodbye to Lenny and explained to Bill the do's and don'ts of hostage situations. Mainly, the don'ts.

"Come this way slowly," Nelson ordered. As I walked into his apartment, he made a turn into a darkened hallway that led to his kitchen, the shotgun still trained on me. "Go sit down." I was surprised by how much control he showed. He was as large as Lenny, and I wasn't sure I could overpower him. I had the advantage of training and the disadvantage of a back held together by surgery. He had the advantage of at least fifty pounds, youth, and a mind unbounded by reality.

I could clearly see outside, and that meant thirty officers could see us as well. I didn't know if that was to my advantage or not. The department at the time didn't have a sharpshooter squad, and a lot of eager rookies were nervous and unpredictable.

"Well, you're here, are you happy now?" Nelson asked with sarcasm. Shards of glass littered the floor, mostly from the windows, but also from picture frames, ash trays, and figurines he had shattered. What was really weird was that he was barefoot—crunching on all that glass without any indication he could feel the cuts other than shifting his weight from one foot to the other. His blood was everywhere, not only from his feet, but from his left wrist where he had slashed himself.

"I'm here to help you," I said. "You need medical attention and I would like to escort you out of this apartment without anybody getting hurt. So far you haven't done anything drastic, and I would like you to think things over and permit me to help you."

I said it as if I only intended to be his companion, but I was thinking over ways of taking him down. The long barrel of the shotgun would be easy to grab if I made a rush at him. It was a distinctive weapon, a 12 gauge Browning automatic with a barrel capacity of five rounds. Hunters were permitted to chamber only three and buy a "plug" that took up the space of the other two shells. I knew how heavy it was from personal experience, because I owned one. When I was hunting pheasants and rabbits, I never thought I would be at the other end of the barrel one day.

I had to assume the gun was loaded. Did he have three rounds in the chamber, or five? Thoughts raced through my head. Double '00' buckshot shells contain eight .32 caliber lead pellets, the kind used in police work. On the other hand, the gun could be chambered with slugs. A single, two-ounce piece of lead at close range would be capable of destroying my entire chest cavity.

"You killed my cousin and now I'm going to kill you and two more policemen," Nelson announced with a frightening calmness. That was one of his strings of illogic. He knew that Nuccio had killed Ronald and I was not Nuccio—and yet he didn't, not now. His rage had made all policemen a target. As he spoke, he took up a shooting position, angled his head, closed one eye again, and looked at my face down the long black barrel.

If I show fear, he'll kill me. If I look tough, he'll kill me.

"At least give me a chance to talk to you," I said. "You let me in here to talk, and I haven't had a chance to say much."

He didn't utter a word, but I could see that my ploy worked. Nelson lowered the shotgun, picked his nose with his free hand, and told me, "Go ahead and say something."

"There are a lot of policemen out there and they have heavy equipment, and I can assure you they will do something if you don't agree to walk out of here."

"Get rid of them. Tell them all to go away!" His voice quivered and his eyes darted in agitation.

"They won't leave, no matter what *I* tell them. They will be there until you're safely out of here. You just said that I killed your cousin, but let me tell you something. That case was a tragedy. You know that Richard Nuccio killed your cousin, and Nuccio is no longer a policeman. He's serving time in the penitentiary."

My rambling was an attempt to distract him. Right now we had a common link, neither Nelson nor I knew what he would be doing next. I knew his arms must be getting tired from carrying that heavy weapon. Maybe I could wear him out even though he clearly wasn't listening.

"If it wasn't for you policemen, my cousin would be alive right now."

His two young friends at the front window trembled in the summer heat. They looked at me in terror. If I got killed, they would be next, if not by Nelson, then by the blazing gunfire from the officers outside.

"Could I have a cigarette?" I asked. "I left mine in my jacket out there." There were three in a pack on the cocktail table directly in front of me. I hoped he would come closer.

"Sure, you can have one. They're right there in front of your nose."

As I reached for the pack, I sat on the edge of the couch. That would make me less of a threat to him. I shook out a cigarette and tossed the pack back on the table. I could make a leap and catch him by surprise, but the table might impede me. What if I tripped on the glass covering the floor, and my falling set him off? I could imagine three shotgun blasts, and then a barrage from outside.

Dr. Kolb's words echoed in my mind. *Don't do anything that will hurt your back.* My thinking had only been goal-oriented, but now I began to wonder if my wrap-around corset could keep my spine fused if I made a dash for the gun. *And what will your duties be if you returned?*

Clerical office work, answering phones, reading reports, things like that…

I remained where I was and lit the cigarette. Was Nelson trying to read my mind? I had to keep him off guard. So with the smoking cigarette between my fingers, I said casually, as if to a friend, "You know, I have to be fuckin' crazy."

He narrowed his eyes. "What do you mean?"

"What am I doing in this apartment trying to help you? I have a wife and three small children, and you keep pointing that shotgun in my direction. And why? I have done nothing to hurt you or your family. I volunteered to come into your home and talk to you and listen to you…"

The words I used were intentional—"children," "family," "home," "listen …"

"Just shut the fuck up," he interrupted. I don't know if he

saw through me or if the soothing words just mixed him up further. "I know I'm in trouble and I know I'm going to have to blow your head off and I'll take a couple more policemen with me!"

The more he babbled, the more his shotgun lowered. A quarter of an inch, half an inch, an inch, two inches … His rage took over and for this one moment he forgot that I was a threat. His free hand moved up to pick his nose again. I made a snap decision to take advantage of the opportunity.

I shot to my feet, oblivious of the cocktail table and the broken glass on the floor, and raced at him. Nelson had drifted into his own world and couldn't get out. He screamed, attempted to raise the gun, but then he turned away like a frightened little boy in a tantrum. I landed on his back, then swooped one arm around and grabbed the stock of the weapon as he ran toward the kitchen with me on his shoulders! Still riding him, I slapped my other hand close to the barrel. There were four hands on the gun now—he pushed one way I pulled the other. The pressure equalized, and the shotgun pointed straight up.

Shrieking, Nelson was unable to twist and throw me off. I clung to him like glue, holding on to the gun at the same time, hoping to keep my fused spine in one piece. I wasn't trying to wrestle with him, just struggling to keep the gun out of firing position until the swarm of officers outside decided to do something.

Then he stopped and faced a window with the green shade drawn all the way. It was the only one in the whole apartment that hadn't been shattered. He no longer screamed, and I had only one notion in my head—put him through that window, even if it meant going down with him. While still on his back, I planted my feet on the kitchen floor and shoved. I shoved him repeatedly against the window, breaking the glass and the frame, but I couldn't hurt him because of the strength of his temporary insanity.

Under the battering, Nelson realized he was no longer in control. Every driving force within him simply collapsed. All that fear, rage, and madness—he just went limp. Not that I realized it—my juices were up and I was prepared to ride him down to hell if I had to. Then, other hands were on me and I overreacted, not realizing that the hostages were coming to my aid. I thought for a moment that because they were Nelson's friends they were trying to pull me away so he could finish me off.

The room exploded in sound as police broke down the door and crashed through the jagged teeth of the windows. Several officers reached for Nelson's shotgun, but I wouldn't let go of it. My question of whether or not it was loaded was answered when I braced the stock against my hip and jacked off three live rounds of double-aught buck shells.

By then, the kitchen and hall were filled with policemen. I handed the gun to one of them, and others left with Nelson in handcuffs. The hostages embraced me in gratitude. Officers patted me on the back and congratulated me. For some reason, though, I disregarded their praise and didn't have the euphoria that usually came with a good arrest. Something was wrong and I couldn't figure out what it was. Lenny sensed this when he returned to the trashed apartment after escorting Nelson to the patrol wagon outside.

"You crazy son of a bitch," he said. "Why did you go in unarmed like that? How could you do that to me?"

I didn't answer. I felt pain in my arm and held it. "I think I broke my arm pushing him through the window frame."

"You think you broke your arm? I think I did something to my shoulder breaking the door down to come and rescue you. You didn't even say thanks!"

"You could have rung the bell," I said flippantly. "Come on, let's go to the hospital and see what's wrong with us."

We walked into the emergency room of Ravenswood Hospital and were greeted by some of the biggest fans of police—nurses and doctors. They even ignored some of the paperwork just for the honor of patching us up. I saw Nelson sitting on a bench. His bloodied feet and slit wrist had been wrapped in preparation for suturing. He was normal again—just a heavy, middle-class young man with all the wrath worked out of him. Only the sadness was left. At least I felt some sense of accomplishment that I was looking at him in the hospital instead of the morgue.

"Thank you," he said.

I think he meant it.

The doctors put a soft cast on my fractured left forearm, and they treated Lenny for a dislocated and severely bruised shoulder. There were more congratulations when we returned to the Area Six station to finish our watch. My main concern was whether we had brought back all the heavy equipment, even though none of it had been used. I typed up a short report for my lieutenant and was finished at midnight.

Lenny and Bill suggested that we stop for a cocktail after work, but all I wanted to do was go home, kiss the kids, and sleep off my strain. My wife was waiting for me—but not with congratulations.

Rosemary was always loving and supportive, but this time it was as if I had betrayed her. She didn't know the full story from the ten o'clock news, but she knew enough.

"How could you do such a thing?" she asked. "Why would you jeopardize your life for the City of Chicago? Did you forget that you have a family?"

She was right. Cops' wives were usually right. But cops keep being cops just the same.

At the annual police recognition ceremony the following May, Police Superintendent James Conlisk presented me with one of the department's highest honors, the Award of Valor, for disarming Nelson without a loss of life.

I began writing these stories after my retirement. I thought I would run the Nelson case by Lieutenant Jack Kennedy, who was in charge of the Hostage/Barricade/Terrorist program, which was set up in late 1979. What he had to say might be a good reminder for all police officers in a similar situation.

"Your case is one of the reasons the HBT Unit was formed," Kennedy said. "You could have very well been a dead hero."

Looking straight at me, he added, "A police officer should never volunteer to become a hostage, and that is exactly what you did. The risk of injury is enhanced because killing a police officer is more prestigious than killing an ordinary citizen. The subject will feel more of a threat from a trained officer, and the officer might feel duty-compelled to disarm him—and that is exactly what you did. Your case was one of many we reviewed to determine if the HBT Unit was necessary. You helped us learn by your mistakes."

He pointed out, "To begin with, the captain made a series of mistakes that violated all the rules of negotiations. The use of civilian negotiators—like members of the subject's family, friends, or clergy—presents a high-risk situation. I could go on and on about the mistakes the captain made, but the main fact is that getting control of the scene is most important."

Lieutenant Kennedy said that in the unit's first twelve years, it negotiated 140 hostage situations across the city and "tactically resolved" forty more, either with tear gas or by assault after buying time to plan for a safe resolution. Yet not one hostage was harmed and not one shot was fired by the police.

"John," he said, "you were indeed a hero and you were willing to sacrifice your life with the best intentions. There have been times when officers were awarded the Medal of Valor when they should have been fired. Rewarding officers for stupidity prompts other officers to do the same thing with the hope of receiving a police medal."

Kennedy's critique of the case was well received, but my wife had put it in its proper perspective the night I came back from Nelson's home.

2

"JUST WATCH US!"

Police Superintendent Matt Rodriguez recently mentioned that in my thirty-three-year career, I always "seemed to be where it's happening" in the second largest police department in the country. I could never make up my mind whether that made me the luckiest or unluckiest policeman on the force.

My father believed that "hard work never killed anyone," and he had the thick calluses on his hands to prove it. He reached the age of ninety-one after living a very healthy life. My dad's world was Chicago's South Water Market, the produce center just west of the Loop. He began as a potato hauler, the hardest job in the market, loading and unloading sacks weighing a hundred pounds. When I was a child he sometimes took me with him as he made truck deliveries all over the city.

With my dad, family always came first. We ate and dressed well, and he sent me to the best schools. He always let me know that he wanted me to go to college and not be just another laborer like some of his friends. During the beginning of World War II, he used his life's savings, borrowed some more, and bought a business that did the exclusive hauling of fruits and vegetables for all thirteen Goldblatt Brothers department stores within the triangle of Chicago, Joliet, and Hammond, Indiana. He worked extremely hard to keep the business from failing, and that meant replacing the antique, worn out trucks that had come with the business.

Over the summer when I was sixteen and about to become a sophomore at DePaul Academy, my father arranged for me to have a commercial driver's license in order for me to relieve his ten regular drivers while they took vacations. Dad woke me at three o'clock in the morning and we drove to the Market for a four o'clock start. Those crates of fruits and vegetables weighed nearly as much as I did, and it was more than the equivalent of a daily workout in the gym. I often thought about the hardships my father must have endured, especially while raising a family in the Depression, but he never complained about anything in his entire life. I have been proud to tell anyone that my dad was not only my father, he was my best friend as well. I find it astonishing that we never had an argument. He taught me about family values at an early age, and his lessons proved invaluable throughout my life.

Dad never mapped out my future for me, but when I told him and mom that I intended to become a lawyer, I could see he was pleased, to say the least.

At the uptown campus of DePaul University, I majored in psychology because the course literature showed me that the human mind is fascinating. I took the standard two courses in logic and followed up with courses in metaphysics, epistemology, and rational and irrational psychology.

I was enjoying college and part time truck driving for my father, and even doing the payroll for several firms at the Market. Then President Truman ordered a "police action" for Korea, and my naval reserve unit was activated. I could have filed for a student exemption, but I wanted to be with my reserve group as it was heading for boot camp at the Great Lakes Naval Training Center in the north suburbs.

Accustomed to early rising, I was always up two hours before anyone else and was able to shave and shower at my leisure, and then relax amid the mad dash for six a.m. reveille. I spent two boring years at the training center and missed going overseas, but entering the service had changed the course of my life.

After my discharge from the Navy, I re-entered the pre-law program at DePaul, but the requirement for entering the law school had been expanded from two years of college to three. That meant I had a year to go, but at least the G.I. Bill took care of my tuition. I went back to work for my dad on a part time basis.

During this year I met the love of my life, Rosemary. When a trite emotion hits you, it always seems as if you are the only person who has felt that way. I courted her for a year before we were married in April of 1955. We had planned a romantic honeymoon in Acapulco, but our family doctor, who often went to Mexico, told us of a bulbar polio epidemic that had killed two honeymoon couples. Against our better wishes, we canceled our plans and went to a lodge in Wisconsin instead.

I continued with two more semesters in college while working for my father, and I took outside hauling jobs for a market company that needed a driver with a strong back. The dream of becoming a lawyer was getting fainter by the week.

Then one day my dad had a talk with me, and he broke the news straightforward. Frozen foods had just come out, and he knew that the contract with Goldblatts would come to an end. He suggested that I find some other career or continue college and go to law school.

I just happened to read in the newspaper that the police department was accepting applications. More or less as a lark, I picked up an application form. I didn't really like or respect police officers all that much, but the job security and health benefits seemed attractive. I used a little deception when answering the questions. After "Why do you want to become a policeman?" I, like a lot of young men, put down, "to serve the public." Quite honestly, serving the public didn't seem all that important to me then. I hadn't really seen the public in need, those very real people desperately looking to the police as their only hope. I just wanted a job, with the intention of some day entering law school.

My sixteen weeks of training began in a former West Side high school ready for the wrecking ball. Instructors taught forty recruits in a classroom plastered with graffiti. As I was studying for tests, I was surprised when some men who had scored even higher than I did on earlier exams came up to me and asked for help, sometimes while tests were in progress! They admitted they had made top scores because they were given the test booklet in advance by political friends.

We transferred to training in an elementary school when a teenage girl named Judith Mae Anderson disappeared. Thanks to my typing skills and my eagerness to get into police work, I was one of the recruits brought in to help search for her near the school. Instead, her body parts were eventually found in two metal drums floating in Lake Michigan, shocking the city.

The detail shortened my training by at least three or four weeks.

After graduation in July 1957, we were given a two week furlough. Two of my police training classmates used the time to rob a gas station, but they were soon caught and sent to the penitentiary. I can't deny that some officers became corrupt from the seductions and frustrations of the work, but many of the ones who got in trouble were bad to begin with. After all, the nature of the work draws people with a craving for action, and no police department is a cross-section of the community.

Because of my years working for my father at a produce market, training was less grueling than for some chair-jockeys. When my class was sworn in, the department was considerably different from now. The cars were invariably black Fords, there was little coordination between police stations, and the Miranda decision was still in the future. Some officers thought the best way to gather information was by force and threats, because that was the way they were brought up and a lot of the old-timers did it—it was faster.

The department was still suffering from the reign of the Six Old Men. In the 1940s, for example, the panel refused to order walkie-talkies for beat officers because they were newfangled contraptions. Detectives had to work out of converted apartment buildings and former bus garages because there were no buildings designed only for the police, there were few minorities, and officers could not conduct formal lineups until real stations were built in the 1960s. There were no female officers, and crimes by women, apart from streetwalkers, were so infrequent that the only washroom for a woman in custody was at downtown headquarters.

Some of the old-timers seemed to take pride in their ethnic insensitivity. I hadn't realized it, but when I became a policeman

I found myself scorned because of my Italian name by a few officers who punctuated their conversation with references to what they called Dagos, Polacks, spicks, niggers, and kikes. These usually were the patrolmen who became detectives because of department friends in high ranking positions or politicians who took an interest for the sake of money.

My first assignment was the old 33rd District, called the Derelict District. The "derelicts" were the cops themselves. Nothing much happened on the Northwest Side around O'Hare International Airport, so the powers that be assigned rookies to work among the lazy officers, the pension-treaders, and the burnouts. Perhaps the theory was that rookies would get over a certain trigger-happy tendency if they worked almost exclusively on burglaries, family disturbances, youth problems, and suicides. I was disappointed when I drew the assignment. Many of the officers there were known to be like broken down race horses put out to pasture, and I wanted something faster. Even so, the 33rd, along with every other district in the city, still had a lot to teach.

My penchant for always seeming to be "where it was happening" may have started early in my career while I was assigned to a three-wheel motorcycle. I monitored a police radio call about a body in an apartment off a street called Northwest Highway. I didn't have to respond, since in those days the department realized that motorcycle cops could hardly hear the calls over the sounds of their own motor and other traffic, but I headed for the address out of curiosity. The paddy wagon had just pulled up and the officers saw me jump off the cycle.

One of the old-timers yelled, "Just watch us, kid. Just watch us." Words I will always remember.

I followed the two veteran cops up the stairs and immediately smelled death. That was something you have to force yourself to get used to, but I knew I had to start sometime. Some officers smoked cigars to cover up the stench or placed their hands over their mouths, but nothing really helps. I could see maggots crawling in and out from under the door. The two partners kicked it open and discovered the blackened body of a huge woman lying on a bed, her remains alive with tiny worms.

The veterans kept calling me "kid" as they sprinkled the body with an essential item for any police wagon—a box of ordinary table salt, to kill the maggots. I think the old-timers enjoyed the look on my face when the granules caused their instantaneous death.

The veteran cops used the sheets as a hammock and were about to swing it onto the stretcher to avoid touching the body, but the rotting cloth—half dissolved by the leaking body fluids— gave way, the corpse dropped two feet and *exploded* on the floor. The flesh and digestive acids sprayed the room, splashing on the officers' uniforms and horrified faces.

"I'll see you, *kids*," I mocked and quickly went down the stairs for some fresh air. Then and there, I decided that never— *never*—would I let myself be assigned to wagon duty. Not even when I was a homicide detective did I ever see anything quite as ghastly, although a number of cases came close.

Some officers develop a flippant attitude toward bodies to cover up their real feelings, but instead I found myself deadening my senses.

A few weeks later, while I was still on motorcycle duty on a cold wintry night, I saw a crowd gathered around a man whose head had been crushed by a bus. The flattened head, with blood draining into the corner sewer, was a sight that no one should ever see. I radioed communications and calmly borrowed a tablecloth from a restaurant to cover the horrid remains until the assigned officer from the traffic detail arrived.

In my days of training, I had envisioned myself in the usual kind of cops and robbers situations, but that wasn't what life was like in the Derelict District. When a woman walked away from a nursing home and was hit by a train, it was my job to get the bushel baskets from the nearest grocery store and distribute them to other officers and firefighters, and then we began picking up the pieces. I did it by hand; the firefighters used shovels.

That winter, I was working the midnight shift. My partner, *[1]Tony Bongliardi, said on our first time out, "This district is a

---

1. An asterisk (*) in front of the first appearance of a name means that it has been changed from the original.

ghost town on midnights. We'll write out a couple of tickets to please the bosses, and then head for the Hole." I thought he might have meant a restaurant.

The three a.m. streets were virtually deserted, but we found a few traffic violators. Then, to my surprise, Bongliardi drove our squad car to the cemetery. Our headlights made the headstones glow as we cruised down the winding road. Bongliardi made a slow stop, left the motor running, shut off the headlights, put the heater on high, pulled his hat over his eyes, slouched down comfortably in the seat, and said, "Get some sleep."

I looked at him in disbelief when he reached the snoring stage. I was wide awake because I had slept the day before, so all I could do was stare at the night and watch the dawn as it rose. I would have welcomed the appearance of a ghost. After three and a half hours, more than I had slept the day before, Bongliardi awoke with a stretch and a yawn. "That felt great," he said. "Let's hit the streets."

That shift I chalked up to experience. When the same thing happened the next night, I had no intention of wasting our time when people might need us, especially since I was still on department probation. The squad car seemed to have eyes of its own as it found the entrance to the cemetery, pulled in, and traveled the same route as before. Bongliardi even used the same words as before—"Get some sleep."

It took me an hour, but I thought of a plan.

I waited until my partner couldn't possibly snore any louder, then I slapped the flat of my hand against the door to create a booming noise. Bongliardi's head snapped forward, and I pulled my hand inside.

"What was that?" Tony blurted, jarring awake.

"What was what, Tony?" I asked, pretending to be groggy.

"The noise! The noise!"

"I didn't hear anything. Get some sleep, Tony." I crossed my arms and slouched down.

Within minutes, Bongliardi was snoring again and I knocked on the door to create a different sound. Once again he snapped awake, only now he looked even more agitated.

When I assured him I didn't hear anything, he started the car, grabbed the wheel, and zoomed to Belmont Avenue.

"Are you sure you didn't hear anything?" he asked.

"You must have had a nightmare."

"I could have sworn ..."

Nothing happened for the rest of the watch. The following night, when I knew the cemetery visits were over, I said, "Teach me the streets, Tony. I really want to learn this part of the district."

At about three-thirty a.m., after half a foot of snow piled up, I noticed beer cans scattered near a parked car with two figures inside. "Let's make a U-turn and see what's up," I suggested.

We pulled up behind the car, got out, and each of us went to a door. Bongliardi knocked on the driver's window and asked for identification. All I expected was that we would ask the two young men in the car to pick up the cans. The driver, a small guy, got out and was polite. His much larger passenger, however, was belligerent. When I asked him to identify himself, he snarled, "Fuck you, I didn't do anything wrong!" He stepped around me and started walking across the street.

At this point I made what I considered to be a career decision. One of the first things an officer learns is to maintain control in all situations. You can be kindly to nice people, but you have to be firm with the obnoxious ones. The officer at that moment is not an individual but rather the embodiment of the law. He has to make the other person know that he demands or at least deserves respect. I knew that if I let this man go, I would always be letting people walk away from me.

I ran after him, slipping and sliding in the snow, and stopped him in the middle of the street. He gave me a slight push before I could say anything. I tackled him and pinned him down. My new hat had fallen in the slush and my uniform was turned into ruin as I wrestled the man to his feet and got him in the "come along" hold that they taught in the police academy. At no time did my partner offer to help. He stayed safe and sound watching from thirty feet away.

Since Bongliardi didn't think we should bring the guy in, and I realized the incident would look petty to my supervisors,

I decided to let the man go—after the two young men cleaned up the littered street. As soon as we returned to the squad car, I told Bongliardi what I explicitly thought of officers who would not come to the assistance of their partners. He actually shook while I was talking to him.

There was no fourth night with him. Bongliardi, a senior officer, apparently requested a different partner, hoping for one who preferred cemetery naps to getting in trouble. So my next assignment was to work with *Ronnie Basumdarth, a "seasoned" officer of ten years on the force. Unfortunately, what he had to teach me was something I did not want to learn.

After an old man drove his automobile through a *yellow* light, Basumdarth turned on the siren and the red Mars light, and then gunned the motor. I thought, *what was wrong with going through a yellow light?* My partner pulled over the elderly driver and asked for identification. There was a dispute that lasted at least ten minutes, with both of them pointing to the ever-changing traffic light. Finally, Basumdarth returned to our car with a smile on his face.

"Well, John, I convinced him he was wrong," he said and took the wheel. As he started up, he showed me about a dollar and a half in coins. "Count it up and we'll split it."

I threw the coins at his feet.

"You're a mope," I said. "I guarantee you that this is the last day we'll ever work together."

It became very quiet and routine for the rest of that tour of duty, and the next day I found myself on foot patrol that lasted a couple of months.

When I was back on squad car duty, my own personal Halloween came in the spring. A woman called the station one evening to report that her "boy" was missing. We thought he might be some runaway kid, but then a woman in her seventies opened the door when we arrived at her place. Her boy turned out to be a onetime well known jockey in the 1950s. The woman was alarmed because, for the first time, he had not come home the night before.

At the academy, we were taught that many missing

children were still in the home, hiding in unusual places. Why not missing jockeys?

While my partner interviewed the woman and made out a report, I went up the back stairs leading to the attic. I opened the door and was surrounded by blackness. My flashlight beam quickly dimmed and went out. I flipped the switch several times and slammed it on the heel of my other hand, but the glimmer didn't return.

I groped for a light switch but couldn't find one. I went into a Frankenstein stance, holding my arms out in front of me to avoid hitting anything, and hoped my hands would hit a string to turn on a bulb. My brain told me to go down and borrow my partner's light, but I continued to move five to ten feet forward in the dark. I stopped abruptly when my hands became entangled with a form swinging against me. At first I was confused, and then I realized I'd found the missing middle-aged son. I was holding on to a pair of legs.

I went down the stairs two steps at a time, tapped the screen door, and motioned for my partner to come out on the porch.

"What's up, John?"

"We'll need your flashlight, my batteries ran out. I think I found the son in the attic."

The body was still swinging from my accidental encounter when we entered the attic. The jockey had hanged himself with an electrical cord that he'd wound around his neck and a beam, and then kicked away a chair he'd been standing on. I wanted to cut him down, but my partner said, "That won't help; he's been dead for hours. Go to the car and radio in the notification for the detectives, and I'll console the mother."

There was a suicide note of sorts. In the man's pocket was a newspaper article about his glory days at the track, before he'd fallen on hard times.

Even stranger was the time a different partner and I raced to the call of a stabbing. A number of people were outside the house, all pointing upstairs and speaking Greek. Not knowing what to expect, I drew my gun, rushed up the stairs, and entered a well-lit kitchen while my partner kept behind me. He didn't like rookies, but he didn't mind if they were attacked first. We had nothing to worry about, though. Waiting for us on the floor was a young man in his late teens. He sat calmly, his face pale and glistening with tears. The handle of an ancient bayonet was jutting from his chest, and below him was a three-foot ring of blood. The ten inches or more of the blade was jutting from his back, preventing him from collapsing to the floor!

I knelt on one knee and our eyes met. I could say nothing to him, for we both knew he was dying. I couldn't tell whether or not he regretted what he'd done. I crept closer, not caring that my shoes and right knee were now soaked in blood. He raised a hand to wipe his tears, smearing the blood on his face. I grabbed him by the shoulders to steady him.

"Can you tell me what happened?" I asked. "Why?"

He answered only in Greek. I nodded as if I understood and sadly waited for the ambulance crew to arrive. No one wanted to remove the bayonet, which was actually keeping him alive by limiting the flow of blood. Rather than carry the teenager down by his arms and legs, the ambulance men sat him on the stretcher and maneuvered him down the long flight of stairs. What an eerie sight that was, a young man with his life flowing out of him, sitting on a stretcher being held as level as possible by two burly men. At the hospital, I watched a doctor remove the bayonet and at last the teenager could lie down to rest. I saw him take his last breath while he stared at me. He looked relieved.

Hospital workers were able to question family members in Greek. They learned that, while in his homeland, he had received a letter telling him of an inheritance from an uncle who lived in Chicago. The teenager borrowed a considerable amount of money to make the trip. When he arrived, he learned that the inheritance wasn't very much. That left him in debt and humiliated. Death seemed the only way out.

At the inquest, I measured the blade the young man had completely pushed through his body. It was twenty-one inches long.

I don't know if my interest in psychology made me a better policeman, although from time to time, as in the Nelson case, it helped me lock into how the other guy was thinking, and that did not necessarily mean the bad guys. The department was going in another direction and set up an anti-mob unit facetiously called "Scotland Yard." However, the tactics were not the kind you would find in Sherlock Holmes. I had no direct knowledge of such things, but it was said that low level mobsters were hung out of windows at police headquarters until they spoke the truth. The special unit was eventually disbanded—not because of civil rights violations, but because it had tapped the phones of a downtown hotel where Mayor Richard J. Daley was conducting a sensitive meeting.

Such over-enthusiasm was not found in the Derelict District, where some detectives were dumped from the Scotland Yard unit. A few of the officers of the district responded only to their assignments and issued traffic citations. I always preferred looking for trouble and letting sober drivers off with a warning, which led some of my supervisors to lecture me about how traffic control and citations were among the most important duties of a good officer. In other words, they were trying to tell me that politicians in City Hall felt that more revenue could be squeezed out of traffic violators than burglars and robbers.

In fact, Lt. John Connors one day called me into his office to haul me over the coals. He was a strong advocate of traffic tickets, and when he learned that I wrote very few citations he decided to talk to me about it. When I told him I made a sizable number of misdemeanor and felony arrests, he researched my stats and told me to forget about the tickets and keep focusing on crooks.

Throughout the department, there were always older officers who liked helping out newcomers if they showed any special spark or talent. The fact that I made arrests and typed up my own reports and court papers attracted the interest of Detective Hugh Phillips. He came over to me one evening while I was processing an arrest and suggested that I "get out of uniform for a while." Without notifying me, he recommended to District Commander Russell Corcoran that six uniformed officers be assigned to a special "burglary detail," mentioning my name and a few others. Burglary investigations were done by detectives, but there were always more break-ins than they could handle in the 33rd District, the quietest as well as the largest in the city. Captain Corcoran was a class act and saw the sense in the suggestion. I couldn't have guessed it then, but this was the turning point in my career. Detective Phillips worked with us in the first weeks as an informal training officer. He never mentioned it, but he had been given the department's highest honor for bravery, the annual Judge Lambert Tree Award. Even so, not all his valuable advice concerned sleuthing and dodging bullets.

One day he said to me, "John, I want you to remember something for the rest of the days that you serve as a police officer. If someone is ever concerned about what you think of a certain person, I want you to give it deep consideration before you answer. I would suggest that if you really like the person you're being asked about, your answer should be, 'He's a nice guy.' And if you really don't like the person, then your reply should be, 'He's a reallllly niiiiice guy.'"

I understood what he was saying, but didn't understand why he was saying it.

"If you think the guy deserves to be called a bad name," he continued, "and you simply said that he's a reallllly niiiiice guy and that terminology gets back to the person you were asked about, *and it will*, then you will never be accused of name-calling. Don't worry, the good people will understand what you mean."

I was still skeptical about his advice. To me at the time, the police department should be like a family, with the members sticking together to accomplish the common goal of protecting the citizens. This was my introduction to real life, though, and the realization that not all politics are found in City Hall. Hugh Phillips' suggestion would come into play many times before my retirement.

Our informal detail made a number of arrests for offenses other than burglary. Since we were still new, whenever we made an arrest, the old-timers told us, "That was a lucky pinch." As time went on we learned that sometimes luck was involved, but more often it was common sense and staying alert.

Each week we would go to the district station before quitting time to fill out our weekly "humper," a form itemizing the cases handled for the last seven days and then channeled to the ranking officers up to the district commander. A lot of the "derelict" officers schemed, lied, and made up phony assignments to fill their humpers. Being a new plainclothes officer, I usually had to add a page or two to put down all our activity for the week.

While we were filling out our humpers on a frigid Sunday afternoon in January, a dentist named *Dr. Arthur Cigo stood in the kitchen of his elderly mother's home and made a call to his estranged wife. His mother lived in one of the new bungalows that were replacing vacant lots in the outer edges of the 33rd District. Cigo had Sunday visitation rights and would drive his children to his mother's house for a family dinner. After brooding throughout the meal, he went to the phone. His mother did not realize that he had slowly and silently gone over the edge.

When his wife picked up the receiver at about 3:45 p.m., he begged her to come back to him. Then he turned to his mother and brother and said, "I can't believe it, she hung up on me. *She hung up on me!*"

My partner and I were on the last page of our humper at around the time of the call, and we thought we would be heading home shortly.

Cigo dialed again, this time while taking a .32 caliber automatic pistol from his waistband. He asked his mother to get his children, *Charles and *Arlene, into their snowsuits. On the phone, he told his wife, "Either you come back or I'll kill myself and the kids."

He fired a threatening shot into the floor. His mother and older brother jumped but thought that when he calmly hung up that it was all over. His mother dressed three-year-old Charles in the living room and was zipping the snowsuit of five-year-old Arlene when Dr. Cigo approached them. The woman didn't see the gun, she just heard a shot and saw the little boy drop to the floor.

Cigo's mother shrieked.

The dentist slowly went over to Arlene and put the muzzle to her head.

"No! No!" his mother yelled.

Another shot, and the girl fell into her arms.

Cigo's brother ran in from the kitchen as the dentist raised the gun to his own head. The brother was able to grab the guy's wrist, but it was a second too late. Cigo pulled the trigger and dropped to the floor.

My partner, Ray Wagner, and I were just district officers working in plainclothes for a burglary detail, but the detectives who should have gone in were nowhere to be found when the call came in to the station. Ray and I raced to the home in five minutes. We threw open the unlocked storm door, and then stopped abruptly at the sight of the three people lying on the floor. We both stepped on Cigo's quivering wrist as a precaution and took the gun from his hand.

Ray examined the victims. "I think the little boy is dead, but the girl is still breathing."

I scanned Cigo for signs of life. "Ray, I can't understand it. This guy has a T and T [through and through] gunshot wound, temple the temple, and he's still breathing." Ray did not answer and probably didn't hear me. I didn't know what private anguish caused the dentist to shoot his children, but I had a momentary desire to kick him.

"Oh my God, oh my God," the elderly woman said while standing over the victims. We took her and her other son to the kitchen table as the wagon men arrived. The woman returned to the living room, picked up one of the throw rugs that bubbled with blood, and carefully carried it to the kitchen sink. She did this with the others, not allowing one drop of blood to drip on her white carpet. Pushing the horror from her mind, she began to scrub the rugs.

Crime lab technicians made their sketches of the scene and took photos. Ray and I helped them find shell casings and slugs. The steel-jacketed, high-velocity bullets had passed through all three skulls and ricocheted around the room.

When we returned to the station, I was surprised to see that the detectives had done us a favor by contacting the dentist's wife and her mother. I found myself staring at *Emily Cigo as the detectives questioned her in the squad room. Her little son was dead, and her daughter and husband were near death, yet she showed no emotion at all. I had seen people act calmly in tragedy because they were struggling to keep from falling apart, but this was different. To me, she didn't care.

Emily's mother seemed most concerned that no one blame her daughter. "I did the right thing," she said. "I called the police right after my daughter was threatened on the phone. The police called me back and told me that they sent three squad cars to Arthur's home, but he wasn't there."

We went to Resurrection Hospital and were surprised to learn that Cigo and his daughter were still alive six hours after the shooting. I questioned the doctor, who answered more in Latin than in English, and he ended his dissertation by stating, "They will die, it's just a matter of time."

The girl died at ten minutes after midnight, and her father followed five minutes later. The paperwork could now be completed—two murders and one suicide. Case closed and cleared.

I was naive then—the nation was naive—and I was shocked at what had happened because I couldn't comprehend it. Where was the logic in the act? If Cigo was angry with his wife, why shoot the children? Maybe logic is just an illusion. Maybe we all run on currents that always elude us.

3

A WITNESS TO CREATION

During the six p.m. to two a.m. shift at the Derelict District, we heard from communications about "a guy who keeps telling us he's going to commit suicide." They said, "We're trying to trace the calls, but he always phones from a different location." Currently he was at a phone booth at Foster and Harlem. "He might not stay there long."

Ronnie Kelly and I were in plainclothes that night. We had a store-bought police frequency receiver and were driving one of our own cars, since the bad guys were adept at spotting unmarked department vehicles. We sped to the phone booth in time to yank out a man in his twenties. We searched him, cuffed him, and threw him in our car. Officers needed to be careful with possible suicidal cases because they might want to take a policeman with them, but we were young, hot shot cops and thought we knew everything. We were certain that if he really wanted to kill himself, he would have done it without phoning communications repeatedly for several hours.

We were processing the man when Lieutenant Paddy Diggins entered the room. Diggins usually ignored the regulation that lieutenants should be in uniform for routine duty; he preferred well-tailored suits, even though he spoke very much like a gruff, hard-edged Chicago cop.

"So you're the fuckin' fruitcake who's been callin' in and tying up our airwaves to scare everyone that you're goin' to commit suicide," he said to our prisoner.

Without waiting for a response, Lieutenant Diggins whipped

out his snub-nosed police special from his holster and slapped the revolver on the table.

"We'll see if you really want to do it," he said.

The man grabbed the gun. A strange expression formed on his face, as if he seemed grateful. He put it to his head. Kelly and I stood frozen as he pulled the trigger on empty chambers and did not give up until testing number six.

Diggins, who had unloaded the gun before coming into our office, took it back and gave us a look I will never forget. Without a word, he indicated that we should always take people seriously when they threaten suicide, because you never know. That lesson stayed with me throughout my career.

Sergeant George Murphy was the "Bull Dick" of the old 33rd District, working in plainclothes to monitor the activities of the station detectives. He assigned John Coughlin and me to a crime pattern in which three women were beaten with a tire iron and then raped. John and I went to the police academy together, became fast friends, and coincidentally were assigned to the same district. We two Johns almost immediately became partners and worked well together because we thought a lot alike.

We began by studying the reports in hope of finding a common denominator. Each woman had been attacked when she left a Belmont Avenue bus in a sleepy residential neighborhood. When the victims cried out, the man beat them repeatedly with the tire iron and dragged them into an alley, where they were assaulted. The age of the victims didn't seem to matter, they were from nineteen to forty-five years old. The attacks were so savage that one almost lost an ear from a blow to the head, and the others suffered arm and leg fractures.

Sergeant Murphy suggested that we follow Belmont Avenue buses from eight p.m. to four a.m., well within the time period of the assaults. John and I used my personal auto and stocked it with sandwiches and a Thermos of coffee for what could be a long night. We stayed about two blocks away from each bus going down Belmont, traveling two miles from Central Avenue to the end of the line and heading back again. The riders had no way of knowing that they had their babysitters with badges watching out for their safety.

Since the runs were every fifteen minutes, we were able to get back to our starting place before the next one came along. After ten p.m., the buses came every half an hour. John kept looking through binoculars, continually calling out license plate numbers and describing the clothing worn by women passengers so that I might keep track of them once they got off. Most of that was just to keep us awake and alert.

At 12:30 a.m., I looked at the odometer and saw that we had gone over sixty miles in our up-and-back trips. We had terrible visions of maintaining this boring assignment for weeks and pondered why we were selected when we were normally assigned to a burglary detail.

We saw the brake lights of a white Chevrolet as a bus pulled over, but the passenger that got off was a man. The auto could have passed the bus, but instead it continued following. Suddenly, both of us were a lot more alert than we were a moment before. John tried to jot down the license plate number and keep the car in sight through his binoculars. When a woman stepped off the bus, the white car quickly veered to the left and passed it. I gunned the motor and peeled rubber to catch up, but when we turned the corner where we last saw the car—the Chevy was gone.

"Shit," I said. "We had a bite and then we lost him."

We circled the block and made sure the woman who got off the bus reached home safely. For fifteen more minutes we cruised the area, but couldn't find the Chevrolet. We were a little frantic and decided to go back and wait for the next bus, hoping the car would return.

"But then what?" I asked John. "We can't arrest him for following a bus."

John and I decided that we wouldn't want to wait for him to attack a woman before we arrested him, that was just common sense, but suppose we took him in and none of the victims could identify him? Then he might move on and start all over again. Most importantly, what if this guy driving the white Chevy had nothing to do with the attacks? We agreed that if we saw the same car following the next bus, we would take the driver in on the presumption that we had probable cause.

The bus appeared, and sure enough, the white Chevrolet showed up to follow it. We did not want to follow too close, but at a distance we could not see the license plate. The bus went to the end of the line without discharging any passengers, and within a few minutes we lost the car. The sense of frustration we felt was like a small explosion.

An hour later I could see a bus approaching in my rearview mirror, and then it sped past us. Twenty yards behind was the same white Chevy. Yeah, we got probable cause, I thought to myself.

"It just can't be we'd be this lucky the first day out," John stammered as he marked down the license number.

When the bus stopped for the red light at Austin Avenue, I pulled alongside the car and John jumped out to announce the arrest. That trapped the Chevy between the bus ahead of it and our car beside it. John had his star in one hand and his gun in the other. Everything had gone off exactly as we had hoped it would—something that doesn't always happen. We could have filmed the arrest for the police academy as a classic example of a street shop.

My exhilaration faded when I saw that the driver looked familiar. When he got out of the car, I felt a jolt. The young man was *Lewis Burke—I had played football with him at DePaul Academy and we sat in the same classrooms for four years. He had seemed to be a good student, well-groomed and well-mannered, but he was rather distant and never smiled. We graduated together, and when I went to college I even pledged at his fraternity until I was kicked out over the paddle incident. In fact, I suddenly remembered that he had been there during that particular ceremony. Lewis was a little heavier now, but there was no mistaking his long, dark eyebrows and thin lips that gave him that strange, forlorn look.

I was so certain we had caught the right man that I didn't feel I needed to ask him anything—not his name, not whether he was guilty, and not why he had attacked those women. He, too, kept silent, but I knew he recognized me.

John snapped on the handcuffs and placed our prisoner in my car, lightly shoving Lew's head down to make sure he didn't hit it on the frame and to keep a good grip on him if Lew tried to bolt away. Then John got behind the wheel of the Chevy and headed alone for the station. As I followed, I saw John stick his arm out the driver's side window, waving a tire iron he had found under the seat. I looked at Lewis. He looked at me. Still, not a word passed between us, but he put his head down. That was more convincing than a signed confession.

I typed the report at about 1:45 a.m. when a detective—one of the dumped "Scotland Yard" sharpies, a reallllly niiiiice guy who later became a high-ranking police official—said, "John, I don't think you got the right man. What have you got? That he was driving by a bus and had a tire iron under a seat instead of in the trunk. That's not very much. This guy's a college graduate, for Christ's sake, and he's never been arrested before. Do you know that you and your partner stand a good chance of being sued if you don't release him?"

"I'll take that chance," I said coldly. "Lew's locked up, and he'll stay locked up until he's viewed in a showup by the victims."

Yet part of me didn't want to admit that someone I knew was a vicious rapist. The detective's words of "I don't think you got the right man" kept playing in my head when I went home. There was no doubt in my mind that Lewis was our guy, but I was wondering whether we might have been too hasty, or "too lucky," by arresting him on the very first night of our surveillance. After all, the detective who told me we likely had the wrong man had been working on the case for three months.

John and I showed up at the station at nine a.m., an hour before the first showup. We both could have used a few more hours of sleep, but we felt a little better when Murphy and Captain Corcoran complimented us on the arrest. The first showup was for the woman who had nearly lost an ear in the attack. Since we had no lineup facilities, a suspect was placed in a line of other people at the back of an ordinary room. Each was told to say a few words, and then all the men faced the wall. The witness was asked to step toward the attacker and point a finger at him. Sometimes victims got carried away and started hitting the suspect, but usually they were shaking and barely able to speak.

After taking one look at my high school classmate, this woman screamed loud enough to be heard outside the station. I had never heard such an unnerving, terrifying shriek. The scene was reenacted at the two other showups that morning, each time with a different victim trembling as she pointed at Lewis without hesitation.

This wasn't one of those arrests that made an officer feel proud. All I felt was relief, and I was glad I wouldn't have to grill my one-time casual friend because the showup identifications were enough. Our fellow officers at the 33rd called us "lucky guys" and the detective formerly of "Scotland Yard" avoided us. We were recommended for awards and promoted to patrolmen first class, which meant a thousand dollar raise that we would not have normally received for three full years. We also were recommended for promotion to the rank of detective.

However, John Coughlin became a detective and I remained behind at the 33rd as a patrolman. There were no hard feelings, and there never would be between John and me.

Lewis pleaded guilty and was sentenced to ten years in prison. He served his time, and through periodic checking over the years, I was pleased to learn that he was never arrested again.

Although I wanted to stay with the action that was developing at the 33rd District, I was chosen to serve for two months as the chauffer of the deputy chief of patrol, Robert "Jitterbug" Ryan. He was a great guy and taught me the city I thought I knew so well.

What you see going through the city at night is just a fraction of what's really going on, but the commentary by Deputy Ryan made certain buildings and neighborhoods come alive as he relayed his experiences to me.

When I was back in the 33rd as a plainclothes officer working with a detective in a felony car, the Chicago Police Department underwent its greatest scandal.

It began with a holdup on Jewelers' Row. That's the name for part of Wabash Avenue downtown, where numerous jewelry stores operated throughout commercial and office buildings. The getaway car was traced to a policeman in the Summerdale

Police District on the far North Side. As we learned later, thieves that same morning looted a tire and auto supply store and loaded the items in the back of several cars containing Summerdale District officers.

At the center of the gang was Richard Morrison, a burglar, safecracker, counterfeiter, and con man. He started by bribing officers with some of his loot. The men then began placing orders for television sets, sports equipment, and other spoils they fancied. In time, eight officers—including one from my police training class—told Morrison where and when to hit, and some of them even helped him out by serving as lookouts.

The spree ended in July 1959, when Morrison was arrested after breaking into an apartment by himself. Before long he entered Chicago fame as the "Babbling Burglar" for telling authorities all they could ask for and more, simply because his confederates did not post his bail. The officers were rounded up after ultra secret search warrants were given to a team of detectives and members of the state's attorney's staff at a hush-hush meeting in the Urban League Club.

The station commander at Summerdale resigned rather than undergo a lie detector exam, although it was believed that he may have been unaware of the burglars in blue. As a symbolic act, Police Commissioner Timothy O'Connor—the man for whom the police academy was later named—stepped down and served out his career as just another department captain.

Mayor Richard J. Daley promised to reform the entire police department. He felt the only way to regain public confidence would be to bring in an outsider as the leader.

A committee was formed to consider applicants from across the country, chose its own chairman, Orlando W. Wilson, a former California street cop, army colonel, and criminology professor.

Wilson took the title of superintendent rather than commissioner and began his clean sweep in the early 1960s by moving his office out of City Hall and to police headquarters a mile south of downtown—further away from politicians.

In time, his changes included phasing out foot patrols in favor of a motorized and computerized department. He also changed the colors of beat cars from the standard black to blue and white for a more visible police presence.

In addition, he let black officers transfer to predominantly white neighborhoods. Since Wilson had no ties to the city, he did not care what the officers or the powers that be at City Hall thought of him or his changes. He had a job to do, owed his allegiance only to the mayor, and was given a blank check to do it. New divisions were created, new ways of thinking instilled, new offices appeared, and O.W. Wilson brought in his own personal staff to assist him in making the drastic alterations.

Plaster flew all over police headquarters. Some inner walls were torn down to make way for a communications center with an unheard-of thirteen frequencies, eleven more than before Wilson arrived. No longer would citizens wait hours before police arrived. The dilapidated motor maintenance building adjacent to the cramped headquarters eventually was turned into the crime laboratory and other needed offices.

I was painting our ceiling at home on a Saturday when Rosemary said there was a Mr. Goldstein on the phone. This man I never heard of told me that I would be off that day and the next, and then I was to begin work in the superintendent's office for a temporary assignment at 0900 hours [nine a.m.] Monday.

That morning, I shaved as close as a baby's bottom, put on my best uniform, and arrived for work half an hour early. I found myself sitting in an outer waiting room with another policeman who was all spiffed up.

"I wonder what's up," Officer Hugh Heraty said to me after explaining that he had received a similar phone call.

At last Goldstein came out, introduced himself, and led us to his office, where he promptly bounced questions off us like a ping pong ball, and then he surprised us by explaining that our job would be to answer calls from the public. That didn't seem like much of an assignment, but I believed that I could always transfer back to a felony car. I decided to wait and see, and that maybe the work would be more interesting than it sounded.

The impressive superintendent's office occupied the entire fourth floor. Goldstein introduced us to everyone there at the time, including four consultants from the International

Association of Chiefs of Police, the renowned IACP. Introduced to everyone, that is, except Wilson himself. That struck us as odd.

Then we noticed something else strange. We were there to answer phones, right? Then why were two other officers directly behind our new desks also picking up phones?

We took our places in another spot out of the way and began answering calls. All kinds of calls. One irate woman said, "I want to talk to the superintendent about outlawing Bingo," the virtual eighth sacrament at a lot of parishes.

"I'm sorry, ma'am, the superintendent is in a meeting right now, but perhaps I can help you," I said, and then my ears were blasted with the vilest vulgarities.

Usually Hubie and I promised to relay their concerns to the superintendent, but we never did, and we weren't supposed to. Part of our job was to make sure O.W. wasn't pestered by cranks. Sometimes Hubie circled a finger around his temple to let me know he was listening to a weirdo, and a short time later I'd be the one circling the finger. Every now and then we'd see Goldstein write things down in a small notebook and smile. Then, on that first day, he told us to go home at 3:30 p.m., two hours early.

On Tuesday, Goldstein conducted private interviews with each of us for about two hours. He asked me everything from details of my police assignments to my family life.

At lunch, Hubie made an astute observation. "Something's up, but I don't know what it is."

We decided to buy a couple of tailored suits from the uniform store just around the corner on Wabash. Ours was just a temporary assignment, but we wanted to make a better impression than anyone else assigned to the superintendent's office.

After lunch we resumed out jobs of lying to the good citizens of Chicago. Since most never called back, we assumed they were happy at getting something off their chests and so we probably were doing a service after all. The officers behind us let us have access to their "Strange Book," an alphabetized list of frequent callers with odd requests, who had long stories to tell, or who made veiled threats.

On Wednesday and Thursday of our week at the phones, we were assigned to various unrelated projects, but it was all just busy work. Then it dawned on us that we were being analyzed and evaluated. Since these odd jobs did not relate to police work, Goldstein must have been deciding whether we had any gray matter between our ears. All he said, though, and with a grin, was how presentable we looked.

Little did we know that Wilson was testing the life skills of a number of young officers whose names had been drawn from Goldstein's IQ list, which he had obtained from the Personnel Division. Another criterion was that the chosen officers would have to reside reasonably close to where the superintendent had recently purchased a home.

Then, on Friday of that week, Goldstein, looking pleased about something, led us to the inner sanctum—the private office of the superintendent. There, sitting at a large desk, was Wilson himself. His dour face, heavy jowls, and droopy eyes gave him the look of an aging bloodhound. Despite the bags under his eyes, his pale skin was drawn tightly over his forehead and chin. Under that no-nonsense attitude of his, we were to discover a Norwegian impishness.

He reached across his desk and gave me a firm handshake, saying "Nice to meet you, Jaaahn!"

Then he shook Hubie's hand and sat. For fifteen minutes he told us—in his way of pausing between phrases—that he had surrounded himself with people of the best credentials and, with their help, he intended to make the department the greatest in the world. Then he approached the subject of why we had been under scrutiny for the past week.

"I inherited the chauffer/bodyguards that I now have from former Commissioner Timothy O'Connor ... and quite frankly ... I don't like them ... or their personal habits. I gave Herman Goldstein an assignment—find me two ... young ... capable officers to replace the drivers I now have, and ... seated before me are two men ... who I sincerely hope ... will accept the positions of chauffeurs ... and bodyguards for me."

We both said we would be honored, but "baffled" would

have been a more honest word. Then the superintendent, bearing a broad smile, introduced us to his aide, Colonel Minor K. Wilson, a British friend of his who was of no relation.

O.W. permitted Hubie and me to agree on our schedules, but he made a declaration before we made up our minds.

"I don't care if you choose … two days off and two days on … or five days off and five days on … as long as I have one of you … every day of the week."

We immediately settled on two days on and two days off, for no particular reason, but we also realized that those days could run from early morning to early morning. We knew that the superintendent was not only working long days in his official capacity, but he was obligated to attend wakes, parties, and other functions suggested by the mayor. The superintendent had us flip a coin to see who would start first, and Hubie lost. That gave me four days in a row to finish painting my home, and do a lot of thinking.

On my first day as Wilson's driver, I got snarled in traffic in the less than two mile drive from police headquarters at 11th and State to his appointment at City Hall. On my next day, since I wouldn't be needed for a few hours after taking Wilson to work, I timed a test run using a longer way—Wacker Drive. The route didn't make sense, except that it took half the time.

The next time Wilson had a City Hall appointment came a few days later. I didn't let him know about my route discovery. Imagine his confusion when the shiny black Cadillac dipped under street traffic to the shadowy caverns beneath the city usually used for heavy trucks. "Jaaahn, do you know that we have … a scheduled meeting at City Hall?"

"Yes, sir, and I think that you … will find this route to be … time-saving with less traffic." *Holy smokes*, I thought, *I'm starting to talk like him!*

He was impressed that I was correct about the route.

As Wilson's driver and confidant, I learned that exceptional people like him were not merely qualified. They were dreamers and visionaries. Chicago sorely needed reform, and Wilson's hope was to change an entire police department. What had been idealistic goals a year before were becoming a step-by-step reality. I was thrilled at being, literally, in the front seat at the creation.

Some of his changes may nowadays appear to have been misguided—such as ending most foot patrols in favor of mobilization—but they were what the city needed then.

Most of the officers I knew disliked Wilson, and they asked how I could be working for an outsider who was "ruining the department." That is, he was making them work harder and keeping them honest. "Wait and see," I said. "You'll learn to like him."

Not everyone did. He was hated by many, including aldermen of wards where district stations were being merged into others for consolidation purposes. Some officers conducted daily picketing, and the president of the Chicago Patrolman's Association went on television to denounce O.W. Wilson and his regime—making a fool of himself. On one drive heading home, I asked Wilson how he coped with criticism every day while directing so many changes.

"Absolutely no problem, Jaaahn," he responded while reading his newspaper in the back seat. Nothing bothered the man, absolutely nothing, as far as I could detect. Although drawn from California, Wilson was genuinely interested in the city and would punctuate our drives with questions regarding buildings, the lakefront, or anything that struck his curiosity.

"Jaaahn, is that a cathedral?"

"No, sir, that is the Medinah Temple—a convention center, and it's sometimes used to host the circus."

He even asked for suggestions on police matters and wanted to know the feelings of the patrol officers in order to gauge the morale of the department. I tried to give him straight answers, even though some were not to his liking. I was pleased to learn that he adopted a few of my ideas regarding the elimination of certain forms and filing unnecessary follow-up reports.

Once at a luncheon, the taxicab drivers' union leader, Joey Glimco, was overly eager to be photographed with the superintendent. Wilson saw no harm in that, not knowing Glimco's reputation. I drew Wilson aside and told him that Glimco was not a man of good character and that it would be unwise to have his photograph taken with him. In a diplomatic way, Wilson explained to Glimco and the photographers that he would rather not have his picture taken that day, and I received glares from quite a few people.

There was certainly no question about his integrity. One day, at his request, I brought him a box from a hot dog stand at Milwaukee and Central Avenues. I handed him the hot dogs and the ten dollar bill he had given me and explained that the owner refused to take money from a uniformed policeman, even after I insisted. The next day, I received a fifteen minute lecture.

"Jaaahn," Wilson started, "whenever a police officer receives something for nothing, he then becomes ... obligated to the person or business." Yet his fatherly tone made his remark seem like words of wisdom rather than a dressing-down. He proved that he meant what he said. Every Christmas, he sent letters to merchants asking them not to give gifts to him or any police officer. He never again sent me to purchase hot dogs.

For a while, O.W. made appearances at station roll-calls, and naturally Hubie or I would be present when he made his presentations throughout the city. The officers were invited to say what they thought about the changes, with no fear of being disciplined or other repercussions. Instead of constructive opinions, all Wilson heard was bad-mouthing from the troublemakers that were always in every district. I suggested to O.W., to improve morale, that these sessions be scheduled weekly in his office with a selection of officers from each district. We decided to choose officers from Goldstein's IQ list and, as a result, the meetings were well-received, relaxed, and instructive. The chosen officers would offer their suggestions or complaints, have coffee and doughnuts in Wilson's impressive office, and then go back to their districts and spread the word. Morale improved!

After some time Wilson became tired of bobbing up and down in acknowledgment whenever people recognized him, which was quite often by then, so he asked me whether there were any nice restaurants reasonably near his home that had some semblance of privacy. I suggested one in the suburb of Niles that I had been to once while I was working in the 33rd District. The restaurant had good food, and I thought the atmosphere would be to O.W.'s liking. I dropped him and his wife off there, went home, and then picked them up about two hours later. They both said they liked the food and the restaurant, but the owner had refused to take their money! This was miles from the city, and the owner could not possibly expect any favors in return. I didn't respond to Wilson's hushed statement, but I thought to myself that perhaps I should have asked around before I made the recommendation.

It wasn't long before a newspaper began to dog the heels of Wilson's administrative assistant, suggesting that his trips to Rush Street night spots made him look like a bagman for police officials on the take. Wilson shrugged off the constant questions posed by reporters and assured them that his assistant was merely gathering information.

"You can't find thieves in a church," he said, which became a famous quote.

As I was driving Wilson somewhere months later, when everyone had forgotten the newspaper hints, he asked me, as if in passing, whether I remembered the nice restaurant in Niles.

"Yes, sir, I do," I answered, and I named the restaurant.

"Do you know ... that Marshall Caifano hangs out in that place ... along with other notorious hoodlums?"

I almost slammed on the brakes, but instead I was fast with an answer.

"Superintendent, believe me," I choked, my throat dry, "if I knew Caifano or other Outfit people hung out in there, I never would have suggested the place. How did you learn about him?"

"A day after we ate there ... I was informed that the restaurant was under a stakeout ... and that *this* car was observed there. Deputy Superintendent Morris insinuated ... that you may have intentionally recommended that restaurant for questionable reasons." My heart nearly stopped. He added in his fatherly way, "Jaaahn, if I thought ... that you had any knowledge that unsavory characters ... patronized a restaurant that you intentionally suggested, you ... would not be driving this car right now."

This wasn't the first time some idiot had suggested I might

have mob connections just because of my Italian name, and it certainly wouldn't be the last. But this time it was made by a high-ranking police officer—the former head of "Scotland Yard," and who was elevated back to a high position in the department—against the wishes of the mayor! The people who usually made such snide remarks and innuendoes never thought twice when Italians became judges, business leaders, baseball heroes, mayors, movie stars, and just good, decent folks. I stewed over Morris' remarks and later, as you will see, let him know how I felt when I met him face to face.

Hubie and I worked out of the fourth floor of police headquarters, but our real office was the gleaming Cadillac. We decided to make it the best police car we could, and half the fun was not informing our boss.

Hubie had the men of the motor maintenance division put in behind-the-grill flashing lights with switches hidden under the dashboard. Then I went in and had a new type of double-winged siren installed. I could hardly wait until we sprang our surprise, and it didn't take long.

Wilson's wife was such an old-fashioned woman that she refused to go anywhere by plane and hated being in a fast automobile. I was the only driver that she permitted on the expressways or the portion of Lake Shore Drive that Chicagoans fondly called the Outer Drive.

That March, a tornado ripped through the South Side, and Wilson and I learned about it while I was driving home after a long day at headquarters. Wilson sent me home to have dinner that evening and told me to return to his house at a specific time to pick up him and his wife in order to survey the damage. Upon arriving at the devastated area, I decided that was the time to impress the pants off my boss.

I flipped on one hidden switch and a flashing blue light went on. Then I hit another switch and the horn became an extra loud siren. The officers working around the rubble and the clutter of fallen tree limbs instantly realized that this was the superintendent's official car, even if they had never seen it before. O.W. was pleased to see the barricades removed and the officers saluting him like a general.

On the way home, taking the Drive as waves died along the beach, we saw two cars weaving in and out of their lanes, playing games. I hung back, hoping that they would just go away or speed father ahead, but a hunch made me turn on the hidden police radio to warm it up. The young drivers took the off-rampat Peterson, the same one I took to drive the Wilsons home.

At the first stop light, we found ourselves behind the two cars and saw the guys inside shaking hands through rolled-down windows. Then they recklessly peeled rubber in a drag race.

I already had recorded their license plate numbers but was reluctant to play traffic cop, or request permission from O.W., because the timid Mrs. Wilson was in the car.

"Jaaahn," O.W. said, surprising me, "get them."

For the second time that night, I activated the siren and flashing lights. I called for assistance while gunning the motor past ninety miles an hour. The first car pulled over immediately, but I decided to get the second one because that driver was trying to outrun us. When he gave up and pulled over, I walked over to the driver and said, "Guess what, you mope, that's the superintendent's car that's been chasing you."

The clean cut teenager lowered his head and mumbled, "Holy shit."

I requested only a single squad to write a traffic citation, but somehow suspected that every officer and his brother would respond to any call from the superintendent. My fears of overkill were soon realized as police vehicles swarmed around us from the 33rd and 17th Districts, and even the suburbs of Skokie and Lincolnwood.

"Just write him a ticket going sixty (miles per hour) in a thirty," I insisted, although several officers were strongly suggesting that the young man in the expensive car be charged with everything possible, including eluding the police, reckless driving, and drag racing.

"Just sixty in a thirty," I repeated, wishing for the first time that I still had my ticket book from the 33rd District.

Wilson didn't say anything that night, but he discussed it

the next morning while on his way to headquarters. He said he thought I handled the situation well, but added with a laugh, "We sure scared the hell out of my wife!" After I drove for perhaps a minute longer, Wilson added, "Jaaahn, that was the most fun I've had since I've been in Chicago."

We both got a surprise when we walked into the office and the reporters were waiting to interview us about the late night incident. The high speed chase had made the front pages of the newspapers, and details would be heard on the radio and TV for the next two days.

Once again I learned a lesson—O.W. was so newsworthy that the media would be all over me if I ever slipped up.

The full story did not come out until much later at a party, when Wilson, pleasantly tipsy, told the guests that his wife "peed in her pants because of the excitement."

4

WINNING A BADGE

My weekdays as chauffeur/bodyguard were especially long when O.W. was the toastmaster for an officer or a staff member who was leaving or being reassigned. The superintendent frequently became soused, meaning that Hubie and I sometimes attended the parties on our days off so the two of us could walk him up the stairs to his home. Ruth would meet us at the doorway and say she'd take care of him. She had a lot of practice.

I dreaded driving Wilson home some days when he would tell me to pull over and buy him a bottle of bourbon. Mainly I was bothered by the idea that I was buying liquor while in uniform and with the Caddy parked outside. I was always concerned that some newspaper reporter might be tipped off. Chicago didn't need another scandal, even a minor one.

Months later I drove Wilson and his wife, along with Colonel Wilson—the British friend of no relation—and his wife, to Washington, D.C. for a police chiefs convention. Wilson asked me to accompany the others for dinner at our hotel when we stopped in Columbus. At first I declined, knowing I would be the odd person joining two couples, but O.W. insisted. I ordered a Coke when the waitress took the cocktail order.

"Jaaahn," O.W. said, "we would like you to join us … in a cocktail for the … various toasts we have to make … and you will have no excuse … not to. You will not … be driving tonight, and we … will all get a good night's sleep … before we continue our journey … in the morning."

In order to give everyone a little jolt, I looked up at the waitress and said, "I'll have a vodka martini on the rocks, with an olive and a twist." I kept a straight face and then gazed at the menu, noting from the corner of my eyes a smile on everyone's face.

Fall colors surrounded us as we neared Washington, but Minor K. Wilson, the British gentleman, was more intent on doing crossword puzzles. He needed four letters for the location of the Taj Mahal, and "India" was five letters. The location just happened to be one of the things that stuck in my mind from reading it somewhere, and I had to bite my lip not to blurt out the name, and hoped someone would ask me. After ten minutes of silence between the two couples, O.W. asked whether I might know the answer.

Like Wilson, I paused for a few moments before answering, "Yes, sir, the Taj Mahal is in Agra." Then there was silence.

Colonel Wilson was not one to speak his mind right away, and he held off expressing his thoughts all the time we were in the capital, but he had made a note of me, as you will see.

I loved all the free time I had to roam the white buildings and learn the streets as part of my job, anticipating that I might be called upon to drive someone someplace. It was distressing when I repeatedly had to pry O.W. from party bars at the hotel. He was having a good time, but I saw that some of his old-time and new-found friends were providing him with extra drinks and making fun of his imbibing behind his back.

"Not now, I'm having too much fun, Jaaahn," he said as I guided him away at the request of his wife.

Once we were back in Chicago, Minor Wilson called me into his office and asked me in his British accent how I knew about Agra. "My hobby is reading encyclopedias," I answered as a joke. Some people would bite, just as you could tell a fish was about to swallow the bait.

Impressed, Minor said, "And Hubie told me that you have never been beaten in a chess game, is that true?"

"Yes, sir, that's true," I replied. I saw no need to add that, as Hubie knew, I had never played chess in my life. Then I excused myself and pretended I had an assignment so I could leave his office before I burst out laughing.

Within a month, O.W. announced that there would be a detective's examination in February 1961, and he asked Hubie and me to start studying for it. I was ready to move up, really ready, but mentioned out of courtesy to O.W. that I would like to stay on as his driver.

"Jaaahn," he said, "you *will* take the examination."

Not only did Hubie and I study whenever we had free time, we studied on weekends when we were off and made a competition out of it. We had always been like partners—we confided in one another, helped each other whenever necessary, and played little practical jokes on each other—and we most certainly did not want one of us to be promoted while leaving the other behind.

Unlike exams before Wilson's reforms, this one was super-secret. Well over five thousand officers took the test in high school classrooms across the city. The questions for the four hour test were as carefully guarded as the original Declaration of Independence, and the four hour exam was monitored by high-ranking supervisory personnel. We were even fingerprinted before the test to make sure no one was represented by a brainy stand-in, and the exam papers were fingerprinted at the time of grading. This was a test that would soon be labeled "the O.W. Exam."

The questions were so tough that some officers looked them over and walked out without putting a mark on the page. A few years before, such officers would have won promotions through their aldermen and ward committeemen. The rest of us toughed it out and hoped for the best as we stood at the test station just outside the classroom while high school teachers graded the papers, monitored by the supervisory personnel. Unlike any other test given by the department, nothing else was factored into the score, such as personal interviews, evaluation marks, or seniority.

The highest citywide score was 114 points out of a possible (and impossible) 133. I scored 92 and felt great, and Hubie topped me with 94. As I told him later, he got those extra points just to show off. Our passing made the front pages—again, simply because O.W. continued to be newsworthy and he would soon lose both of his hand-picked chauffeurs.

In mid-spring, O.W. threw one of his renowned "departure parties" for us. As toastmaster, the superintendent, as usual, was full of liquor and accolades. He mentioned many detailed accounts of the habits of Hubie and Jaaahn and that he regretted losing two "speed demons." Wilson concluded the speech by fondly congratulating us on posting within the first hundred of the five thousand officers who took the exam.

The two of us went through a one month detective training course, but frankly, what you really need to know can never be taught. We were not fully aware of it, but we were in the first batch of a new breed of detectives—chosen on merit and determined, as a group, to abide by standards that all too often had been shrugged off. We would often be in conflict with the detectives who used the old-school ways of threats and the third degree, but we found that the criminals were more open to us because they trusted us. We also learned that, for public safety, the old ways sometimes *had* to be used. Eventually the older detectives learned from the new, just as the new learned some practical skills from them.

The one hundred dollars more a month as a detective really came in handy. I was already the father of two young girls. A few weeks after attending detective school, Rosemary and I had our third child, a boy. Somehow the Wilsons found out about it and showed up at our door with a silver rattle as a gift for our new son. The Wilsons were low-profiled and generous, judging from their previous visits to our home bearing gifts for our little girls, along with hand-made wreaths of pine cones and evergreen cuttings from the farm of O.W.'s sister near Peoria.

To this day, I cannot tell when my admiration for him as a superintendent left and my affection for him as a friend began. In time, I came to realize that working with O.W. would alter my entire career. To me, he was the most capable, educated administrator in the history of the department. Having served at his elbow for well over a year, I was never afterward intimidated by any supervisor.

When Wilson reorganized the detective division, he did away

with having district officers work in plainclothes without detective training. He established plainclothes tactical teams for the districts and divided detective work into specific fields such as burglary, robbery, homicide/sex, and general assignments, with the goal of making specialists of the newly promoted detectives. Once again, he was criticized for changing something that had been in place for so many years, but the men gradually accepted the new specialty assignments. In time it proved to be well-received.

A few months after I was assigned to the Northwest Side Burglary Unit, I received a call from my friend from the 33rd, Bill Duffy. Things had changed quickly for him in the two years from when I met him—he had been promoted to sergeant, lieutenant, captain, and then head of the prestigious Intelligence Unit—perhaps the most rapid advancement ever. He was one of those people you remember long after you first meet—in his late forties, talkative, weighing over two hundred pounds, with red hair parted down the middle like a bartender of a bygone age.

Duffy loved to talk. If you asked him what time it was, he just might explain how to build a watch. He decided to bring in officers that he personally had confidence in, assuring us that service in his unit would enhance our careers and allow us to spend more time with our families. I had no reservations about saying yes and considered it a compliment that he asked me to be a part of the intelligence division, but I thought there was something Duffy might not have considered.

"Bill," I began, "it sounds great, but some of the other guys are going to think that since I'm Italian I might—"

He interrupted me at the right time. "John, do not even consider what they may think. What they think about you, and what you think about them, has nothing to do with your job. All of the men I've picked have merited my trust."

The Intelligence Unit and the newly formed Investigations Division (which later evolved into the Internal Affairs Division) were set up in a former park district field house in the South Side's Washington Park. The old building later became the DuSable Museum of African American History. At the time I started, in January 1962, the place was surrounded by bare trees and the bleakness of winter. Making it worse at the inception was that many officers thought the units sharing the building were the same, and that therefore my job was to spy on them, which wasn't true at all.

James Zarnow and I were assigned to make record checks and background investigations on businesses and people suspected of shady dealings. Zarnow was a good cop straight from *Dragnet* and not very communicative. In fact, having a mixture of patrolmen and detectives assigned to the same unit kept all over conversations brief and to the point. The unit also had more than its share of backbiters, from supervisors on down, all trying to make points with the boss. I know for a fact that two of the investigators told Duffy that I must be supplying confidential information to the mob, just because my name ended in a vowel. These two officers happened to be detested by everyone in the unit, so that did not particularly bother me. Besides, Duffy knew better.

The captain, we soon learned, worked in mysterious ways. During the weeding out period, he sometimes assigned the same case to two or three squads but arranged for them to work at alternate times so none of them knew about the others. Some of the reports turned in by the loafers were complete fabrications, which was obvious when Duffy compared all of the submitted reports.

One of the better supervisors in the unit was Sergeant Don Lappe. Rumor had it that he came from a rich banking family, but he just liked police work more than reading the *Wall Street Journal*. He certainly seemed to keep himself busy all the time. Lappe assigned me and Officer Mike Carone, a good friend from my days at the 33rd District, to investigate "policy" and the "numbers racket."

"I have to let you know, sergeant, I know absolutely nothing about that stuff," I said.

"That's okay, you will," Lappe assured me. "Everything will be fine. So snap to it, get busy, get started, let's go. Start your assignment and report to me once in a while."

Oh well, I thought. It was the Intelligence Unit.

When I caught up with Mike, my second partner in two

weeks, I asked him if he knew about "policy" or "numbers." Mike—a friendly guy who always laughed and fooled around—just shook his head.

"How about if we take a ride and get some coffee," I suggested. "I want to think this thing over, and we should talk about it."

What I really wanted was to ask Captain Duffy whether or not I should go back to the Burglary Unit, which was something I understood. But ignorance about an assignment is a bad basis for any transfer request.

"Hey," I said to Carone over coffee, "since neither of us knows anything, let's start reaching out to people who do and see what we come up with."

The numbers game was an illegal lottery involving printed sheets. We visited a friend of mine, Mario, a printer who was a police officer working in the reproduction and graphic arts office at headquarters. Smoking a pipe and wearing an ink-stained apron, Mario told us more than anyone needed to know, including the fact that officers historically went in the wrong direction in cracking down on the rackets.

Mario was just a lowly cop and printer, but he was smarter than all the brass who ever tried to shut down the illegal lotteries. He said white officers especially had trouble making headway in such investigations in the solidly black neighborhoods of the South Side, where the rackets thrived. As a result, police merely arrested the policy runners and never came close to the top echelon. That was like stopping a flood with a mop.

He explained that the game involved pre-printed slips that were sold in paper books listing a variety of numbers, and the winners were selected by spinning a wheel. The operators used a special kind of press that numbered backwards, and the device used on the printing press was called a "numbering machine." Mario planted a seed by telling us that printing presses, and especially numbering machines, break down often when used continuously, and there were only one or two businesses in Chicago capable of fixing them.

We went to the yellow pages book, let our fingers do the walking, and located one of those companies in the Loop. We visited the business and interviewed the owner, *Mr. Gallager, who was very cooperative and helped us learn the names of firms that printed the list books. He also told us he was expecting a backwards-counting machine to come in for repairs from Detroit, and that he had serviced and returned one to a Chicago firm just a week ago.

The next day, we went to see Captain Purtell, the commander of the document section at headquarters—a really nice guy.

"As soon as you learn that Mr. Gallager has received those numbering machines in need of repair, bring them to me," he said in the formal way police adopt after years of writing reports. "I will be able to notch certain numbers on the machines that will positively identify them as gambling paraphernalia when the list books hit the streets. Are you specifically assigned to the investigation?"

"Absolutely," I responded. "Sergeant Lappe assigned us."

"Well, for many years the department has been going about it the wrong way," he said, echoing Mario's words. "But you could be headed in the right direction."

We then learned from a company not far from headquarters that a north suburban printer had an unusual order—20,000 list books, fifty sets to a book, and the pages printed in triplicate but without any company imprint. In addition, the material was to be shipped in plain cardboard boxes. The man who placed the order came in an unmarked truck and paid cash. The printing company owner, *Mr. Haughton, admitted the transaction was "very mysterious."

We knew we were getting closer to the bosses when we interviewed a *Mr. Bentley, owner of a printing and paper manufacturing company. He was cooperative—but nervous— as he answered our questions. We assured him our interview would be strictly confidential, but he looked as if he knew we were lying and that everything he said would be written in our reports.

After we had enough preliminary information to compile a report on the numbers operations, we turned our attention to policy. The name came from the observation that many poor people wagered what should have been their insurance money. Policy slips were similar to adding machine paper, but they are wider and thicker, almost like construction paper. We obtained samples that had been discarded on the streets of the South Side, and then went around to printing companies. Again, officials at the companies gave us the names of firms that continuously placed large orders for that kind of distinctive paper. The cooperation we received was unbelievable, as if the companies genuinely wanted to disassociate themselves from illegal activity, even if it meant losing business, or for reasons that we were too naive to assume.

We submitted a thirty-eight page preliminary report to Sergeant Lappe. Carone and I ridiculously imagined that we had provided enough information to begin making arrests, and headlines flashed in our minds. We thought we might even get a pat on the back. Lappe perused our report as we stood in anticipation, but he didn't say a word. Carone and I looked at each other. What was wrong? Why no questions? Then Lappe just walked away. This was indeed the Intelligence Division.

The next day Sergeant Lappe told us that we were being reassigned.

"What about Captain Purtell, what about the numbering machines?" I asked, and received no answer.

"Stick around, get the car washed, have lunch, waste a couple of hours," he said in rapid fire speech. "See you at three o'clock."

All sorts of questions rushed through our heads. To begin with, why had two inexperienced men been assigned to a major investigation out of their field? Carone had something to say but he held back, so I said it for him.

"Maybe we put too much in the report that they didn't expect us to find out." It definitely seemed that something dirty was going on.

We returned at three, and Lappe had us do insignificant things with a week to finish them. I thought they were burying the investigation.

Later, while working alone, I was assigned to do some work concerning Manny Skar, the crime syndicate hanger-on who had opened the Sahara Inn, a Las Vegas-style show lounge near

O'Hare Airport. A very pretty "harem girl" waitress named Rose Martino, whom Skar had fired because of a quarrel three weeks before, was found dead in her home in a new development in Schiller Park.

Sergeant Walsh told me that he would supervise the investigation on orders from the director. He said I should take three hundred dollars from the unit's contingency fund and rent an apartment in the same suburban complex in order to learn what I could. *Lordy, lordy,* I thought, *this is the kind of police work that was right up my alley.*

I decided to establish a fictitious identity by using my membership card from Teamsters Local 703 and told my dad to claim, if anyone called to check up on me, that I was still working at his South Water Market cartage company. The department gave me an undercover blue Pontiac with the police radio in the glove compartment, and from then on, I was on my own.

For research purposes I drove to the morgue and talked to the chief pathologist, *Dr. Wagner. He told me that not all of the toxicological tests were in but that he had no doubt the young woman had died from an overdose of barbiturate sleeping pills. "Probably a suicide," he mused. I wondered out loud about the funeral arrangements, and the doctor gave them to me off the top of his head. Why would a chief pathologist know details of the funeral home and the time of the wake? But then, maybe I was becoming knee-jerk suspicious.

At the Schiller Park police station, I routinely identified myself and asked to see the police reports. Suburbs almost always opened their files to us and were glad to help out. This time, though, the officers flatly refused, and they said no again when my sergeant made inquiries on his own. I was beginning to feel the stonewalling that accompanied anything even remotely connected to the mob.

I parked in the lot of the beautifully landscaped Howard Gardens subdivision in the northwestern suburbs, and the grounds gave me a feeling of unreality. The carefully trimmed lawn was covered with beautiful young women tanning themselves. I had a smile on my face as I opened the door of the renting agent, all prepared to use my cover identity to look at an apartment and sign a lease. As soon as I entered, I saw a man I knew casually.

"Hey, John, how the hell are you?" Bill Smith asked. He was a friend from a police hangout (not a cop), but I'd lost track of him. Now he rented out apartments. "I just asked Jimmy Jack about you the other night and wanted to know how you were, and he told me you were transferred to the Intelligence Unit. Congratulations!"

I felt as if I'd ventured outside in my pajamas, slightly ridiculous and not quite knowing what to do, I decided to wing it with honesty.

"Bill," I said, "I'm not going to bullshit you. I'm here about the Martino girl, and maybe you can help me."

"Sure," he replied. "I'm the one who found the body."

As I sat in his office, he gave me everything an investigator could hope for except a reason she would want to kill herself or someone might want to murder her. "Neighbors told me they hadn't seen Rose in a couple of days, you know how it is. Neighbors watching out for neighbors. She was a good-looking kid, usually seen going in and out a lot. I knocked and found the kitchen door was unlocked. I opened the door and called out, but I didn't get an answer. I saw a burner was on and a frying pan was on the floor, so I knew something was wrong. The wall was spattered with food, and there was a bowl on the floor with some pancake batter in it. As I walked a little further in, I saw Rose on the living room floor, dead for awhile, dressed in a muumuu. The dress, or robe, or whatever you call it, had some batter on it, by the shoulder. Oh, I almost forgot the most important thing—her dog was outside. Why would that be? She always locked her door, always, even after letting her dog out, but this time it was open. No blood or anything, and nobody around here knows what happened, because I already asked around."

"Anything else unusual?"

"The TV. It was still on, on the upper level, and it was pretty loud."

By now, I was familiar with suicides, and this definitely didn't sound like one. No suicide note was found, and it was apparent that the Martino girl was in the process of fixing breakfast when she was killed.

That day and the next, Bill showed me around and introduced me as a detective to people who lived in the complex, most of whom were stewardesses. He also introduced me to former boxing promoter Bernie Glickman, a low level mob figure. Glickman was a frequent gin player who bragged about his association with syndicate boss Tony Accardo.

"Hey," Glickman told me, "I rented Rose the apartment myself. Bill had to go someplace when she walked into the office, and she told me that she worked at the Sahara for Manny Skar. I didn't want to rent the place to her because we been tryin' to get all the stews (O'Hare Airport stewardesses), but she was attractive, spoke real good, and she told me she had a real good job. So I says to myself, go ahead and rent it to her." He then added, "Hey, John, do you play gin? How about we play a few games just to see how good you are?"

I thought, *why not?* As we played, Glickman said, "I know you're a copper, but that's your job. Do it good! Do you know the Martino girl was close to *Peter Franklin? He owns a hot dog stand but drives a Lincoln Continental, so something's not on the up and up, you know what I mean? He came here the other night wanting to break the coroner's seal and get into the flat. Bill wouldn't let him in. Franklin thinks he's a tough motherfucker. If only he knew the people I know, John, he'd shit in his pants. They'd make mincemeat out of him."

"What do you think?" I asked, since Glickman seemed to be telling the truth. "Do you think she was murdered?"

"She didn't seem down, you know what I mean? Not to me she didn't, and I saw her practically every day. But who might have done it and why—I was hoping you could tell me. If you find out, be sure to let me know."

Glickman was my first mob acquaintance, and I was surprised at how pleasant and helpful he was. I met my supervisor every day to go over the bits and pieces I'd found out, without leasing an apartment, and he must have thought the department at last was gathering evidence in a mobster case, or at least developing enough information to fill out a lengthy report. Lengthy reports, I would soon learn, were the most important things that the Intelligence Unit personnel do.

However, a completely different Bernie Glickman testified at the inquest.

I was shocked when he said, "Miss Martino was in low spirits and expressed a desire not to live."

Even the phrasing sounded coached, and it was apparent that someone got to him since I talked to him last. Tony Accardo and perhaps other syndicate members were backers of the sprawling apartment complex. Maybe Rose learned too much about the people who hung around with Manny Skar and the former mayor of the suburb, who supposedly had a financial interest in Howard Gardens. Perhaps a lot of things.

The coroner's jury consisted of eight incompetent, sleepy old men who usually ruled the way the coroner's office wanted them to, so it came as no surprise that they returned a finding of suicide, regardless of the contradictions at the scene.

Afterward, I followed the coroner's investigators as they removed a seal on the door and went through Rose's duplex. Schiller Park police arrived minutes later and conducted their own search like vultures. We found the apartment just as Bill Smith had described it, with the floor spattered with pancake batter, but who knew what secrets and clues might be awaiting us? This was my first time working in tangent with suburban police. I had reason to be suspicious of them, since they included the two detectives who had refused to let me see the police reports. I should have followed them to see what they might be grabbing, but instead I made the mistake of trailing the coroner's men. They discovered a closet full of hanging sweaters, and each had a pocket with a hundred dollar bill in it. Was that payment for a favor, or just mad money? Then we heard a yelp from the officers on the lower level.

"We made a large seizure of narcotics," they told us as they quickly bagged the stash.

"Well, what is it?" I called to them as I rushed down the stairs with the coroner's investigators.

"This is our jurisdiction," they said, "and we're taking the narcotics to our station."

They left in a hurry carrying a brown paper evidence bag. I could see why Franklin, the hot dog stand owner, had been so interested in entering the flat before the police did—it was the narcotics, not the money.

The drugs turned out to be a cache of marijuana worth thousands of dollars. The seizure was enough for Sheriff Richard B. Ogilvie to reopen the Martino case, and he put his chief investigator, Richard Cain, in charge. No one knew at the time, though, that Cain, a former Chicago police officer with a dubious reputation, was a double-dealer. He was also working for the mob. His downfall came when he planted fake evidence on a man, along with proof-positive that he, himself, was mob-connected. Cain eventually was killed gangster style, gunned down in classic fashion by masked killers with shotguns at a Chicago restaurant. The syndicate knew how to kill, and it knew how to cover it up.

Maybe I shouldn't be wasting your time by describing an incomplete investigation, but there is something haunting about the death of beautiful Rose Marie Martino. This case could have been solved.

As for Glickman, he turned on the mob when they turned on him. Milwaukee Phil Alderisio, an Outfit hitman, tried to strangle Glickman over a boxing matter, while Glickman was serving again as a fight promoter. The FBI put Bernie under its protection as a cooperating witness in a probe into the proposed heavyweight match between Ernie Terrell and Cassius Clay, who of course became Mohammed Ali. From what I understand, Glickman taught a lot of FBI agents how to play gin before he died.

A short time after the Martino case, Captain Duffy called four of us in the intelligence division into his office to make some pretty startling disclosures— although he didn't start out that way. First he told us some of his wonderful stories of life on the streets. Then he gradually zeroed in on Frank Kenny and wanted him to know just who his partner really had been for the last couple of weeks. Looking more like an Irish barkeeper than a cop, Duffy sat on the edge of his desk and said, "Frank, you didn't know it but that guy had been under suspicion for months. We assigned the two of you to cases that were unrelated to intelligence work and ascertained that your partner was passing the results of your investigation to crime syndicate ties. Don't worry, he will be on the next transfer order and put back into uniform. I only regret that I have no authority to fire the son of a bitch. I apologize that he got into the Intelligence Unit in the first place, but I inherited him and a few others of questionable allegiance."

Then it was time for Duffy to surprise Carone and me.

"Mike and John, did you know that when you were assigned to policy and numbers, I also gave the assignment to *six* other teams? As a result of their investigation—or rather what they *called* an investigation—I can only assume that they have been on the take and probably still are. They're now out, and under investigation by Special Prosecutions."

Duffy added that our efforts weren't wasted after all. The FBI was waiting to trace list books that were run off the numbering machines that Captain Purtell had notched before they were put back on the printing machines. Hopefully, Duffy said, that would lead them "to the top echelon of the mob."

Carone and I looked at each other sheepishly for having doubts about the integrity of the unit and jumping to conclusions.

"I want you two to know that I consider you guys to be my special trustworthy people from the 33rd," Duffy said. "In my new assignment, I had to use you guys somewhat like undercover agents to learn the real truth about what was going on, so you can see why I couldn't tell you. Admit it, John, you probably had your doubts about us and wished you were back at Area Five Burglary, didn't you?"

He didn't wait for an answer that he already knew, but everyone else must have noticed the smirk on my face.

Now that our unit had been given its shakedown cruise, Duffy assigned all of us remaining to the newly formed Special Investigations Unit, headed by Sergeant Lou Sabella.

"By the way," Duffy told us, "there's a card game tonight at Sabella's house on the South Side, and I hope all of you can make it to celebrate the formation of the new squad. We'll have things to discuss, and who knows, maybe you'll get lucky."

Lucky with Duffy? He always won.

Duffy was a firm believer that friends could work together better than strangers, and before long so would I. Maybe that was the origin years later of the Three Musketeers of the Chicago Police Department—Jimmy Nolan, Paul Roppel, and me.

Over a game of poker at Sabella's house that night, with Lou's girlfriend constantly yelling and complaining about the smoke, Duffy told us that our relatively boring days were over and the fun was about to begin. We were going to learn surveillance techniques, including lock-picking and court-approved wiretapping.

"And that will only be the beginning," he said.

5

SPECIAL INVESTIGATIONS

The next day, Sergeant Sabella met us at Washington Park, drove us to breakfast, and then took us to a dilapidated warehouse. He unlocked the overhead door and had trouble pushing it up. We expected something ghostly to greet us but, instead, there were five nice looking autos of various makes and colors. They were nearly new and lacked hints that they were unmarked cop cars. The antennas and other special equipment were hidden so well we had to look for them.

"You will have to fight over who gets which one," Sabella said. "And here are your gas credit cards."

Although the Special Investigations Unit was new, it apparently had been in the planning stage for some time.

"One thing before I go," Sabella said. "The assignment of the squads and who will be designated for the responsibility of each vehicle will be your duty for today. Everyone will have his own squad, even though you will be working with partners. We will need the extra squads for doing details and surveillances to spread out the manpower. Is that understood?"

When no one had any questions, he left with a grin.

Val Ridge stepped in front of the rest of us to make something known from the start. Val, who had been Duffy's partner in the "Scotland Yard" unit and the 33rd District, where they had been dumped, was a character who seemed fresh from someone's overactive imagination. He was a robust man with thinning black and white hair, and he walked with a swagger as if his ample belly was pulling the rest of him along. As usual, he wore a vest and tweed sports coat so that he looked as if he enjoyed living a soft, comfortable life. What he seemed to like most about police work was the theatrics—lying, assuming different identities, and in general just fooling people.

"All of you men are young and skinny," Val said with an exaggeration of his Irish brogue, "and therefore I choose the biggest car."

That was all right with us—all of the cars looked great. We each ran to the ones we had our eyes on and gleefully discovered that there were two radios in the glove compartments. One was a regular police radio, and the other allowed car-to-car transmissions without going through other police channels.

We worked out codes for one another and thought Sergeant Sabella should be designated "Car One."

"Why Car One for him?" Mike Carone shouted out.

"Because Sabella's in charge," someone yelled back.

"Yeah," Carone added, "but look at my name—CAR ONE!" Then he smiles and said he was only kidding.

The next day there was a little thrill hearing Sabella saying, "Three-C [for Carone] and 4-D [for DiMaggio], this is Car One. I want you to meet me at North and Central in forty-five minutes."

"Ten-four," I answered.

At our rendezvous, Sabella just told us to go home and get some sleep because we would be on night detail that could last well into the morning. Before we left, he had us spin the dial of the FM part of our regular radios all the way to the left.

"Perfect," he said as we heard a slight humming sound.

"Perfect?" Carone asked. "We can't hear anything."

"You're not supposed to, but I think you will tonight. Bring a tape recorder and I'll meet you at eight o'clock at the corner of Maxwell and Halsted."

"All right, what will we hear?" I had to ask, knowing it wouldn't be Toscanini.

"Your FM has been de-tuned on that band. It is now on a special frequency that will pick up conversations from a specific mob guy's telephone. One we tapped. We have a wireless transmitter hooked up on a pole and that will work in conjunction with your radio, and that's all you need to know for now. Bring lunch and a couple of empty bottles, because you're probably not going to get out of your car."

When we gathered at the corner that night, Sabella made a test call from a business phone to the subject's house. Even though we were told in advance what would happen, we were amazed when we heard the phone ringing and Sabella's voice coming over our FM radio as he asked the man who answered if a certain person, using a made-up name, lived there. The target told him he had the wrong number.

Everything was working—what could go wrong?

Five minutes later, the sergeant jumped into our back seat and we told him we had heard him "loud and clear." Sabella stayed just a few minutes and left us again, not telling us where he was going. Then we heard our first call, and it came in crystal clear.

"Hello, Frank? This is Joe. I tried to reach you this afternoon, but your phone was busy for two hours."

"Yeah, Joe, that was my wife on the phone gabbing with her girlfriend. I gotta get her a separate line."

In a short time, Sabella sped toward us and slammed on the brakes as soon as he was beside us.

As Mike Carone rolled down the window, the sergeant said, "Get that car out of here, go home! I was sitting in a bar watching the state basketball championship *when I heard that call over the TV*! That means everyone within an area of three blocks will be able to monitor the calls this guy is receiving. Something is wrong with the transmitter. I already called for the take-down team. Get going, I'll explain later."

We were back at the Washington Park headquarters early the next morning, eager to learn the technical facts concerning our assignment. Sabella told us that the department had bought preset transmitters from a California firm for $350 each. The problem was that if the decibel setting was not precise, then the interception interfered with television waves. The radios were de-tuned, or set at a lower band frequency, in order that the general public would not be able to hear the tapped conversations. The transmitters, unless defective, would be set at the same decibel level.

That was the reason why Sabella, or any other supervisor, would leave during a wiretapping. They would go to a nearby business with a television set on, usually a tavern, to monitor the voice reception.

"Now everyone knows we were listening in," Carone said.

"They heard, but that doesn't mean they know," the sergeant replied. "The customers where I was thought it was some type of commercial." We laughed. "Yeah, I swear to God, they were looking at one another and saying it's gotta be some beer ad or something."

We returned to the same corner the next night, this time with a portable TV that plugged into the cigarette lighter. While the TV was on, we were relieved when our subject's voice stayed off the air. The "take-down" team removed the defective transmitter and the "put-up" team rewired a new one.

We could then hear Frank say over the FM radio that he thought his phone was tapped. We tensed, but Frank kept talking anyway, revealing a number of sensitive mob secrets. Experience would teach us that most of the crime figures being tapped would start out their conversations by saying, "I think my phone is tapped," and it was a sentence we became used to.

The tap was taken down after five days and was considered to be hugely successful.

Some of our transmitters were discovered by the telephone linemen and turned over to the FBI. We had a good relationship with the Bureau, though, and the agents always returned them to us because they were doing the same thing—sometimes on the same subject!

We often had more luck with bluff than technology, and learned a great deal from Val Ridge. He loved acting and as a result he could get anywhere he wanted. He collected business cards from dozens of doctors, lawyers, engineers, and consultants, and, when needed, passed them out as his and played the part. If we had to search a certain building without witnesses, Val used one of his best ploys to pose as a utilities inspector using a contraption he called a "gas leak detective device." We never asked whether the machine was real or if Val just put it together with spare hardware from the garage.

Whatever the thing was, it turned out to be the world's greatest door opener. Just tell a recalcitrant business owner that his place was about to blow sky high, and he would go out of his way to accommodate you by vacating the premises.

The men of our unit and six other investigators went to a specialized training course in a rented room at a South Side YMCA. Each morning for three weeks a professional locksmith came by to show us everything he knew. He was quite honest as he told us at the start that only about half the officers in his "class" ever got the hang of it, simply because certain individuals did not care to practice with the variety of locks that they were given to work on. He started out by permitting us to examine an array of locks he had cut in half in order to demonstrate their inner workings. I could hardly wait until I got home to show Rosemary how I could undo all the locks in our house, and that wasn't too smart because she then demanded they be replaced with high quality, high priced dead bolts.

Lock-picking became my hobby, and when I wasn't challenged by the complexity of the lock, I concentrated on speed.

On the afternoons of our three week course, an instructor from Illinois Bell, which became Ameritech, showed us the art of wiretapping until we could put up transmitters on our own by using the old system with terminals of X-boxes, or the color-coded wires being installed across the city.

We put our training to practical use on the day after school finished. My job was to open a door in a basement in order that Frank Kenny could hook up a transmitter. We wore gray washpants and linemen's belts to pass ourselves off as Bell workers. All they told us when they gave us the assignment was that "a bad guy" fresh from prison was living in the house, along with a German shepherd and a sawed-off shotgun for protection.

I felt during our training that I could have tackled the locks at Fort Knox, but I was somewhat nervous now that I was in the real world. I chose a large tension bar and a double diamond-head lockpick, my favorites. The lock clicked open in twenty seconds, just like on television. Then I held the flashlight as

Frank connected the transmitter into the terminal box while standing on the damp, dirt floor. We heard footsteps and creaking overhead. The beam of my flashlight shook a little, probably because the dirt under me moved.

If the ex-con heard us and came down, we were to pose as linemen and introduce him to Val, our "supervisor." The bad guy stayed upstairs, though, and we slipped out ten minutes after I'd started on the lock. We never learned, or wanted to learn, why the tap was set.

Something occurred in early 1963 that threatened my entire career. It started with a call from a friend about an undertaker named *Bradley, who was running for Chicago alderman, even though my friend and many other people believed that he actually lived in the suburbs and had only a mailing address in the city. Since there was no unit in the department that handled such things, I did a credit check on my own and made some requests within my team.

One week later, I was handed a package of documents proving that Bradley did live outside the city. Not thinking much about it, I submitted an official intelligence report to Sergeant Sabella, thinking I was being a good guy and reporting just one more law breaker.

The dirt hit the fan while I was home on vacation in February. Sabella, who was not an excitable man, was more than just wound up when he yammered into the phone, "You're in a lot of trouble! Deputy Superintendent Morris wants to talk to you!"

"Tell the deputy superintendent that I won't talk to him on the phone," I said. "If he feels that the matter is important, I'll drive to Washington Park and discuss it with him personally." I mulled over the situation as I drove halfway across the city and came to the conclusion that the "trouble" might concern the politician. There were true bosses, like O.W. Wilson, and there were idiots that protected their rears at all times.

Finally I was going to meet the brains of the less-than-successful former Scotland Yard unit, and I suspected I would not enjoy the encounter. Morris was capable and well-respected, but he was despised by the mayor. In this instance he most certainly didn't want to lose his prestigious assignment to city politics, and that meant he needed a fall guy. He must have recalled his dump and then resurrection to power during the initial regime of O.W.—at least that was what I was thinking as I arrived.

Sabella met me at the station front door, profusely swearing, and led me down a short corridor to an office with a big embossed sign:

DEPUTY SUPERINTENDENT

Morris was sitting behind his desk when I entered the office. He was a red-faced, white-haired man in his fifties, with a big, bulbous body.

He rose from his chair, glared at me, and pushed his fists on the table, gorilla-like.

"You're a dirty Dago!" he growled, and that was just for starters. "Who do you think you are, making an investigation you were not assigned to?" I just stood there calmly as he threw words at me. "You are a trouble-making son of a bitch, do you know that? That man, that highly respected man, reported that he was under investigation by the Intelligence Division when, in fact, he is not. It was just you, you slimeball!"

As the rant continued, I did some thinking. How could Bradley have learned about the investigation unless there was a security leak in this supposedly super-secret Intelligence Unit? Bradley must have complained, but to whom? Mayor Daley? Superintendent Wilson? Morris? Or Captain Duffy? I would never find out.

"You'll never work in this office again, DiMaggio. You are relieved of your duties."

His tirade over, Morris threw a glance at Sabella and said, "Get this guy out of my office and make up a report for him." When he saw that I was not moving, he asked, with a chainsaw edge to his words, "Do you have any questions, DiMaggio?"

"I don't have any questions, but I want you to know that I am not a dirty Dago, a son of a bitch, or a slimeball, nor do I consider myself to be trash. And with all due respect to your rank, I don't think you have to right to call me those names and I want you to know that I'm not afraid of you."

My memory tells me I spoke calmly, but my friends told me later that they heard me throughout the building.

"I know that I didn't do anything wrong," I continued. "You didn't give me the opportunity to explain."

"Get him out of here!" Morris yelled, growing redder. Sabella tugged at my arm.

Once we were in the hallway, I told Sabella I would type up my own report. I went to the typing desks and clattered away, trying to be as objective as possible. I noticed other unit personnel moving away from me. After I finished, I made Xerox copies of my report and handed the original to Sabella. The sergeant told me to go home and said, "Wait by the phone."

Before I could leave the building, an officer ran up to me and said, "Director Duffy wants to see you."

I walked dejectedly into the office of my friend, who told me, "I'm afraid I can't help you on this one, John. Morris just won't listen to anyone. You know, John, he's the man that made me, and I owe my allegiance to him." In other words, I was going to be ass-kicked but Duffy couldn't bring himself to say the words, and he certainly didn't want to hear my side of the story.

I understood. I probably would be transferred out of the Intelligence Unit and maybe even dumped into uniform and lose my detective rank. What really mattered to me was that a man was illegally running for alderman and no one was doing anything about it. I never could understand politics during my entire career.

Many days later, Sergeant Paul Quinn of the superintendent's office called to offer condolences. "How are you holding up?" he asked. He had been in the frying pan while I was working for O.W., and I suspected he knew how it felt.

"Okay," I said. "I didn't do anything wrong."

"Morris is in the superintendent's office right now about you. O.W.'s asking him all sorts of questions. I'll keep you posted."

Morris not only went to Wilson, but he had the Internal Investigations Division investigate me thoroughly. To the credit of the IID, knowing that Morris wanted a reason to break me, any reason, they concluded their work by stating that I had not violated any regulations. The officers who conducted the investigation mentioned that the Bradley incident should be *investigated further.*

Morris went berserk again.

The administration sergeant who had passed the Bradley documents on to me told me the following Monday that "officials" in the Intelligence Unit were considering giving me a three-day suspension and dumping me to patrol. I couldn't envision myself taking my uniform out of the closet. Because of special assignments and my work as Wilson's driver, I never saw much duty as a patrolman and would not mind street work, but there was a stigma attached to being brought down from detective, as well as a loss of pay.

I told the sergeant to notify everyone that if I lost my rank, I would contact reporters with whom I was friendly and tell them the political reason for my being dumped. The call was immediately terminated.

Three days later, I was again called and informed that a written reprimand would be placed in my personnel file and that I would be returned to the Northwest Side Burglary Unit. That was the best news I'd heard in two weeks. I'd be back in action without being demoted.

A few days after being reassigned to Area Five, I had to pick up O.W. Wilson in order to take him to his new condominium near Lincoln Park. I was absolutely quiet during the ride until Wilson broke the silence. "Jaaahn, how do you like the Intelligence Division?"

I was shocked and so confused by his remark that I had to wait a moment to think of an answer.

"Superintendent," I said with respect, "I was removed from the Intelligence Unit." Then I added, with an unintentional sarcasm, "I thought you knew."

He waited a few moments before posing the next question. "Was that because of that … incident … regarding the politician?"

"Yes, sir, it was."

"How can you be sure of that, Jaaahn?" His voice betrayed some doubts.

"Superintendent, I'm positive. I received an official Police Department written reprimand, even though I was exonerated by the IID, and I was transferred back to the Burglary Unit on a telephone order."

"Jaaahn, I gave Deputy Superintendent Joe Morris ... specific instructions ... that there would be no disciplinary action ... taken against you." Wilson told me that he personally had reviewed the reports and the entire case with both his aide, Minor K. Wilson, and the director of the IID, and they all agreed that there was no basis for a reprimand or any other type of disciplinary action.

Without any other words being spoken, I dropped off Wilson in his new neighborhood and then drove the Cadillac to the home of one of the new chauffeurs, who then drove me to my house. At around noon on Monday, Sergeant Quinn of the superintendent's office called and said Wilson was still chewing out Morris's ass for everyone to hear.

"I never saw O.W. so mad before," he said. "Everyone you used to work with have smiles on their faces."

A great weight was lifted from me when my reprimand was removed from my file, and especially when I learned that it was taken out in the presence of Morris while he was stewing in O.W.'s office.

I never had the occasion to run across Morris again, but when I learned that he passed away, I sent a large floral piece to the funeral parlor—with my name in big letters.

6

TOUGH GUYS

The 1960s were a watershed everywhere in America, and no more so than in the Chicago Police Department. We newcomers were working with officers of the old school like Frank Pape, whose robbery detail boasted of sixteen shootouts that resulted in the deaths of nine criminals. When Wilson instituted psychological testing, Pape refused to go along with it.

"There were these two young guys," he said years later, "and they started asking me how I got along with my wife and my mother, and I told them it was none of their business."

The new professionalism had come with a cost. Criminologists said the higher standards and laws like the Miranda decision were leading to an increase in police divorces and suicides across the country. Modern officers had to put up with more danger than ever because of increasingly violent gangs and drug trafficking. Because of civil rights concerns, they needed to do it showing less emotion. Not everyone can live day after day never letting your guard down. If officers didn't have the right support going into the job, they tended to crack, but the rewards of police work could make everything worthwhile.

A friend of mine called me at home one summer evening to say a woman had told him that a neighbor named Joyce was possibly being held against her will somewhere in the 3700 block of Windsor. My friend, a police officer, didn't quite believe it himself and apparently neither did the neighbor woman, who hadn't bothered to call the police station. Very often police officers routinely disregarded vague third-hand tips since they seldom amounted to anything.

I worked midnights at the old Area Five headquarters, and we usually had a little free time to conduct investigations, tails, or surveillances. Area Five was on top of the 14th District station in an aging, liver-colored brick building that was formerly a Chicago Boys Club. The place was so huge that we never used the third floor, a former gymnasium, although we were constantly being falsely accused of beating prisoners on that level.

When I went to work that night, I told Sergeant Jimmy Janda about the information I'd received.

"Is that all you have?" he asked.

My partner, Steve Pizzello, stepped in. "John," he said, "maybe you want us to start canvassing that neighborhood and find out if someone is being held hostage."

"Yeah, Steve, thanks," I said, with a dawning of the obvious. "You got the idea. We just can't let it drop."

I could see from both faces that they were against the idea, but they agreed we might as well look into it. In fact, Sergeant Janda, who was a detective in the same unit with us prior to his promotion, decided to ride along on our rounds that night, saying that if time permitted we could knock on a few doors and learn if a Joyce Someone live there.

We found no Joyce on the first night out. Rather than attempting to discourage me, Pizzello and Janda were intrigued by the possibility of a phantom woman, so we tried for two more nights in our spare time. At last, around 1:30 a.m., a woman in a second floor apartment told us that her next door neighbor was named Joyce. The woman claimed that, three or four days earlier, Joyce had gestured from the window directly across the way that she was being held against her will. It turned out the woman was the person who originally told my friend about it.

The three of us left the building and discussed what to do as we stood on the sidewalk. As with the man who kept phoning in suicide threats, we had to assume the danger was real but also gave thought to the possibility that it might simply be a husband and wife spat.

We radioed for backup and a friend of mine from Homicide showed up. We asked him to cover the rear of the building, and the three of us from Burglary repeatedly rang the bell for the second floor. When no one answered, we turned the knob of the bottom door and found it to be unlocked. We walked up the stairs, not knowing what we'd find.

After listening at the apartment door for a moment and hearing noises, we knew somebody was inside. Pizzello was a big, coarse-talking detective who had once saved my life from sniper fire, something I'll go into later. He hammered at the wood with his huge hand and growled, "Police, open up!" We stood there for up to ten minutes, but the knob never turned, and our resolve to get in never wavered.

In those long moments there were no voices, but our hearing picked up footsteps and perhaps a chair being moved. What were we to do? Our wait had given whoever was inside the time to set us up and yet we had no evidence of criminal activity.

I disliked officers who walked away from a problem and just wrote a report, leaving the solution up to someone else. Sometimes the decision you made was good, and sometimes it was bad, but taking no action guaranteed to make everything worse.

"Go downstairs and slam the door," I whispered to Pizzello and Janda. That would maybe lead the person behind the door to think he'd fooled us and that we were leaving. If there was going to be any surprises that night, I wanted to be the one making them.

Seconds after the outer door slammed, the apartment door swung open. I had my service revolver held against my chest, but I knew I could be confronting a nice little old lady for all I knew. Out came a rough-looking white man with a shotgun in his hands. He had been so taken in by our bluff that he held the weapon loosely at his hip, pointing at the hallway floor.

"Police!" I aimed the revolver at his chest. "Drop the gun."

Startled, he let the heavy weapon thump to the floor.

I moved toward him and he backed up. He was in his forties, thin-lipped, and compact. He wore a crew cut and, from behind his glasses, his steely eyes watched my every move. I kept my revolver trained at him, but let the loaded shotgun lie on the landing. Once I was two feet inside a dark living room, I said, "That's enough." My main concern was Joyce—whoever and wherever she was—and I hoped she was still alive.

"What's your name?"

"*Pat Deavers." His eyes were like ball bearings. I got the feeling that the few words he let out were coming from an ice statue.

"Why didn't you answer the bell? We know you heard us." He didn't reply. "Do you always come to the door with a shotgun?" He kept silent, acting like a man with a lot to hide. With no evidence to the contrary, I had to treat him as a law abiding citizen. Still aiming my gun at Deavers, I impatiently shook my flashlight beam around the front window, hoping the other officers would see the signal and come running. It took *five minutes*, but they finally came trotting up the stairs, picked up the shotgun, and walked through the front door.

They kept their guns on Deavers while I said, loudly, "Take this guy into the kitchen and question him." I was so angry at my backup that I momentarily forgot my position and treated my partner and sergeant as if I were in command.

Once Deavers was led away, I raced around the apartment, turned on the lights, and glanced into rooms. I flipped on a bedroom light switch and saw a thin woman cowering in a corner, shivering and sobbing, wearing just her bra and panties.

The first thing that jumped into my mind just blurted out. "Are you being held against your will?"

"Yes! Yes!"

"Are you Joyce?"

"Yes, thank God you're here!" I helped her stand. "Pat's killed people and robbed people, and he was going to kill me next!"

Misreading my silence for skepticism, she added, "I can show you, I saved things from people he's robbed, they're in the kitchen, and I can give you stuff on the murders."

"Why don't you get dressed, Joyce, and we can talk about it," I told her. "You're all right now, we'll make sure nothing happens to you."

I asked our backup from Homicide to stay with her as I went to where Pizzello and Janda were questioning the man at a small table against the kitchen wall. Because of what Joyce had told me, we needed to treat him as a potential threat.

"Stand up!" I ordered. "Face the wall and assume the position. Don't tell me you don't know it by now."

I had taken over the investigation without really realizing it. I just blurted out whatever I thought needed saying in typical police style. Pizzello and Janda sprang into action because they could tell by my sudden confidence that I had turned up something. I frisked Deavers, not knowing that Pizzello had already done so, and we cuffed him. Janda had the detective from Homicide take him down to his squad car and follow the standard procedures for guarding a prisoner.

The rest of us stayed upstairs to question Joyce, a pathetic former mental patient who was absolutely clear headed now. She raced to certain parts of the kitchen, such as underneath the pull out cutting board, and removed numerous pieces of identification from robbery victims. What she told us, and what the police and prosecutors were able to piece together later, gave us a picture of a cold-blooded killer— one of the worst I'd ever helped arrest. If we hadn't tricked him into coming out to the apartment landing, I have no doubt that he would have blown me and my fellow officers away. Deavers had absolutely nothing to lose because he was going back to prison for life and would possibly face the electric chair.

One of his criminal buddies, *Chester Blough, was just as ruthless. Blough came up to Chicago after escaping from a Missouri prison, where he had been serving time for killing a salesman. He met up with Deavers somehow and they became fast friends. Blough was caught stealing a car they had planned to use in robberies. While in jail awaiting trial or extradition back to Missouri, Blough developed an arm infection and was transferred to Cook County Hospital, which at the time was so lax in security that it was commonly used as an escape route.

Deavers entered the ward posing as a lawyer and somehow helped Blough get out of his chains and produced a set of new clothes. They calmly walked out and drove away.

What happened next was like a 1930s gangster movie. Joyce nursed Blough back to health, and he grew fond of her. The attraction was so strong that he had to move into an apartment a few miles away just so Deavers wouldn't catch on. The two men held up a tavern, shot a bartender, and ran out after emptying the cash register. Wanting to make sure that no eyewitnesses would show up in court, Deavers went home and told Joyce to get dressed so they could go back and "make sure the guy was dead." The couple went to the tavern and tried to be "curious patrons," and it worked. A policeman at the door said they couldn't go in because someone had been killed.

Joyce could handle the robberies, but when her boyfriend started murdering people it became, as she said, "too heavy" for her. Her growing dread made Deavers even more abusive and domineering. Extremely suspicious, he even had his sister come up from her apartment downstairs to stay with Joyce when he was away, trapping her there.

One of her fears was that if Deavers was arrested, she could be charged with abetting the crimes. Another was that because she was a former mental patient, no one would believe her when she told them about the crimes. For insurance, she began keeping at least one identifying item from each robbery the gang pulled off, such as a victim's driver's license or voter registration card. Each of these she taped to a sliding cutting board below the kitchen counter. The souvenirs piled up.

Deavers' five member gang shot it out with the police after a botched robbery of the Shannon Tavern in western Illinois, after which they hit the Fox Valley Country Club in the outer Chicago suburb of Bavaria. When Joyce heard that the men intended to return there a little more than a month later, she decided to warn the police by sneaking a phone call while Deavers was in the washroom. The Bavaria officers waited for the gang, and there was another shootout. Deavers returned home with bruises and torn clothes.

"You should never worry about us," he told her. "We're smart enough to park our cars where the stupid cops can't find them. We scattered through the woods. They're probably still looking for us there."

Joyce pretended to be pleased, but she really wished he'd been killed. By then she had a new worry—Deavers became suspicious of her and Chester Blough, and she wanted to distance herself from the Number Two man in the gang.

While drinking in a bar with Deavers, Joyce casually mentioned that Blough had asked her to move in with him. She played one against the other, and it worked.

Deavers had wanted to get rid of his partner anyway for talking to others about the bartender killing. So Deavers, who thought himself so clever, took Blough for a ride near Elgin. They stopped by the side of the road to relieve themselves, and then Deavers pumped two bullets into the back of Blough's head and rolled the body into a ditch. One of his gang members witnessed the act. Deavers went home and told Joyce what he'd done.

Joyce might have been a former mental patient, but the daily panic she felt wasn't paranoia. A man who had taken part in two killings might not blink at raising the score to three. Each day the mail that Deavers opened could include her death warrant in the form of a phone bill showing that a call had been made from the apartment to Bavaria a few days before the robbery. Luckily, we came in one day prior to what might have been a fateful mail delivery.

Seeing the relief sweep over Joyce's face was one of the most rewarding moments of my career.

The case was an exciting combination of minimal information, a hunch, and luck. We received the cooperation of all the persons assigned to Area Five in rounding up the entire gang and helping with the voluminous paperwork. In retrospect, even Patrick Deavers had luck, or maybe the judge just thought that one robber killing another wasn't such a bad idea. He gave the frosty-hearted Deavers a term of forty to sixty years rather than the death penalty. Many prosecutors thought he should have been tried for killing the Chicago bartender, but there wasn't enough evidence.

The Chicago Crime Commission knew how important the arrest was. Although Deavers was an independent hoodlum, he was listed as one of only thirteen men convicted of a

Chicago-area gangland murder between 1919 and 1968.

Pizzello and I received department commendations for "perseverance, skill, and ingenuity, coupled with clever exploitation of information, and courage under hazardous circumstances." In other words, for doing what cops do every day!

During my stint in Burglary, I was promoted to sergeant at the age of thirty-two, which was considered rather young to be supervising some officers who were almost twice my age. The head of Area Five Robbery, Lieutenant Walter Vallee, asked me if I wanted to work in his unit, and my immediate reply was, "Yes! But aren't all new sergeants sent to the patrol division?"

"It's rare, but it can be done," Vallee said.

So I found myself in Area Five Robbery as a supervising sergeant. I was well received in the unit, although I thought I might be too young at the time. However, I had confidence that in a short period I would adapt to the robbery investigations in the same manner that I quickly caught on to those in burglary. I knew the neighborhood and most of the personnel assigned to the Area, and I was sensible enough not to let my promotion go to my head. I truly respected the officers I worked with, and they appeared to respect me, too.

Of course, it helped dealing with tough guys if you're one yourself. I still had muscles developed from work at the produce market, and I was known to swing a fist or two in a quarrel when the other guy wouldn't listen. I didn't forget the rights of prisoners, though, as many old timers did, along with younger officers who admired them and tried to copy their styles. Being tough was admirable, but being foolish was just plain dumb.

A short time after I was promoted to detective sergeant, I had a powerfully-built surly black man handcuffed in an interrogation room. A detective came in and started to push and slap him around to "soften him up." He also probably wanted to make a favorable impression on me, not knowing what kind of guy I was.

"You can stop that, *Ben," I snapped. "Didn't you hear me? I said stop it!" He still got in another hit. "Hey! I'm going to see how *you* like it." I reached for my pocket.

"What the hell are you doing?" Ben asked.

"What does it look like I'm doing? I'm taking the cuffs off this guy for a while. If you're going to beat somebody, give them a chance to get beaten without cuffs."

The detective couldn't believe his eyes. He was still staring at me when my prisoner began to pound him with fists forged in anger that had been building up. Fortunately, there were no windows in interrogation rooms, and I found out later that there were a few detectives who would have liked to peek.

The detective, to his credit, got in a few blows, but he didn't have the power that the prisoner could delivery. Those large fists were like pistons. He could have just as well struck out at me, but I think he somehow liked me and I wound up refereeing the bout.

Ben pulled away to reach for his own manacles dangling from his belt, but the robber kept saying, "Fight fair, fucker, no cuffs, no cuffs!"

When I said, "That's enough," the prisoner stopped without giving a final punch, as if I'd rung a bell. He even held out his wrists for me to handcuff him again.

Ben glowered at me after his eight-knuckled lesson in prisoner rights. Fuming was all he could do, and I think he knew if he made any threats, I would have whacked him. If he filed a complaint against me, he would also have to disclose his maltreatment of a suspect and lose face with his fellow officers. Ben left without a word, but the story spread like bad news throughout the building. The message was, "Don't screw around with people the Sarge has in custody." Or, "Don't hit anyone unless you give them a chance to hit back."

Sarge. I was starting to like the title. It seemed to suggest that the detectives and uniformed officers knew I was a boss who would listen to anything they had to say, and that I never forgot I was one of them. Whenever I could get away, I went out with the detectives to take part in the investigations or I gave up my lunch periods cruising the streets.

One week I was filling in for the midnight coordinator of Area Five. The large station became a lonely place as most of the city slept, and I would get the itch to go out and roam the streets. During a pre-dawn lunch break, I signed out for a squad car to take a drive around the Northwest Side instead of eating.

Someone other than a police officer might see only empty avenues and darkened windows, but if you drive slowly and observe rather than just glance, the streets come alive.

On that clear, cold autumn night near Milwaukee and Montrose, my eyes focused on movement down a dark side street—two or three people near an auto parked at the curb, thirty-five feet away. The forms merged, and I couldn't be sure how many there were or what they were doing. Sixth sense— the cop's sense—told me that something was about to happen. If only I had cause for suspicion, such as a fight or a woman screaming, I would have u-turned and sped right in. Even so, I got closer because I was curious, a very dangerous state for an officer.

Rather than draw attention to myself, I went around the block with my lights off, spinning a couple of corners, and pulled up about ten feet behind the car. Their auto appeared empty, but I could see a teenager standing in the darkened alcove of a nearby shop. Not just standing, he was lurking—moving a few inches one way and then the other, all the while watching something. I wouldn't know it for a while, but I had just blundered upon a gang of armed robbers. Their youth didn't make them any less dangerous, as I would soon learn.

I walked up to the teen, quietly introduced myself as an officer since I was in plainclothes, and asked a few typical questions that seemed to be natural by now. "What are you doing here? What's your name? Where do you live?"

He had been drinking, and his answers weren't very clear. Since the kid was under the legal drinking age, I had something to hold him on. I led him by the arm, opened the passenger door of my police car, and guided him in. At the time, many cars had an inside light that automatically went on when the door opened, but the ones in police cars were wired to go on only at the switch to avoid giving us away. I went around to the driver's side, climbed in, and looked around while my hand was on the butt of my snub-nosed revolver.

As soon as I got next to the teen lookout to ask a few more

questions, a man around twenty years old came around the corner and walked toward the other auto. He carried a large, narrow box, the kind sweaters came in, and I watched him open it and toss the cover on the ground. The teenager beside me didn't say a word. He probably sobered up fast, knowing he was in trouble.

From the flimsy box, the young man on the street removed a sawed-off barrel and stock of a shotgun. Not knowing that I was watching him, he assembled the weapon, took cartridges from his pocket, and methodically thumbed them one by one into the chamber. My mind was racing, skimming over all my options and their possible consequences. Suppose I called for backup and the man saw me lift a radio transmitter to my face? That kind of movement and playing safe could prove to be deadly. I had intentionally left my driver's side door slightly ajar in case I wanted to get out fast, and I thought it would be better to act while I could. I quietly climbed out as the man closed the 12-gauge shotgun with an ominous snap.

I stayed for a moment beside the car, revolver in hand, and waited until I saw him place the shotgun on the rear floor of his auto. Then I ran toward him, shoved him hard against the open car door, and shouted, "Police officer!" At the same time, I switched my gun to my left hand, freeing my right to reach in and grab the shotgun.

"You motherfucker," shouted the man, whose name was *Aristo Orlando. I didn't have time to unload the weapon, so I pushed it into my overcoat pocket and kept it in place with my elbow. At the same time, I had to keep the young man off balance by pinning him awkwardly against the door with my left forearm. Then I kept my gun pointed at him as I slowly backed away so that he couldn't grab it or the loaded shotgun in my deep pocket.

A third member of the gang was slouched over in the passenger seat of the car. I couldn't tell if he was playing possum or had passed out. All this time, Orlando filled my face with profanities and a mist of alcohol. He fumbled at something in his pocket.

"Don't do it!" I warned.

How close were we to bloodshed? Closer than you and this page to your face.

Orlando was attempting to slide a pistol out of his pocket, but the hammer snagged on the cloth. Knowing that I had problems and they would probably get worse, I concentrated on Orlando's every move.

Then another pair of hands appeared out of nowhere and tried to yank the shotgun from my overcoat. I had no idea that the teenager I'd left in my squad car would come to the aid of his pal. Fortunately, I hadn't relaxed my elbow pressure on the shotgun. As the teenager tugged and struggled to lift the weapon, I snapped around and hit him on the head with my revolver. The movies made it look as if cops knew exactly how to knock people unconscious, but the truth was you never knew where to strike. Sometimes you gave them a concussion and they blacked out, and other times you just slammed the butt down hard and they kept fighting. This time, the teen dropped to the street, leaving me free to pay undivided attention to Orlando.

Moving drunkenly closer, he said, "Kill me, motherfucker!" That thought crossed my mind as he lunged at me, but I whacked him with my gun and down he went.

I now had a pair of young men on the ground, stirring at my feet, and an oblivious youth was hungover in their car. I called in a 10-1, that a police officer needed help, which usually got cops to drop everything and respond promptly. Ten minutes went by. I waited. In that time, Orlando and the lookout teen were more or less conscious but still groggy. I was able to control them by handcuffing them together, holding both down with my foot like a big game hunter, and keeping a watch on their sleeping friend.

The requested help took a long time coming, which was unusual, but when it arrived the side street filled with officers. I told them to search Orlando because I knew that he had a gun in his pocket. They had to rip the pocket apart to get it out, and they found that it was loaded.

As all three prisoners were cuffed behind their backs, one of the officers threw my set of cuffs to me and casually said, "Nice job, Sarge, but you should have had a partner!"

He was right.

Orlando and the teenager had bumps on their heads but refused medical treatment. They were extremely hostile while being processed. When they appeared before Judge Saul Epton, their attorneys simultaneously insisted that their clients were victims of police brutality, and their fingers pointed in my direction.

Epton was well known as a sympathetic jurist. He was especially interested in giving young offenders a second chance so they might learn to go straight. I will always remember, though, the kindly old man rising to his feet, supporting his weight by gripping the two ends of his court bench, and leaning toward the lawyers. He shouted, his voice quivering, "This officer was out-numbered and should have *killed* your clients, and he would have been justified if he had done so. Sergeant DiMaggio easily could have been killed by them, considering the state of mind they were in! Your clients should be thanking this officer and shaking his hand for saving them."

I had been in Branch 42 many times and never saw Judge Epton so angry. When he was through with his ten minute tirade, he sat, declared a finding of guilty on all counts, and told the packed courtroom audience that, for the first time in his long career he was going to recommend a police officer for a judge's commendation.

Two days later, the three teenagers were charged with multiple robberies after their photographs in newspapers were recognized by the victims.

7

A FIRE IN THE WIND (PART ONE)

You could be sitting on a volcano and not know it was about to erupt, and so it was with us.

Police work had changed since the 1950s. Hippies, yippies, and often just ordinary citizens attempted to rile officers into doing something stupid, and at times they succeeded. It was worse in black neighborhoods, where the police were seen as symbols of oppression. Wherever we went, someone—sometimes young children—would call us pigs, and often they spat at us and threw rotten fruit or rocks at our cars.

Many African-Americans at the time at least had a little reason for distrusting some officers. Chicago had the largest ratio in the country of killings by police, and most of the victims were black. One reason was that white officers in solidly black neighborhoods often felt surrounded by hate and couldn't handle it. Other officers carried over the prejudices of their upbringing into their work and beat blacks after chases and sometimes while the prisoners were in custody. Because white officers had few contacts in solidly black neighborhoods, they at times resorted to cruel treatment for information.

You couldn't blame people for thinking much of the conflict as racial. Police work wasn't just good versus evil in places overrun by drug dealers using street gangs as ready-made distribution networks. Officers were in daily assault on an entire economic system of heroin and cocaine smuggling, manufacturing, recruiting, distributing, and selling. It was one way of life against another, and anything could happen anywhere at any time.

Making the situation worse were the neighborhood black leaders who kept suspicions and hatred alive just to stay in power. Wherever officers went, and no matter how hard they tried to help, people ran from them, refused to talk, or cried out, "Don't kill me, don't kill me!"

This was the reality of Chicago streets when I was promoted. As the supervising sergeant of the Robbery Unit in the huge and aging Area Five building, I assisted rookies, got to know a number of new detectives who were eager to prove their worth, and learned from old-timers who did their jobs without fanfare. Many of them were allowed to work the midnight shift, the least-wanted watch by younger officers, because there was less hassle from bosses and they could work with compatible partners. In time most of the graying officers on the midnight watch came to resemble one another, as if coffee and doughnuts triumphed over genetics.

As with any way of life requiring extra effort, I soon learned that getting police officers to work as a team usually involved babysitting for their egos. The men knew I was not a strict disciplinarian but that I would come down hard if they stepped over the line. If something needed to be said, it was in private so as not to embarrass the officer. My men also knew I would never ask them to do something I wouldn't do myself, and that was tested time and again.

On the lighter side, they may have liked me because I was a relief from Sergeant Dodger Smith, who sent his men out on such "missions" as paying his daughter's fifteen-cent library fine.

In early 1966, I had pins on a map showing that we had what would now be called a serial rapist pattern. Over the course of a year, the attacker had gone from purse snatcher to hitting women on the head slightly in the course of a robbery, and now he was raping his victims at knifepoint. Since the attacks were becoming more frequent and vicious, I was afraid he would eventually start killing the victims.

Making the difficult case more bewildering was the fact that the women couldn't pick out the person from photo albums in the Robbery and Homicide Units. All we had to go on was that the man was tall and wore a ski mask and three-quarter length coat. The mask was a new addition to the offender's attire for the most recent serious assaults. Each attack occurred between 10:00 and 11:30, and one of them happened on the coldest night of the year. Because the rape was committed in a gangway in sub-zero weather, the newspaper people were calling him the "ice cube rapist."

It became obvious that he would wait near bus stops, and then follow women until they reached an alley, where he would accost them. One of the approximately twenty victims recalled, under repeated questioning, seeing an older blue car, possibly a Plymouth, sliding in the snow just a few minutes before she was attacked in a desolate area. She could not be sure that the car belonged to the attacker; it was just something that we tucked in the back of our minds.

We made sure the patterns were discussed at every roll call, but then the attacks stopped. For six weeks, not one new crime fit his pattern. We wondered if the man might have taken his own life or simply moved away.

On March 30th, a very cold night, I was riding with Detective Larry Evans when we heard a police broadcast of a woman stabbed in a three-dollar robbery near Milwaukee and Medina. We rushed to Resurrection Hospital, where the victim was in critical condition with her throat slashed virtually from ear to ear. She would have died had it not been for off-duty Sgt. Charlie Adamson of the Criminal Investigations Unit, who lived nearby. He heard her screams, ran outside in his underwear, and found her lying on the sidewalk. Adamson stopped the flow of blood until paramedics arrived and then rode with her in the ambulance. Doctors took fifty stitches to close her wound and credited Adamson with saving her life.

When Larry and I arrived, the first thing we asked was if the attacker wore a gray coat and ski mask, and we learned that he did. Larry and I looked at each other, and I was sure we had the same thoughts.

Evans was a systematic, blond, baby-faced man with a few pounds on him. He didn't look like a hard-worker, or even a cop, but he was the type of guy that you couldn't pry off a case.

He wanted to stay on after our watch ended though we had already worked a double shift.

One of Larry's many traits was that he was a walking encyclopedia of suspects. When I couldn't remember someone's name, he could rattle off the subject's file in detail. He also knew how to work with partners and personally trained many young detectives.

Once we had stopped a man who had been sticking up mom-and-pop grocery stores. Larry kept a gun to the man's head while I frisked him.

"Sir," the robber said as I stepped back, "you missed the gun. It's in the center of my pants."

He was afraid that if I'd discovered the weapon later, we might put a bullet through his brain to teach him a lesson. I reached into his jockstrap and removed a .38 caliber revolver and was embarrassed at having blown a search that could have endangered both of us. Larry never mentioned the incident, not even as we were joking around with other officers many years later.

As a detective sergeant, I put out an all-call message with every scrap of information we had on the rapist, including that he could be driving an older model blue Plymouth, then Larry and I drove to where the woman was ravaged. Using the last area of attack as a starting point, we circled every block within a two mile radius.

"He's going to hit again tonight," I thought aloud, but intuition had nothing to do with it. The rapist had done a double attack in January and a double attack in February. That was his turn-on and his new M.O.

We were driving along broad Milwaukee Avenue at one a.m. when we saw an old blue Plymouth going north on Elston Avenue. Larry tapped the gas pedal for us to get a look at the driver and, from thirty or forty yards away, we could see the gray coat but not much else.

"Put on the siren, Larry, this is our guy," I said, almost lifting myself from the seat. The siren and flashing lights went on simultaneously; it was no surprise that Larry and I always thought alike.

The driver refused to pull over even though he was moving slowly. Behind us, someone angrily pounded his horn. We quickly learned that it was Detective Louis Clepp of the Homicide/Sex Unit, who had heard the all-call while he was in a squad car and then noticed the Plymouth, too. The target kept on for a few blocks, turned into an alley, and stopped abruptly. We cut off the siren as the driver stepped out, put up his hands, and waited to be arrested. He was a tall, muscular elementary school janitor named *Louis Legrand. Apart from his size, he had the kind of features you see every day without noticing. We had no proof, and yet we knew we had our man.

"What were you doing back there?" Larry asked.

"Just driving around," the man answered calmly.

"Why didn't you stop when you heard the siren?"

I drifted around to the passenger side while Larry questioned him and glanced into the car. There on the front seat were a bloody knife and a purse.

"I was afraid to stop," Legrand replied.

"Were you looking for another woman to rob?" I went back to Larry and whispered in his ear.

"I don't know. I just don't know."

It was all over. We were relieved, and maybe so was Legrand.

Under the seat we found another purse, this one with the identifications of all the victims, including some in suburban attacks we knew nothing about.

We had some trouble handcuffing Legrand because he was over six feet tall, weighed about two hundred pounds, and was a weight-lifter with huge wrists. No wonder he was able to overpower his many victims.

Legrand answered a few preliminary questions as we snapped the cuffs on in front of him, but then he went into his shell. It was as if he entered a coma while still awake; a strange look came over his face.

Clepp took the Plymouth to the Area Five parking lot, and Larry drove our police car as Legrand sat silently beside me in the back seat. He was so silent and rigid that we didn't consider him a threat. While I was thinking of the paperwork that needed to be done, all the victims who must be contacted, and the suburban officers to be notified, Legrand moved his manacled hands ever so slightly to reach the door handle.

Suddenly the door swung open and our prisoner attempted to push himself out and onto the expressway. His intent was certainly to commit suicide, for he wouldn't have survived the jump at the speed we were going. Legrand was halfway out when I struggled to pull the powerful man back inside—first by his clothes, and then by his arm and neck. Once I shoved him back in his seat and slammed the door, he didn't say anything. I did hear Larry mutter, "Holy shit," under his breath.

We couldn't just call it a night, although we needed sleep. We spent hours processing the evidence and rotating the interrogation of our prisoner. Despite his size, Legrand made no attempt to act tough, and he casually mentioned that he had a wife and two-year-old child.

"How many women did you attack?" I asked. He didn't answer right away. "Fifteen? Twenty?"

"I don't know how many. I guess I'm sick."

"Why weren't you ever caught?" Clepp asked.

"I was, once." That surprised us. "*Detective Nelson let me go. It was about a year ago."

The questions came rapidly—"Why would he do that?"

"Did he stop you on the street?"

"Were you arrested and taken in?"

"Well," he said, "I, uh, my family and my lawyer gave him some money. The case really wasn't too bad, I just stabbed the lady in the leg, and I think the lawyer talked her out of testifying against me. Oh, and one more thing, the detective promised that my mug shot wouldn't go in the books."

Now it was me muttering, "Oh shit," under my breath. The bosses and the Internal Investigation Division would be interested in that revelation.

"Louis," I said to him, "we didn't hear of any attacks for about six weeks. Why is that? Were you away?"

"I've been seeing a psychiatrist for two months," Legrand answered. He added that the doctor told him he would have to report him to the police if he kept on attacking women or if he killed someone. We were flabbergasted that a psychiatrist would withhold this information, but we later learned, and did not agree, that it fell under the patient/doctor confidentiality guidelines.

Even though he was now handcuffed from behind, Legrand pounded his head on the office desk. He didn't want to hurt himself, no matter what he'd done, and we certainly didn't want to have him appear in court with bruises that could be blamed on us. We handcuffed him to a chair in the center of the room and assigned an officer to keep constant watch on him.

Bosses from headquarters arrived between six and seven a.m. and garbled what happened as they talked to reporters about the arrest. They said that Clepp had been the first to spot the Plymouth and signaled to Larry and me in the squad car. Clepp eventually got the higher award, but what the hell, we didn't care who received credit as long as Legrand would never rape again.

More than twenty victims identified Legrand in showups, and he was subsequently sentenced to serve twelve to thirty years in prison. The citywide Robbery commander game me an honorable mention.

A criminal investigation was launched into the bribe allegation against Detective Nelson. Every effort was made to indict him, but there was no proof other than Legrand's word, and his family failed to cooperate with anyone. The department settled for Nelson's resignation, and the mug shots of Legrand were placed into the Robbery and Homicide albums.

We were handling a lot of tavern robberies around that time, and the condition of the witnesses invariably ranged from tipsy to a drunken stupor. The patrons were so used to the dim lighting of bars that they went into voltage shock when they entered a brightly lit room for a showup.

One call of trouble brought us to a tavern where the owner was squatting on top of the jukebox, waving his arms and grunting like an ape. The uniformed officers helped him down, eased him into a chair, and placed cold towels on his neck.

A nude woman strolled back and forth along the bar, her arms extended as if she were on a tightrope. The cops gently led her away and covered her up with a couple of tablecloths.

The biggest of the three male patrons swung barstools over his head. Another "swam" on the tavern floor.

The third guy was coherent enough to say that he and his two friends were playing pool with two strangers who had offered to buy drinks. "Then all of a sudden, my friends started going goofy, like they were drugged or something."

"Can you tell us what happened then?" I asked.

"I saw the two men go behind the bar and empty the cash register, but I couldn't do anything because I was too weak."

Detectives Frank Pernice and Dick O'Sullivan didn't know what to make of the case.

"We can't just slough it off to the General Assignment boys as a theft," I told them.

"How can it be a robbery without a weapon?" the wiry Pernice asked.

"Good question." I gave it some thought. "We're going to have to presume that the drug, whatever it is, was used to dope the customers in order to commit the crime, and that would constitute the force necessary to classify this as a robbery."

"You mean the drug was the weapon," O'Sullivan groaned, lightly patting his belly as if thumping a watermelon.

"Correct."

"All right," Pernice responded. "We'll get on top of it."

All the glasses were sent to the crime lab. The immediate testing revealed that the two strangers had pulled off the robbery with LSD. At this time, officers across the country were just becoming familiar with this drug, which was publicized in the 1960s by Timothy Leary. More importantly, the glasses also provided us with matching sets of fingerprints that identified the bad guys.

The case led to long discussions by the assistant state's attorneys, who needed to approve the charges. Fortunately, a judge ruled that the use of drugs rather than a standard weapon did constitute robbery, and the two men were sentenced to long terms. The case was so bizarre that copies of the report written by Pernice and O'Sullivan circulated around the department as a masterpiece.

Working out of the Northwest Side, which was largely Polish, German, Irish, and increasingly Hispanic, I had less contact with some of the racial friction than officers were seeing on the South and West Sides of the city. Chicago was regarded at the time as one of the most segregated northern cities, largely because each immigrant group had staked out its own territory and resisted blacks who arrived later. Real estate agents exploited racial fears by buying up whole blocks in changing neighborhoods amid fears of dropping property values. The term was block-busting.

The tense racial situation was the reason why Dr. Martin Luther King, Jr. chose Chicago for a series of peaceful demonstrations. King and thousands of supporters marched down the center of streets at around 115th and Avenue O as the police kept everyone back and detoured traffic. Each block brimmed with residents screaming vulgarities at the black and white marchers. The police stood ready along the curbs of the entire route, and then sealed off the streets once the marchers passed and escorted the demonstrators.

King sometimes headed the marches, but when violence was in the air, he walked resolutely, surrounded by his supporters to avoid giving the angry crowd a focal point.

At most of the marches, I stayed parallel to King so that I could rush in if anyone tried to jump out of the crowd. Rocks, stick, bottles, and full beer cans were hurled at every step, especially from alleys where young men tossed missiles over the roofs, not caring who they hit. The yelling neighbors couldn't reach the marchers, so they battered me and other officers with everything they could throw, but thankfully the demonstrations never got out of hand.

I never had the occasion to speak to King during his many marches in Chicago, but from time to time his eyes made contact with mine and it seemed as if he wanted to talk. That trait of appearing to direct personal attention toward strangers may have helped make him a leader. America seemed ready for a change, but in some ways, it was moving backwards.

On July 12, 1966, someone illegally opened a hydrant near Pulaski Road and Madison Street, a "ghetto" neighborhood four miles west of the Loop, and that set off a deadly chain reaction.

After an officer turned off the gushing water with a hydrant key he kept in his squad car, a rumor spread that a black child had been hit by a fire truck. Thousands of people who could not afford air conditioning sat outside their homes that sweltering Tuesday, allowing rage to escalate before anyone could fight it.

There had been a few racial disturbances along the borders of changing neighborhoods, but the Richard J. Daley administration took the posture that full-scale riots never happened in the City That Works, and so we were never trained in crowd control and mass arrests.

What we were trained in was the use of machine guns, shotguns, and guns that fired tear gas, mainly for storming buildings in hostage situations. The use of "heavy equipment" was so new to the department that some of the older officers were knocked on their asses from the recoil during practice sessions with the powerful 12-gauge shotguns. We were prepared for war, but not for a civil disruption.

There was a little fighting that night and the next morning, but we were unaware of how bad the situation was until a little before noon, when supervisors in the riot command center called our Robbery Unit commander, Lieutenant Walter Vallee.

"Conditions are becoming worse and policemen are under heavy sniper fire at Lake and Wood." That was a notorious housing project.

We had no specific instructions, but Vallee went with me and two detectives to the epicenter, bringing with us the equipment from our heavy weapons cabinet. Nothing that we had heard prepared us for what we saw when we arrived.

Uniformed policemen were pinned down by snipers for a one hundred yard radius. Soon after we pulled up close to one of the project buildings, our squad car windows exploded from gunfire, matching the other vehicles at the scene.

Sizing up the situation was impossible. Being surrounded by gunfire gave us tunnel vision, and it was directed at the muzzle blasts from the upper floors of the brick fortress before us. Officers stooped behind their cars like settlers in a ring of covered wagons. From habit they fired their service revolvers without realizing the bullets dropped short. The only officer we recognized was Lieutenant Paddy Diggins, who usually ignored orders to wear a uniform when he was at the 33rd District. Times had changed and he was in uniform now, topped by one of the newly issued riot helmets.

Diggins was a character. Once as I was writing reports at the 33rd, a motorist came charging into the station and complained to a desk sergeant that an officer had stopped him and suggested a bribe. "So," the man said, "I gave him five dollars."

Before the motorist could say anything more, Diggins stormed out of his office and went right up to him. "So you're here to make a complaint against one of my officers?" Removing a five dollar bill from his wallet and stuffing it down the citizen's shirt, he added, "Here's your money, you stool pigeon son of a bitch. You're just as guilty as the policeman!" Then he grabbed the man by the collar and seat of his pants and threw him out the front door.

It was a vastly different Paddy Diggins who was inching closer to us as we scrunched for cover behind our parked auto. The air crackled with gunfire.

"These bastards have had us pinned down for three hours, John. Did you bring the heavy stuff?"

"Yeah, but I don't think it's going to help. We have shotguns and machine guns, but we need rifles with scopes. We've got to enter the building and seek out the snipers."

"All right," Vallee said, "let's go." He was known for jumping into situations and thinking about ramifications later, but I'll always give him credit for having guts and making decisions when no one else would take the chance.

To be quite honest, there were times that I felt there must be something wrong with me because many of my fellow officers panicked, sweated, and became irrational when we were under fire. I didn't consider them cowards, because their reactions made more sense than my calm. Now I'm finding out why some officers and soldiers don't feel fear. They tend to ignore the reality of the situation and are more inclined to put themselves in the middle of it. There's even a name for it—"disassociation"—a feeling that the dangerous situation is slightly unreal. Fortunately, such officers can ease their stress at cop hangouts, and we're less likely to have nightmares and flashbacks years later.

I was eager to throw myself into the riot even though there was shooting all around us. Diggins wanted the shotgun, so Vallee and I took machine guns. We shut the trunk, and Diggins quickly led the way. He headed straight for the front doors of the project building and, as he was running, a gallon jug shattered in front of him, splashing water and hitting all of us with glass shards. If the large bottle had landed on Diggins' helmet, it would have driven the lieutenant into the concrete.

He temporarily froze, and then hollered "Those dirty bastards!"

We ran in a crouch toward the building, not yet aware that a number of officers were following us, including two detectives from our Area. All of us by now had a blueprint of the building in our heads, and we knew where we wanted to go. We hit the stairwells and readied our weapons at every landing. Some corridors were empty, and others had a few people who had backed against the wall at our approach, screaming for us not to hurt them. The other residents hid under beds and other furniture that offered protection.

As we reached the ninth floor where the snipers were, Diggins blasted away at a heavy door without warning. We rushed into the apartment and confronted three men standing around a high-powered rifle lying on the sofa and numerous empty gallon jugs. The men threw their hands to the air and begged us to let them live.

We handcuffed all three and turned the rifle over to patrol officers who took them to the nearest station. By then, officers throughout the riot area were rushing buildings and making weapons seizures. The new machine guns must have made a big impression. Word of the heavy equipment spread, and all the buildings were cleared of snipers in an hour of utter chaos. I had a feeling of exhaustion and accomplishment because we'd helped quell the anti-police riot with only a few injuries. I was angry at the city, though, for warehousing people in huge block brick buildings that allowed gangs, fear, and hate to take charge.

The rioting continued as we drove down streets at random.

We went to the assistance of officers we found under fire, being beaten, or running after a gunman or looter. Sometimes we won, and sometimes the rioters won.

The disturbance ended at two in the morning that Friday. In all, two civilians were killed and half a dozen officers needed to be hospitalized for bullet wounds. Many more were grazed and battered in fights. Two hundred snipers and rioters were arrested, many of them school children. You would think that riot-torn neighborhoods would learn that violence accomplishes nothing, but the hydrant riot was just the training ground for both sides.

8

FIRE IN THE WIND (PART TWO)

When news came in that Dr. Martin Luther King was shot to death in Memphis on April 4, 1968, my family was celebrating the birthday of my middle daughter. I was distressed at the restaurant and feared that another deadly disturbance was about to break out. However, that night the streets of Chicago were absolutely silent, and that in itself was eerie.

King's death had brought an immediate void in black leadership, and in Chicago, at least, the dream first died and then turned to anger. Officers were put on twelve hour shifts, and all leaves were canceled, but there was no trouble other than sporadic looting.

We were more prepared for an outburst this time. After the hydrant disruption, all officers were called back to the training academy for a revised course on crowd control, and we had to go to National Guard stations for exercises that included wedge formations to clear the streets. Our riot gear consisted solely of newly issued helmets, some with plastic face shields, but most without. Bulletproof vests were virtually non-existent in the department—most officers hated the weight and resented that the city refused to pay for them. It would take several deaths over the next few years before a suburban attorney raised private donations to supply the vests for Chicago police.

I had reported to the Area Five building at six o'clock in the morning, two hours early. The looting started with vandalizing the shops of white owners, but now the residents were turning upon themselves and the police. Every available officer was called from a duty roster and ordered to report to their assigned areas.

The lieutenant of my Area couldn't cope with the enormity of what was happening and was at a loss for words—and direction.

Despite the much-lauded emergency roster list, a lot of the detectives and patrol officers still hadn't been notified, and nothing was ready. The station was a single roar of yelling, curses, calling out names and assignments, and locker door banging. Some officers around me talked about how this disturbance was going to be a lot easier than the hydrant episode, but I had bad feelings about it from the start.

"Sergeant DiMaggio," the lieutenant shouted to be heard above the noise, "you will be in charge of our heavy weapons car. Pick your three best men." He actually yelled that in front of all the officers, not caring a damn about the morale of those who wouldn't be chosen. I went through the crowd and surreptitiously tapped the shoulders of the detectives I wanted, and they followed me without drawing attention to the fact.

I took them to the unlit, vacant third floor and told them, "I hope you guys aren't pissed that I selected you, because it's going to be rough out there. If you want to back out, do it now and there won't be any hard feelings."

"You can count on us," one of them said for all three.

The men I chose were Larry Evans of the Louis Legrand case; Frank Pernice, who had worked on the LSD tavern robbery; and seasoned detective Richard Riccio. He was the oldest of our four-man team and was an excellent driver. A top driver for a police unit doesn't mean he obeys all the laws. Riccio could pull off Hollywood stunts when he had to, yet he always made sure no one was in danger.

"Larry and Frank, start yanking all the heavy equipment out of the locker," I said. "Empty that sucker—three shotguns, the gas gun, all the ammunition, and the heavy-beam lights. Bring the stuff down the rear stairwell and meet with Rich. I brought my carbine from home, just in case. I hope we won't need a lot of that ammo, but we'll feel better knowing it's there."

I went to our pathetic, stressed-out lieutenant for further

SARGE!   *105*

instructions. "Just hit the streets," he screamed. Just hit the streets. So much for two years of planning.

Where did we get our assignment information? From ordinary radio newscasts! The broadcaster said there was trouble at Madison Street and Pulaski Road, so that's where we headed. We knew the area well because of the large volume of robberies committed in the nearby neighborhoods. It had gone from virtually all white to all black in about four years. The blacks who moved in brought with them a hatred for their white shop owners and landlords. Some sort of riot was due, maybe overdue, and the killing of King could be the excuse to set things off.

Evans felt the same way, but we kept our thoughts to ourselves because we hoped we were wrong.

All we saw were a few broken store windows when we arrived at the scene. I could hear a sigh of relief in our car, and Pernice made a comment that our supervisors might decide to cancel the twelve hour shifts. Riccio, being a coffee and doughnut man, suggested that we get something to eat. That turned out to be a great idea, because we wouldn't have anything else for a long, long time. We went to a fast food place in a solidly black neighborhood at Madison and Cicero Avenue, and the manager did not have to ask why four white men in suits had entered.

"How's it going, officers?" he politely asked.

"Fine," Pernice replied, "just fine."

"It may be just fine now," the kindly looking man in his sixties said, "but you better be prepared for a mighty busy day." What he knew, he could not tell us. Just a feeling. Something was out there.

We saw a few squad cars slowly pass the store windows, and the ominous feeling returned. As we left the small restaurant, I asked Riccio to open our trunk so we could keep our batons with us in the car. "And let's keep the car windows closed, just in case someone decides to throw something in our direction."

Early that morning, Board of Education officials had wrung their hands over what to do and decided to let classes resume as if nothing had happened, but the students who showed up were so unruly that the board abruptly closed down all the schools without notifying anyone, even the police department.

We climbed into our squad car and heard the tail end of a newscast saying, "… and the students are being let out of school early."

"Holy shit," said Evans, summing it up properly.

Thousands of angry teenagers, feeling betrayed by the assassination, went on a wild spree of arson and looting. Soon hundreds of people— from little children to senior citizens— joined them in the most wide scale disturbance the city had even seen.

We were in the 4200 block of West Madison when a mass of people swarmed the sidewalk and street. They saw us, they knew we were cops, and they didn't care. *Pow, pow, pow*—large plate glass windows were being smashed all around us. The crowd shoved itself through the now-broken windows and the doors. They were not robbery gangs or snipers in a high rise. The enemy was an entire neighborhood. There were children and a few elderly people out there, along with street gang members and thieves, but normally good people who had let go of their restraint because everyone around them had. We couldn't stop them, and we couldn't arrest all of them. In fact, we were totally helpless.

Frank Pernice broke the silence. "Let's *do* something."

"And do what?" I asked. "If we get out, we'll lose the car and get separated, and then it would be each one of us against the mob. What good could we be then?" There was no answer.

The police radio came alive, and the flow of instructions to units across the riot area would be non-stop from then on. The windows kept shattering in an ugly staccato. We did the only thing we could—put on our helmets, locked the doors, and watched the incredible scene unfold. We couldn't even attempt to press our car through the waves of people surrounding us.

There was no sense of grief in the crowd for the murder of King. Instead, there was chanting and jubilation as if the people had won a victory. They were taking whatever they could grab, as if by right.

"Look at that," someone shouted, and the horde darted in another direction. Look at that and that and that. Chairs, television sets, even a large couch being shouldered by two young men were carried off. All the while, we remained trapped in our squad car as we watched in disbelief.

Perhaps half an hour of angry helplessness passed and then I told Riccio, "Hit the siren, hump the curb, drive through the empty lot, and try to get to the alley." Retreating without a shot was our only option. Using our guns would just make the situation worse.

Crowds flowed through garbage-strewn alleys as we headed back, but at least there was room to pass them. No one tried to stop us or hide their looting from the rear windows and doors of the shops.

"Hold up, Rick," Pernice called from the back seat. "We just passed two guys trying to flag us down." Riccio slammed on the brakes.

Balding, white-haired Caucasian men hurried to our car. They apparently worked at or owned one of the stores. "Help! Please help us!" they implored, blood dripping from their faces.

We jammed the two men into our car. There were six of us now, along with my carbine and our night sticks, as we headed for the nearest station. Then we heard a rock go *chunk*. The looters thinned out as we drove north, and the streets were clear before we reached the station. The place was buzzing with officers moving about and citizens waiting for help, most of them cut and bruised. Other officers hauled in prisoners, and soon every lockup was crammed. We directed the two shop people to a patrolman and decided to return to the streets.

Just two minutes after we resumed driving, we saw a fifteen-year-old boy chopping away at a telephone booth with a long axe to remove a coin box. Riccio aimed the squad car directly at the boy to scare him, and then we lurched to a stop and jumped out. We grabbed the boy and saw from the inscription on the axe that it had been stolen from a fire truck.

We knew we'd be going nowhere by making one arrest at a time. I asked for suggestions, and Pernice said we should go back into the thick of the riot and try out the wedge tactic we had learned. He wasn't serious, considering that we would be four against more than four thousand, but the idea was the only one that came close to making sense. On our way, Riccio thought the problem over and saw a way of applying it on a more practical basis—using the wedge in some alleys and fringe areas, attacking the mob a little at a time along its perimeter.

"Let's grab two, three, or four at a time, shoehorn them into the car and bring them in," he said. We all agreed, not knowing at the time how drastically our strategy would change as time went by.

Mayor Daley toured the scene by helicopter, seeing children running with stolen clothes and inky smoke shrouding the center of the city he thought he owned. Daley ordered Police Superintendent James Conlisk to "shoot to kill" arsonists "shoot to maim" looters. Conlisk refused, and so did all the officers assigned to riot duty.

By now, the police radio was jammed with messages and no one could get through, even if they needed help. The overlapping voices made it impossible for the front line troops to understand anything.

"Clear the air, clear the air," someone at headquarters said. "You're all jumping in at once. Clear the air for emergencies!" But no one cleared the air; forty to fifty cars were trying to transmit at the same time.

I switched our radio frequency to Citywide Four as a test and was surprised when a radio operator answered to my call number, 7520, and asked for my message.

"God damn you son of a bitch, why isn't this channel being used for emergency transmission?" I growled. To hell with FCC regulations against profanity.

"We don't have the authorization from the command post to open this frequency, Sarge."

"Then you better as hell call the command post and get authorization, it's total chaos out here!"

Not ten minutes later, every squad on the street was told to use Citywide Four for all emergency messages. I switched to it and talked to the operator again, telling him to broadcast our number on his band and inform us if we had any emergency calls or requests for heavy equipment.

The Citywide Four band kept a semblance of order and for

the most part was utilized strictly for emergency calls. Now at least a squad operator could get through if he needed us to bring heavy weapons to a sniper building or someone decided to use the riot as a cover for a major robbery.

"It's always the policemen on the street that handle the problems," Riccio complained, "and if they fuck up, the bosses have someone to blame."

"It's still early," I said. "The supervisors will be out here, you'll see. They did a lot of pre-planning." Sometimes I was as wrong as could be, especially when I had faith in the command ranks in the department.

We expected to arrest looters and window smashers, but we soon realized we needed to rescue victims first. We were constantly stopped by weeping and battered store keepers and sales clerks, black as well as white, asking just to be taken anywhere safe. Some were splattered with blood.

Time and again they said things like, "I told them to take everything, just not to hurt me, but they kept hitting me," or "They took everything, what am I going to do now?"

We stopped a few robbers who were beating people in the alleys and taking their wallets. Knowing we had just a few seconds to made an arrest before rioters would get to us, we would spring from our car and use our clubs with as little force as possible, and sometimes throw a robber into a car next to a bleeding victim.

At times, we rescued a victim who would point out a rioter a block or so away as the man who stole his wallet or wrist watch. Riccio stayed at the wheel and one or two of us hopped out and gave chase. There were so many arrests made that sometimes we just had the robber give up whatever he took and return it to the victim rather than tie up station officers and ourselves processing an arrest. The victims wanted to forget the nightmare and not press charges, and most of the time we didn't have room in the squad car anyway.

Baby-faced Larry Evans chased down a kid with a gun and brought him back to our car. For no reason, the kid punched Frank Pernice in the nose, sending a spurt of blood down his tie and white shirt. Pernice had fire in his eyes, but he didn't strike back. Hauling the teenager into the Fillmore Station at least gave us a chance to call home and say we were all right. We also told our wives that since all other neighborhoods were drained of officers, they should protect themselves and the children. We didn't have to say more. Our wives knew where we hid our extra guns.

We had been on duty for eleven hours when we heard a dispatcher announce that shots were fired at police a few blocks from us at Kildare and Madison. We headed there, our tires cracking over broken glass. Riccio skidded to a stop almost in front of the building, popped the trunk, and threw the shotguns and ammunition to the rest of us. Across the street, a shotgun or high-powered rifle blasted away from the third floor. Citizens, some holding merchandise they had stolen from stores, hid behind bushes, trees, and parked cars as they were pinned down by gunfire along with the police. Shots repeatedly fired with brief pauses as the sniper reloaded. Riccio and I fired from behind our car while Pernice and Evans covered our backs by staying close and behind ready to fire in the opposite direction.

I took aim and shot at the window. Carbines were fairly small, but their discharges sounded like explosions. Although I was a good marksman, night had fallen and I doubted that I could hit an unseen sniper through a window across the street and thirty feet up. I had to use my hearing and some calculated guesswork before I squeezed off a few more rounds. Then there was silence. I never learned if I'd hit the gunman or just scared him into giving up.

I returned to the car and radioed, "Police fire was returned to terminate the incident. We're back up for assignments."

Rather than being told to go home, we were given another assignment, and another, and several more. We learned that Superintendent Conlisk had decided to make shifts from midnight to noon and noon to midnight, regardless of the officer's starting time that day. That meant sixteen hours non-stop for us except the doughnut break, and fourteen hours directly in the riot.

"Jesus, that's super," I said.

We climbed into our car and went back to the street war.

Over the police radio, we heard, "Shots fired at police at … send us a wagon for prisoners at … we need help at … where's our fucking relief? Where's our fucking relief? Where's our fucking relief?"

We smelled smoke and saw flames in the night sky. Soon there wasn't sky anymore, just smoke rolling across the West Side as a neighborhood destroyed itself.

At two o'clock in the morning, our relief came.

"Hey, Sarge," Riccio said as we left the squad car for our private autos in the well-lit lot of the Area Five station. "I want to show you something." There was one bullet hole after another on the passenger side of the squad—the side I'd been on.

"Yeah, Rick, a lot of holes, four broken windows, and a lot of dents, but it still runs. Remind me to make out a 'damage to police vehicle' report tomorrow." Tired, I added, "I'll see you guys in the office at eleven o'clock. Get some sleep."

By then, Mayor Daley had issued a call for six thousand National Guard troops, but the administration had decided that for the image of the city, these men would not actually be deployed during the active stage of the unrest. They would sit around high school auditoriums and armories playing pinochle or something. We sure as hell could have used them.

I opened my front door that early morning and didn't want to move or say anything, and Rosemary understood. "Take a hot bath, DiMaj," she said. "I have some food for you, and then hit the sack. We'll talk about it tomorrow."

It was only a few hours later when I arrived at Area Five, in uniform for the first time since my days as a driver for O.W. Wilson. I carried a cooler Rosemary had packed with sandwiches and pop, but not exactly for a picnic.

A command post was set up at a West Side factory. Coffee was brewing, and there was a tray of doughnuts for the supervisors. Riccio filched a few without being seen. The citywide Robbery Commander, Earl Johnson, told us to keep up the good work, but neither he nor anyone else knew what we had done the day before, since the only paperwork being filed was on major arrests and heavily damaged police vehicles. Johnson said the worst was over, and the neighborhood would be back to normal Monday.

For a few hours, it seemed that way. Some untouched stores were now protected by private security guards, and others had large signs emblazoned BROTHER. The streets were fairly quiet, but we saw maybe twenty people carrying bundles of clothing still on store hangers. Riccio made a U-turn, stopped the car, and we told them to halt. All of us jumped out and prepared to make a mass arrest.

"Hey, man," one of them yelled. "We didn't steal this stuff. The man's just giving it away."

"Yeah, sure," Pernice said, his nose still swollen.

"God's truth! Down at the Robert Hall store, they giving away everything, they just don't want their place torched." The others nodded and gave the same story, and, crazy as it sounded, we believed them.

"All right, go on," I said, "behave yourselves." Then I asked Riccio to take us to the Robert Hall store. We saw scores of people pouring out, smiling and carrying clothing pulled off the racks. The manager of the chain told us he had been assured the placed would be spared if he let them have everything.

"Shit," Evans said as we left, "we're selling the farm."

"I hope the place burns down," I muttered. I wouldn't have thought that the day before, but that was what came to mind as I looked in disgust at all the stores being sacked and torched. The rioting was dehumanizing more than just the residents.

As we tried to keep a presence in the neighborhood, we discussed all the things we should have done the day before. Our one solid accomplishment was to prove that all the training and manuals were inadequate for handling a spontaneous outburst of mass behavior. The geniuses that designed the programs must have never lived through one. The instructions looked good on paper, but for all practical purposes they stank.

By four o'clock that afternoon, the streets filled up. You didn't need to be a genius in tactical warfare to know that blockades should have been put up at major intersections and all alley entrances, but no, the supervisors were sure the riot was over because they willed it to be so.

The police radio droned on with steady calls of: "Send me a wagon for … we have two prisoners at … looting near …" but at least there were no more calls of "Where's my fucking relief?"

"Rick," I said.

"Yes, sergeant?"

"Get this car out of here so we don't get squeezed in like yesterday. Let's see if we can come from behind the crowd. And, all of you, no more 'sergeant' shit. We're working as a team, and we're going to use our common sense to get through this."

"Good idea," Larry said. "*Sarge.*"

Some trapped police cars had been overturned by the looters, and the officers were pounded and kicked as they tried to crawl through the door openings. We sped to a report that rioters had thrown a brick through a squad car window to get at the men inside, and when we got there, a group of people were on top of the officers, pummeling them. We jumped out, grabbed the attackers, and threw half of them into our car and the rest into the battered policemen's auto. Then we sped out of there before the mob swallowed us up.

At least one hundred and twenty officers started marching *en masse* down Madison Street from the command post, all wearing helmets and holding batons at the port-arms position. Lieutenants and captains directed them from the street, and pulling up the rear were three patrol wagons and a variety of marked cars and three-wheel motorcycles.

The sight made a nice picture, but after fifty yards, the officers forgot their instructions and broke ranks to make arrests among the people hurling bricks and bottles at them. So much for the training in wedge formation!

"Shit," Evans said, "it's out of hand again."

We stopped at a gas station out of the riot zone to get our heavy weapons out of the trunk and place them inside the car with us.

Lieutenant Governor Samuel Shapiro, acting in the absence of Governor Otto Kerner, had urged the White House to send five thousand U.S. Army soldiers. They arrived by cargo plane from Texas and Colorado, only to sit at the Glenview Naval Air Station, far from the disturbance.

This second day of rioting saw the systematic destruction of small stores, pawnshops, jewelry stores, and the businesses that supposedly were guarded by private security. Fires were set in at least one commercial establishment per block for miles. A police officer who had never worked riot duty will never see as many fires in his entire career. Even youths not yet in their teens filled bottles with gasoline, lit old rags as wicks, and hurled them at shops with apartments upstairs. Families, good people hiding in terror, ran screaming from their homes as the flames spread.

Perhaps the outbreak was worse for the firefighters, for they had no guns or training for fighting back at snipers. When fire trucks arrived, gunmen shot at the generally white firemen for trying to put out the blazes and save lives. Black firemen were targets as well because a riot has no mentality other than attack with vengeance. We had to give up making arrests because we were needed to run convoy for their equipment. It got so bad that at the first shot, battalion chiefs ordered their men back into the pumpers and ladder trucks. The firefighters watched the buildings burn one by one, heartbroken that they were being forced to stop what they were trained to do.

To my knowledge, not one black alderman or civic leader came out to call an end to the madness. Some ministers went about telling people to stay inside their homes, but we didn't hear of anyone asking the rioters to stop or the looters to give back what they stole.

The radio carried a report of the Robert Hall store going up in flames. My remark of a few hours before seemed stupid to me then, and I was sorry I'd said it. Gunfire, smoke, muzzle shots from roofs, flames, sirens, looters running with anything they could grab, people fighting over stolen goods, neighbors beating and trampling neighbors—it was all an unreal daze.

"Squad 7520, take in sniper fire at … squad 7520, report to shots fired a police … squad 7520, policeman needs help…"

We couldn't respond to all the calls directed to us. We did what we could, not much more than record the requests for service and give them priority, which wasn't easy. We heard so many messages from officers running out of ammunition that I decided to call them all together and distribute some of the supplies from our trunk. The officers showed up at our meeting place behind a station, some in torn uniforms and a lot of them battered. They told me what hell it was out there with no way to stop the snipers. Pernice didn't think giving up our supplies without authorization was such a good idea. Actually, what he said was, "Don't step on your prick." After a little arithmetic, we decided to limit the supplies to six rounds per man, enough to fill up their service revolvers. We served eighty-three men and had two bullets left besides what we had for ourselves. Then it was back to the streets.

From time to time, sniper fire whistled around us and we could hear bullets pinging off squad cards. Our radiator was hit and began leaking badly, and two tires were shot out, but my men never mentioned being scared. I don't think they were. Being surrounded by two days of anarchy had made them fatalists.

We were relieved a little before two o'clock Sunday morning. My uniform smelled of smoke and burning produce, and I had to scrub the soot from my face and hands. I saw some officers turn animal that night and witnessed them beating people who were looting and tossing Molotov cocktails, but the officers didn't kill them. As the kindly Judge Epton might have said—they would have been justified in doing so.

At the Area station the next morning, Riccio told me Commander Johnson wanted me to call him at the command post about giving away my ammunition. Riccio advised me not to lose my temper and added, "We're all a little hyper now." I was prepared to defend myself, but after explaining it all to Johnson, he complimented me for using good judgment.

When I hung up, I saw concern in Pernice's expression. From my end of the phone conversation, he couldn't tell what had been said. After Johnson ended the call, I shouted into the phone, "Well fuck you, I don't care whether you like me or not!" Then I turned to Pernice and said, straight-faced, "It's all right, I told Johnson it was your idea to take all the ammo without my knowledge and sell it."

Pernice, always serious, may have believed me. I know he didn't smile when I told him that!

When we returned to the command post, Riccio walked off with a bag of doughnuts that was intended for the supervisors. He was prepared for another rough day, but the neighborhood was different now. The army troops and National Guardsmen in all their splendor and imposing vehicles had barricaded the major streets during the early morning lull. The appearance of soldiers in full uniform, fully armed, made a strong impression on the would-be rioters. They had no quarrel with the army, and the sight of .50 caliber guns mounted on olive drab vehicles made a lot of people think twice. You could feel the tension, and most people outside had expressions suggesting that they were wondering what could have happened if the troops had not been posted.

The soldiers had been brought in only when there was little left to steal and burn. All electricity and natural gas to the West Side was shut off, and people were speculating about the number of businesses that decided over the weekend never to move in to where shops were looted, vandalized, and set afire. Entire miles were economically abandoned, and the area looked like a bombed out city of World War II.

More than 250 buildings were looted, and many of them had been torched. Police made more than two thousand arrests. Nearly 400 of the prisoners were children. Most of the youngsters had been sent by their families to loot stores because police and soldiers were less likely to fire at them. At least 500 people were injured. Officially, nine people were killed in the riot. We knew there were more, because several bodies of apparent snipers were found in burned-out buildings with rifles at their sides. Maybe one of them was the man I'd been shooting at on Friday. Every action we took was justified—we had been under fire in war conditions—and there was no remorse.

On the day the disturbance ended, we saw a very large safe protruding invincibly from the concrete foundation of ruins in the 3500 block of West Roosevelt Road. I joked that we should wax and polish it as a monument to the riot. Several days later, a police sergeant who we knew very well momentarily lost his mind from the strain of that terrible weekend. He got out of his car and attacked the massive safe with a long-handled axe in broad daylight. People just stared at him as he kept hacking at the dial, and in a few minutes several officers arrived to persuade him to lay down the axe, and lead him to an ambulance.

Just one of the many casualties of the 1968 Chicago Riots.

9

INTRUDER IN THE NIGHT

Charles Percy promised to be the golden boy of Illinois politics. He was a handsome millionaire who saw nothing wrong with stepping out of Republican ranks to vote on some issues supported by Democrats. His mellifluous voice breathed confidence in the future at a time when the escalating Vietnam War was spreading pessimism. His special interest lay in foreign affairs, and some people thought he would someday make a viable candidate for president.

Like many political leaders, Percy was supported by a strong-willed mother, a Christian Scientist who had taught him that "evil must be overcome with good." He and his family began each day with Bible readings and study.

During his 1966 campaign for the U.S. Senate, Percy was being helped by his attractive twenty-one-year-old twin daughters, Valerie and Sharon. They smiled into the cameras and flashed two-fingered victory signs. Valerie worked with her father more often because her sister was unofficially engaged to John D. Rockefeller IV, who was running for the West Virginia legislature.

Before dawn on Sunday, September 18, an intruder cut through a patio screen and glass section of the French doors in the seventeen-room Percy mansion in the exclusive Chicago suburb of Kenilworth. The girls' stepmother, Lorraine, awoke to the tinkle of glass. Then she heard clicking sounds like someone walking on the tile. When that stopped, all she heard was the Lake Michigan breeze rustling through the elm trees that kept the house in seclusion. She thought Valerie or her thirteen-year-old sister, Gail, had knocked a glass tumbler off a bed stand and went back to sleep. Next, she heard a low moan coming from Valerie's room.

"Valerie?" Lorraine called out uncertainly as her husband slept soundly. Mrs. Percy slowly walked down the dark hallway. She saw a light coming from under the door, turned the knob, and was startled to see a shadowy figure standing over her daughter's bed. The intruder was a dark-haired man, about five feet, eight inches tall, and who probably weighed around 160 pounds. She could see his checkered shirt under his light jacket. Before Mrs. Percy could order him out or call for help, he turned the bright beam of his flashlight into her eyes, momentarily blinding her.

The man pushed her out of the way and ran down the corridor. Mrs. Percy raced to her bedroom, woke her husband, and pushed a button in the master bedroom, setting off a burglar siren mounted on top of the house. Charles Percy rushed to Valerie, found her battered and bleeding, and then ran back to his room and grabbed the telephone by his bed. After calling a doctor and a Christian Scientist practitioner, Percy thought he might still find the prowler. That would leave his wife and two other daughters unprotected, though, if the man was still inside the large house, and then a thought came to him that there might also be an accomplice. His fear was greater because this was just after one of the worst crimes in Chicago history—the methodical murders of eight student nurses in their South Side townhouse by a skid row drifter named Richard Speck.

When the English houseman came to take over protecting the family, Percy looked everywhere for the man his wife had seen but could find no trace of him. He turned off the wailing alarm when the police arrived. One of the officers felt Valerie's faint pulse, but the young woman died moments later. Filled with rage, Percy pounded the alarm button again and let the siren do his screaming for him. By then the killer had fled, possibly down the private beach.

An autopsy showed that Valerie had been hit several times with a heavy instrument that left peculiar pine cone-shaped dents in her skull. The police believed that the weapon could have been a ball-peen hammer with one end sharpened to a point, resembling a tool used by jewelers or silversmiths. The young woman also was stabbed fourteen times in the face, neck, and chest with a narrow two-edged blade.

The family was frozen in grief. Popular Senator Paul Douglas offered his condolences and immediately canceled his campaign against Percy for the mourning period. The eleven member Kenilworth police had never handled a murder before, and they called out for all the help they could get. In time, nearly one hundred officers from the Chicago, suburban, and state police departments were working on the killing, as well as the State's Attorney's Office and agents from the FBI. However, nothing in the seventeen bags of possible evidence provided a clue, and hundreds of phone tips just muddied the waters and led investigators in various directions.

Making the investigation more difficult was that there was no clear motive. Valerie had not been sexually molested, and the killer left without taking her jewelry or the money that had been left folded on the dresser. Police could not even be sure if Valerie had been the intended victim. Suppose the man had come to kill Sharon and got the wrong daughter? The other twin had come home from a date at 11:30 that night, spoken with Valerie for a few minutes, and then gone to bed in her own room.

Police compiled a list of 285 people to question, and the description of the killer was too general to be of much help. Neighbors reported seeing a man on the driveway looking at the house just four hours before the murder. A turbaned man from Bombay, India, drew suspicion when he refused to be fingerprinted for comparison with the dustings at the house, and for a while the officers suspected a young man in Percy's campaign office who had angered a lot of people by his fast promotions. Percy also told of receiving a crank letter a few months before, saying:

Just be careful what you say from now until June.
THE BOYS FROM OUT OF TOWN

A youth told police in Arizona that a stranger had paid him seventy-five dollars to kill anyone in the home, and several other confessing "murderers" came forward to claim they had killed Valerie.

The most promising lead was that the intruder might have been the cat burglar who had been prowling around Evanston, a suburb between Kenilworth and Chicago. He had attacked a nineteen-year old woman in a similar way, but she survived. The leads were very slim in that case.

One of Chicago's most active police officers, Bernie Sako of the Shakespeare Avenue District, received tips from a hardcore criminal named *Oscar. Being a uniformed officer, Sako had limitations in verifying certain information he was getting. He chose to do what he had done many times in the past—he went upstairs to my office in the Area Five building and talked over what he had picked up from his informer.

Oscar, who had been in jail at the time of the killing, said he'd read about the crime in the newspaper and that the method of operation was similar to an ex-crime partner of his, Fred Malchow, alias James Nykaza. The name was familiar to me, but I had never arrested him. I knew what he looked like because police bulletins had been published with photos of him and the men and women who were his accomplices. He was blond, middle-aged, stocky, and had a deceptively innocent face. Malchow was a member of a loosely-knit robbery gang that specialized in early morning home invasions of wealthy people. The informant, hoping to claim Percy's $50,000 reward, said Malchow had spent five years in a Wisconsin prison for raping a young socialite he had tied to the four corners of a bed during a robbery. He also was arrested under an assumed name somewhere in California.

I notified my unit commanding officer, Walter Vallee, and he asked me to notify the citywide Robbery Commander, Earl Johnson. Knowing that the tiny Kenilworth police department was inundated with leads to follow up, Johnson suggested that I choose a partner and verify the new information on our own.

"You two will be unofficially assigned to the Percy case and report directly to me," he said.

I picked Richard Riccio, the great driver, because he was a good investigator and Johnson already had assigned us to work on some home invasions, which were always considered to be prestigious assignments because of the flashy nature of the crimes and the often dramatic arrests.

The Percy case started out as just busy work for Rick and me. Who could trust the word of a reward-hungry semi-reformed burglar? I went over Malchow's record from the FBI and did not find anything to suggest he was a cold-blooded person who could murder a millionaire's daughter. He was arrested for vagrancy in Appleton, Wisconsin, but there was nothing about a supposed Wisconsin rape charge. We did learn that in 1950 he served a term for tying up and raping a seventeen-year-old girl in upstate and upscale Hamburg, New York. Malchow was discharged from Auburn Prison in 1955, and by then his wife had divorced him. He also served a year back in Wisconsin for jail break, and his arrest sheet revealed a variety of other charges nationwide.

I typed up a few letters to authorities across the country to learn a little more about Malchow instead of relying on the arrest records that had few details.

In 1965, citizens in Anaheim, California, caught him prowling while his fly was open and he had a tube of Vaseline. He jumped bail, which had been posted, suspiciously, by a wig maker who disappeared after her place had been burglarized.

Malchow emerged from these dry reports as a brutish man who apparently had expensive tastes and stocked his apartment and garage with stolen property. We learned that some of the commercial burglaries apparently had been "put-up jobs" arranged by the owners for the insurance, which might explain why he was all the way in California and why a burglary victim had posted his bail.

This possible link to the Percy case became more interesting, but what the hell, he was just another suspect among hundreds.

We located Oscar's brother, *Paul, who knew even more about Malchow. Paul, who was also in jail at the time of the Valerie Percy murder, told us that Malchow always seemed kind of goofy. "He might be carrying an antique revolver with an extension on the handle that looked like a blackjack," he said, something the Shakespeare District officer had known but forgot to mention. "Oh, yeah," Paul added, "he always carried a knife along with the gun."

Was Paul just adding the knife because he'd read that Valerie was stabbed as well as beaten? I was dubious because I had found that criminal informants added lies and guesses to the truth if just to keep in practice. Still, Riccio and I kept listening.

Paul said that whenever Malchow went on a score, it would have to be a high class home or he wouldn't bother. He staked out the house for up to a month, sometimes even climbing trees to watch the activities for hours. That way, he learned what times the lights went out and when the last person retired. Malchow, envying the rich, may also have received gratification from spying on the wealthy and feeling more powerful than them.

Paul added that Malchow had burglarized a mansion in Lake Forest, near Kenilworth, in June, and stole thousands of dollars in jewelry. The intruder had defecated on the floor and wiped himself with a silk scarf, as if expressing contempt for his victims. I had investigated numerous burglaries in which the thieves did something similar, and during questioning they always attributed their actions to nervousness while committing their crimes.

Malchow, though, went further than just defecating. On a score in another North Shore suburb, he killed a cat in the yard, slipped into the home, and, after stealing the valuables, placed the animal's body alongside a sleeping woman. Once, while he was in a mansion out of state, he masturbated into a condom, knotted the top, and placed it in a woman's purse.

At least, this was what Paul said Malchow enjoyed telling his cohorts, and these despicable acts had the ring of truth. The imagination behind the acts must have been tied in with anger and half-disguised sexual feelings. Not that I could ever explain what went on in Malchow's head. His emotions were all mixed up, and he might not even have been aware of the feelings that drove him to what he did and the reason he bragged about his exploits.

Riccio and I drove to Lake Forest to start verifying or discounting Paul's information. The officers we spoke to asked us, "How did you know about the defecation and the scarf? That information hasn't been disseminated to anyone." The officers were deeply concerned. We received a similar response from Winnetka police about the cat incident. That meant the wild stories Malchow told his partners in crime were true. We were aware that the Malchow connection was just one more possibility that would have to be pursued by the small army of investigators spread out across the Midwest, but he started to look like a better suspect as the days went on.

Once I had corroboration about the soiled scarf and the dead cat, I drove to police headquarters to turn my information over to Commander Johnson. He listened intently and just glanced at the confirming letters. "John," he said, "you have reached a point where I believe you should turn over all of this to the Kenilworth task force. I really think you have something and still want you and Riccio to maintain contact with the informants, develop all subsequent leads, and, most importantly, try and locate Fred Malchow. Let me know when you succeed."

As I left Johnson's office, curiosity led me to the corridors of the crime lab. Chicago had the oldest crime lab in the world—the original version was set up at Northwestern University during the Capone era and was then copied by Scotland Yard and the FBI. While being ignored by technicians passing by in white coats, I was drawn to the glass cabinet of confiscated weapons, each chosen for its age or unusual design. These were considered the most interesting guns of the thousands seized over the years. I knew what I was looking for, but since I had never seen one, I didn't expect to find it—an old revolver with a blackjack handle extension, as our informant described. Then, I found myself facing it. Locked up behind glass was a gun similar, and perhaps identical, to what Malchow could have used to kill Valerie Percy.

As I stood in front of the cabinet, I saw the murder played out in my mind. Malchow and a partner prowling the silent mansion with a flashlight. Valerie awaking and screaming while her room is being searched. Malchow bringing the blackjack portion of such a unique weapon down on her head repeatedly, knocking her unconscious and perhaps killing her. Then whipping out his knife and stabbing her while receiving sexual gratification from his savagery. His partner turning and running out of the house, leaving Malchow to finish his butchery as Mrs. Percy enters the room.

Someone tapped me on the shoulder while these thoughts raced through my mind. I turned to see the crime lab director, former citywide Homicide Commander Frank Flanagan.

"Oh, hi, boss," I said. Flanagan was a fine administrator and he had a great personality. Well-liked by everyone.

"Why the interest in guns, John? I've been watching you stare at the cabinet for the last ten minutes."

"Well, to be honest, I guess I was day-dreaming. I'm looking at the pine-cone pattern along the handle that looks like a blackjack on that gun." I pointed it out to him. "Don't you think something like that could have been used to strike Valerie Percy on the head?"

For a moment Flanagan joined me in peering at the weapon and mentally matching it with the coroner's descriptions of the wounds. Fascinated by the possibility, Flanagan invited me for a cup of coffee so he'd have someone with whom he could talk it over. He put an arm on my shoulder and asked one of his technicians to unlock the cabinet and bring the gun to his office.

"What's up, John? Have a seat, haven't seen you for a while," Flanagan said, setting down his mug, a crystal cup etched with a map of the world. He picked up the gun and felt its weight and balance, and held the handle to see how the extension could be used as a club. "Amazing," he said, and then he mentioned how the curved indentations might fit the impressions beaten into Valerie's skull. Since I had not yet worked Homicide, I was unfamiliar with some of the terms he rattled off.

"Out of all the weapons and tools we examined, I would have to say that a weapon like this is the one most likely to have been used to kill Valerie. Why didn't we consider this? You probably have an informant on this, don't you?"

"A couple of them. They're pointing the finger at a certain

individual who supposedly has a gun like this. So far, everything they're supplying seems to check out."

"How would you like to come work for me on the Percy
case?" Flanagan was no headline grabber, difficult cases just
intrigued him. He would do anything to solve a case personally,
and he thought nothing of giving credit to someone else.

"I'm sorry," I replied, "Commander Johnson has already put
me on it full time."

Flanagan shook my hand and said, "Well, anything you
need, come down and see me."

Riccio and I discussed our plan of action, and then we
conferred with the man in charge of the Percy task force, Bob
Lamb of the Illinois State Police. Lamb, one of the nicer guys in
the business, listened to us more with patience than interest.
He told us of the possible suspects the task force members were
running down, including someone who lived in a "wayward
home" not far from the Percy mansion. Dropping his voice
practically to a whisper, he confidentially told us that the Percy
children had entertained some of the wayward youngsters. It was
obvious that Lamb was attempting to discount our information,
and he seemed to be reluctantly recording Malchow's name in
his notebook.

Lamb came from his background in police work, and I came
from mine, and my experience told me that the wayward home
lead would prove a dead end. Malchow may or may not have
been the killer, but I was sure that the murder was committed
by someone fairly like him.

So Riccio and I began building a case against Malchow.
From time to time I wished I had taken up Flanagan's offer,
knowing that I would then have access to everything besides
police and coroner reports, but at the same time we could
feel the Malchow trail heating up. At last we learned from
an airplane baggage ticket and other information that he and
home invasion specialist Harold James Evans had been hanging
together and had positively been in the Chicago area when
Valerie was murdered.

Now we tried even harder to locate Malchow. We went to
the Chicago Police Intelligence division for credit checks in

hopes of learning his address. We inquired at post offices in Chicago and suburbs for forwarding addresses. We checked on Malchow and Evans at the Secretary of State's office, but they had no record of issuing a driver's license to either man.

We spent five months interviewing acquaintances, poring over files, making telephone calls, writing letters, and crossing out possibilities that led nowhere. We wished we had the cooperation of the Percy task force.

By November, though, we learned that Malchow and his teenage wife, Edna, had been living in the west suburb of Addison. We rushed there and found a string of look-alike townhouses on North Avenue. A husband and wife identified Malchow's mug shot and said their daughter used to babysit for our man's two young children until the couple moved out in August. Two things were odd about their home, the family told us—the furnishings looked very expensive, and there were wigs all over the place.

"When did they move in?" Riccio asked.

"Sometime in April," the woman answered hesitantly. April—the month Valerie was killed. "They took over Mr. Harrington's lease. They really had nice tastes, but we, uh, never found out what they did."

"We thought he was from the syndicate," her husband jumped in. "People around here just don't have that kind of money to throw around. My God, their baby had necklaces with big diamonds, a karat or more—a baby! People like that, you just don't ask them what they do. But they didn't work!"

With the woman and her husband aiding each other's memories, they said Fred and Edna owned two new Oldsmobile's, one a gold 98 and the other a dark maroon with a black top. The man who had sub-leased the home after Malchow, *Jim Jeffords, was only too happy to give us information about him. Jeffords received a phone bill for a call in his name to a New Jersey Holiday Inn in August. From that motel, we learned that the couple had stayed there under the names of Mr. and Mrs. Carl Jeffords from the Chicago suburb of Villa Park. Their new Ford had the license plate issued to a Chicago man who drove a four-year-old Chevrolet. The real Mr. Jeffords told us that Edna picked up the couple's mail from him the week before, saying they were expecting something important and would be back. She never returned or called after that, though.

Riccio and I thought we might have enough information to find Malchow with the leads we developed, but we didn't have any firm indications that he was the killer.

By then we were receiving feedback that certain bosses thought the two of us were off on a tangent and wasting a lot of time. Despite the trust of Commander Johnson and crime lab chief Flanagan, the chief of detectives ordered us off the case. Only he knew why he intervened, but maybe our work was getting too much notoriety, since some of the letters and calls in answer to our inquiries were directed to police headquarters rather than to Area Five. The chief gave the case to the Criminal Investigations Unit, which reported directly to him, and ordered us to supply CIU with all the reports and information we had cultivated. That made everything simpler—so simple that the investigation went nowhere from then on, and no one asked to speak to our informants.

On the other hand, what did we really have? A lot of paperwork and little patterns that we thought we'd found but had not yet come together. I retained copies of the more interesting reports, and we followed up the loose ends whenever we had time between our robbery investigations.

We almost were to the point of agreeing with the detective chief that Malchow was nothing more than an ordinary burglar, but in the late winter of 1967 our informants, Paul and Oscar, called and said they had bumped into Malchow at a restaurant. They learned that he and his sometimes-partner, Evans, were on their way to Pennsylvania for more mansion break-ins. Even though we'd been taken off the case, we excitedly brought our new information to the chief, CIU, and to Bob Lamb and his task force. They simply were not interested and still discounted Malchow as a possible suspect.

In April, Malchow and Evans were being held without bail on charges of raping a moderately wealthy housewife in Wynnewood, Pennsylvania, and stealing $15,000 in furs and jewelry during a home invasion. Malchow was also charged with two earlier robberies, one of which was in the home of the daughter of a former treasurer of the National Democratic Party. The daughter was tied up while Malchow took $98,000 in jewelry.

Officers from units across northern Illinois called us, wanting to know if we had connected Malchow to the Percy slaying, and all we could do was refer them to Lamb or CIU. Riccio and I wanted to go to Pennsylvania so badly we could taste it. Since Malchow always bragged to his underworld friends about the bizarre aspects of his crimes, we felt confident we could get him to trip up. Even if Malchow didn't admit his involvement, we thought that we could talk to Evans and present the personal information we had developed regarding Malchow, such as the gun, and get him to inform on his partner. We also would be the perfect people to talk to the suspects, or so we thought, but the FBI became interested as well.

There were some police officers who admired the FBI, and although the agents did have a military efficiency, the Bureau was not known for cooperating with the local police. The agents usually seemed to step in at the wrong time, come in with their own agenda, and take the credit when something went right. When it went wrong, they stepped away with clean hands and blamed the other agencies. Most often, time proved to be a benefit to the FBI, and they waited until a major case was close to being solved, and then stepped in to finalize the investigation.

In possession of our reports and believing that they could solve the Percy case, two FBI agents set up separate jail interviews with Malchow and Evans. We don't know what went on, but later learned that Malchow admitted that he knew something about the case, but he insisted that Evans did it. Evans, grilled separately, repeatedly said he was innocent, but that Malchow had admitted the murder.

According to an FBI report, Evans said Malchow claimed that Valerie Percy had kept trying to get up, and that was why he had to stab her so many times. The agents, according to my reliable information, concluded that they had enough information to solve the case, and wanted the men to be sentenced for the Pennsylvania home invasions before making a deal with Evans. Then they'd officially announce that Malchow was being charged with murder. It made sense; they must have felt that they had all the time in the world, considering that the pair was safely locked up.

The interview they conducted turned up the heat on Malchow, who was already facing heavy time for the Pennsylvania home invasions. Confirmed sources revealed that he and Evans remained friends because both had "beefed" on the other to the FBI, and the disloyalties canceled each other out. Or they might have had other plans. Both men were convicted of the Pennsylvania crimes on June 26 and sentenced that same day to serve 199 years in prison. As they were led away, they managed to break free and run in different directions, doubling their chances of escape by thinning out the number of guards after each man. Evans climbed over the barbed wire fence with clothing over his hands for protection. He outdistanced the correctional officers and disappeared.

Malchow took the direction of the Schykill River flowing near the Montgomery County Jail. He was a good swimmer and thought the guards with tracking dogs would never find where he emerged, since the water would erase his scent. But the river was muddy, and he didn't realize how shallow it was. He leaped head first into the rock bed, plunging with such force that his head drove into his chest cavity. Malchow died instantly.

We wanted the FBI to comment on what Malchow might have said, but the agents in charge in Chicago and Philadelphia, embarrassed at having blown one of the worst murder cases in the country, denied that federal agents had ever questioned either man. Then why did the agents file "302 reports,"— documents filled out by agents after interviewing people who were willing to make a statement? They were similar to written confessions, but the suspects or the people being interviewed don't sign them.

I also have personal information that Bob Lamb interviewed Malchow in jail, and the suspect admitted being in the gangway of the Percy home but denied killing Valerie. He may have been the man some neighbors saw acting suspiciously four hours before the murder.

In 1991, long after the crime, John O'Brien of the *Chicago Tribune* quoted Lamb as saying about the homicide:

"To this day I am convinced that Freddie Malchow was the killer and that he acted alone. We considered Malchow our prime suspect for several reasons: (1) He was a professional burglar who specialized in nighttime home invasions, (2) We were able to place him in Chicago at the time of the murder through an airline baggage ticket, and (3) At least two of Malchow's underworld associates have said that Freddie admitted the murder to them."

How about that? Lamb and many others were convinced that after police interviewed an estimated 10,000 people and investigated 1,200 possible suspects, Malchow was the killer.

A frequently arrested home invader, Francis Hohimer, also told authorities that Malchow, a one time member of his gang, was the killer. A jailhouse informant claimed Malchow had told him he was afraid the police might find a pair of trousers that could link him to the slaying. Agents, believe it or not, located the pants, and they did have blood stains on them. According to the FBI, though, the stains were too old, and lab testing at the time couldn't determine if the blood was human or animal.

Evans was arrested two years after his escape. All the agencies were soon on top of him for information about his late partner. Evans' polygraph examinations suggested that he was with Malchow when Valerie was killed but that he didn't take part in the murder. His wife's polygraph results suggested that her husband had told her that he was with Malchow when the murder occurred.

A lot of police officers who worked on the case continued to walk around with snippets of information in their heads that they never divulged. There's something about the investigative mentality that makes some cops think that what they've dug up is their personal property, and they don't share it unless they have to.

I feel proud of the fact that I worked on the Percy case and surrendered all the information that Riccio and I uncovered, and

I feel proud that Officer Bernie Sako, who originally received the information, turned it over to me.

It was my firm belief that the truth of the Percy case would finally emerge if all of the agencies that worked on it came together and assembled the parts of the puzzle. That's the thought I carried with me ever since the investigation was dropped, especially when I read Lamb's quote in the newspaper. The case should be cleared for the anguished family and the sake of justice.

And because Valerie's voice is still calling out from the grave.

From left to right: Group # 10   1957

Bottom row: W. Proctor; P. Callotta; R. Collins; F. DeMauro; J. DiMaggio;
              J. Madison; J. DeLopez; L. LaPaglia; M. Darcy; T. Campagna
Second row: Sgt. C. Jaeger, Instructor; F. Owick; D. Drnek; W. Dinse; J. Casey;
              C. Odierno; J. Kosminskas; R. Desmond; L. Clark; J. Lucchesi;
              E. Shields, Instructor
Third row: J. Coughlin; R. Somerville; L. Stomp; L. Cammon; B. DelPrincipe;
              A. Gaudio; E. Divito; L.Dorsey; R. Bychowski; A. Clements; C. Deasy;
              H. Kielbasa; T. Corcoran
Top row: D. Drake; N. Defilippis; K. DePaula; W. Bassie; C. deVyver; W. Connolly;
              W. Gename; J. Carroll; H. Dozier; T. Cannon; R. Drake

(*below*) John DiMaggio's first year in the Chicago Police Academy
(*back row, far right*).

(*second row, third from the right*) John DiMaggio pictured with his fellow officers.

SUPERINTENDENT OF POLICE

CHICAGO

19 May 1961

TRIO ADMITS 25 BURGLARIES; 2 INVOLVE FIRES

Three men in custody yesterday admitted 25 burglaries, two of which resulted in fires which destroyed the buildings, police said. They are Joseph Giffee, 22, of 4108 N. Keystone av., Kenneth Kneitz, 24, of 3851 N. Oakley av.; and George Ikmanis, 24, of 93 Edward st.; Northlake.

Detectives John DiMaggio, Charles Swaner, Walter Carter and Charles Peop, investigating the burglaries, found torn fragments of checks taken in the burglary of a meat market at 1472 Milwaukee av. in the basement of a building at 1859 N. Mobile av., where Giffee formerly lived.

Giffee was arrested and named his companions. Ikmanis was arrested yesterday when he appeared in Felony court on another burglary charge. The burglaries which resulted in fires were at the B & G grill, 7191 Addison st., and the Overhead Garage Door company, 3824 N. Harlem av.

Dear John:

Nice going! Keep up the good work!

Sincerely,

Superintendent of Police

Detective John A. DiMaggio

HU 9-2352-53

CHICAGO POLICE DEPARTMENT
DETECTIVE DIVISION AREA 5

BURGLARY UNIT   J. DIMAGGIO

'For Skill, Courage'

Cite Two Who Solved Killings

TWO DETECTIVES from Area 5 burglary unit have been awarded department commendations for work leading to arrest of a suspect in two homicides and several robberies.

Cited for "perseverance, skill and ingenuity, coupled with clever exploitation of information, courage under hazardous circumstances and good police methods" were Detectives John DeMaggio and Steve Pizzello.

They were commended for an investigation that led to arrest of Frank O'Connell, an ex-convict since charged with the Aug. 21 holdup-murder of Frank Sullivan in a tavern on Elston and the subsequent slaying of Charles White, his alleged accomplice in the robbery.

THE PROBE started Sept.

18 when Pizzello and DiMaggio learned that a woman was being held against her will at Windsor and Avers. After three days of surveillance, the officers pinpointed the apartment and learned from other residents that the flat was also occupied by O'Connell, an ex-convict known as an associate of White, whose body had been found near Bartlett, Ill.

O'Connell's car matched that used in the Sullivan murder.

Entering the apartment, the detectives separated the woman from her captor, and learned that she was being held against her will.

The woman told police that O'Connell had killed White because the latter was discussing the Sullivan murder too freely. She also gave a detailed account of other crimes, which led to clearance of nine armed robberies.

CHICAGO POLICE DEPARTMENT

presents to

Detective

John DiMaggio

Detective Division Area 5

this

DEPARTMENT COMMENDATION

for

an outstanding act or achievement which brings credit to the Department and which involves performance above and beyond that required by the member's assignment.

PRESENTED BY:

Deputy Chief of Detectives

DATE: 20 November 1964

(below) John DiMaggio (second from the left) & partner Steve Pizzello (second from the right) accepting their 1964 Department Commendation Awards.

Station on the corner of Damen and Grace closed in 1975, and was replaced
shortly thereafter with a new fire station.

(*above*) John DiMaggio (*back row, fourth from the left*). (*below*) John DiMaggio (*front row, far right*) with Mario Maida (*top row, second from the left*).

(*above*) Detective DiMaggio in a rare playful moment in his backyard.
(below) John with his wife, Rosemary.

31 MAR 66 CHICA

Arrest Janitor as Slasher of Twenty Women

Police early today arrested a board of education janitor believed to be the slasher of at least 20 northwest side women.

Taken t...
Shakes p...
avenue ...
was G...
Hall,...
3807 N....
Par...
janito...
Gregory Hall   Far...
school, 5414 Linder a...
Hall, married and ...
of a 2-year-old so...
rested in his car ...
street and Milwa...
shortly after Jane...
32, of 6145 Thorn...
slashed and rob...
home.

She was tak...
tion hospital, ...
50 stitches ...
close an 8-i...
neck and b...
purse contai...
taken.

Victi...
Miss I...
the car h...
drove off ...
car was ...
Sgt. Joh...
Evans.

In j...
huntin...
mitte...
mey...
T...
pur...
20...
attacu...
cember. Accor...
of the 20 were raped.
DiMaggio said Hall admitted attacking "many women, but I don't know how many. I guess I'm sick."

Hall will be placed in a show-up today before many of the 20 victims.

Quizzed on Schuesslers

Police said he also will be questioned about the 1955 murder of John Schuessler, 13; his brother, Anton Jr., 11, and Robert Peterson, 14. Bodies of the youngsters, students at the

Slasher of 20 Women Caught After Attack

31 MAR 1966

BY TONY SOWA

(Picture on back page)

A young man was captured by police on the northwest side late last night shortly after, they said, he had slashed and robbed a woman. They said he apparently is responsible for at least 20 similar assaults on women in the area since last fall.

Greg Hall, 26, of 3807 N. Central Park av., a machinist, who is married and the father of a 2-year-old son, was arrested. His victim, Miss Jane Fechtmeyer, 32, of 6145 Thorn-... rushed to Resur-...

more

[TRIBUNE Staff Photo]

Greg Hall at Shakespeare avenue police station.

block. Adamson stopped Miss ...'s bleeding and ...bulance.

As Wolf enc...
bank, he saw another ...
pulling out of his parking space.

It was being driven by a woman who said she had been parked there, "for a few minutes.".

Wolfe, 43, was mystified as to how his auto which was equipped with a burglar alarm, could be hijacked with ...

than 20 ... said. Sgt. DiMaggio ... admitted the other attacks, as well as that on Miss Fechtmeyer.

The policeman said some of the victims were raped.

He said Hall admitted being

LICENSE CI... BY DETECTI... NETS SUSP...

Linked To 15 H... At Cleaners, Can... Shops Here

Robbery Unit dete... this week reported a ... charged with at lea... armed holdups of N... West area cleaning's... and candy shops d... the past month will ... trial in Felony C... April 1.

The suspect is Dona... LaReaux, 35, of 1911 ... ner, who is arreste... detectives Mar. 15 at Ad... and Broadway in an auto ... in the Mar. 9 holdup of a ... ing store at 5328 W. Mad...

Police said in addition ... the string of area holdups ... ...ed to LaReaux, ... — victim...

...
...old ...
ng P...
yn P...
ey. F...
09 La...
Stockho...
...ton, F...
...ake Sh...
d., Feb.

mont, Me...; Dutch N...
Candy Store, $245 Bryn Maw...
Mar. 3, $10; Leader Cleane...
2824 Diversey, Mar. 4, $...
Leader Cleaners, 3300 Lawren...

Larry Evans (far left) and John DiMaggio (second from the left).

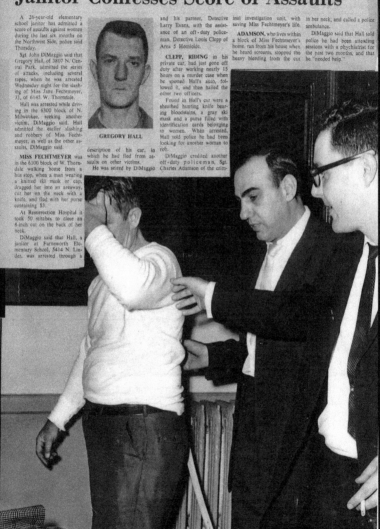

24 ☆   CHICAGO DAILY NEWS, Thursday, March 31, 1966

Janitor Confesses Score of Assaults

A 26-year-old elementary school janitor has admitted a score of assaults against women during the last six months on the Northwest Side, police said Thursday.

Sgt. John DiMaggio said that Gregory Hall, of 3807 N. Central Park, admitted the series of attacks, including several rapes, when he was arrested Wednesday night for the slashing of Miss Jane Fechtmeyer, 33, of 6143 W. Thorndale.

Hall was arrested while driving in the 6300 block of N. Milwaukee, seeking another victim, DiMaggio said. Hall admitted the earlier slashing and robbery of Miss Fechtmeyer, as well as the other assaults, DiMaggio said.

MISS FECHTMEYER was in the 6100 block of W. Thorndale walking home from a bus stop, when a man wearing a knitted ski mask or cap, dragged her into an areaway, cut her on the neck with a knife, and fled with her purse containing $3.

At Resurrection Hospital it took 50 stitches to close an 8-inch cut on the back of her neck.

DiMaggio said that Hall, a janitor at Farnsworth Elementary School, 5414 N. Linder, was arrested through a

GREGORY HALL

description of his car, in which he had fled from assaults on other victims.

He was seized by DiMaggio

and his partner, Detective Larry Evans, with the assistance of an off-duty policeman, Detective Louis Clepp of Area 5 Homicide.

CLEPP, RIDING in his private car, had just gone off duty after working nearly 15 hours on a murder case when he spotted Hall's auto, followed it, and then hailed the other two officers.

Found in Hall's car were a sheathed hunting knife bearing bloodstains, a gray ski mask and a purse filled with identification cards belonging to women. When arrested, Hall told police he had been looking for another woman to rob.

DiMaggio credited another off-duty policeman, Sgt. Charles Adamson of the crim-

inal investigation unit, with saving Miss Fechtmeyer's life.

ADAMSON, who lives within a block of Miss Fechtmeyer's home, ran from his house when he heard screams, stopped the heavy bleeding from the cut

in her neck, and called a police ambulance.

DiMaggio said that Hall told police he had been attending sessions with a psychiatrist for the past two months, and that he "needed help."

142

John DiMaggio (*second from the right*)

CITY OF CHICAGO / **DEPARTMENT OF POLICE**   1121 South State Street   Chicago 5, Illinois   WAbash 2-4747

RICHARD J. DALEY, *Mayor*
O. W. WILSON, *Superintendent*

Ⱶonorable Mention

10 May 1966

Sergeant John DiMaggio
Detective Division
Area 5, Robbery

   I would like to take this opportunity to commend you for
your excellent performance in the investigation and arrest of Gregory
HALL, charged with 2 Rapes, 3 Armed Robberies and 1 Aggravated Battery.

   On 30 March 1966, at 2200 hrs., a 32 year old single woman was
returning home from bowling and got off the Milwaukee Ave. bus and was
walking to her home when she was grabbed from behind and the man attempted
to drag her into a passageway, at which time she put up tremendous resis-
tence and screamed. The offender then slashed at her with an 8" hunting
knife. The offender took her purse and fled.

   Your leadership and careful analysis of this crime which you
associated with a previous crime pattern and your determination, resulted
in the arrest of the perpetrator several hours after he committed this
most serious crime. Your actions in this case are in keeping with the
highest traditions of the Police Department and are deserving of recognition.

   You are hereby awarded an Honorable Mention. My sincere thanks
and appreciation for a job well done.

   A copy of this letter is being forwarded to the Personnel
Division for inclusion in your personnel jacket.

Earl R. Johnson
Robbery - Commander

CPC-11.194 (1/63)

(*below*) John DiMaggio (*far left*) with Richard Riccio (far right).

Police Nab 'Bonnie and Clyde' Pair

A bandit team who said they were inspired by the movie "Bonnie and Clyde" used a trick the other couple never thought of.

During a 2½-week robbery spree, the female member of the team, Margaret Quinlan, 36, of 721 Belmont av., had her

Peter Bianchi   Margaret Quinlan

flaming red hair trimmed in crew-cut style, and wore men's clothing. The pair are suspected of committing 20 or more robberies.

Miss Quinlan and her companion, Peter Bianchi, 36, were arrested separately last night, but both admitted they were aware the law was closing in.

Surrenders at Headquarters

The woman went to police headquarters at 1121 S. State st., surrendered, and admitted her part in the robberies, according to Sgt. Richard Riccio.

She also said Bianchi could be found at the home of his estranged wife at 2414 Cullom av., but other detectives were already on his trail, and found him hiding under a pile of dirty clothing.

"Don't shoot. I'm unarmed. I threw my gun in the river, he said.

Feared Being Slain

He later said he didn't try to resist "because I didn't want to end up like Clyde."

Clyde Barrow and Bonnie Parker, who gained fame as bank robbers in the 1930s, were shot to death in a police ambush.

Riccio said the pair had been sought since April 3 for gas station, grocery, and tavern robberies that netted them more than $3,000.

"The trouble was we thought we were looking for two guys," Riccio declared.

Seized in Dope Case

Bianchi and Miss Quinlan were tripped up when they were arrested Tuesday night by federal narcotics agents, for allegedly selling narcotics.

They were released on bond, then rearrested last night for the robberies.

Judge Daniel J. Ryan in Felony court today set $60,-000 bonds for each on six counts of armed robbery. The case was continued to May 8.

The pair were identified by six victims last night in a s h o w u p after their arrest. Others will view them later.

Police said Bianchi had a record dating back to 1951, including convictions for strongarm robbery and burglary.

Bianchi and Miss Quinlan carried .32 caliber revolvers on the robberies, but never fired any shots, detectives said.

Questioning of Bonnie and Clyde ensues.

CHICAGO POLICE DEPARTMENT

VOLUME 7, NUMBER 198
17 July 1966

DAILY  BULLETIN

O.W. WILSON, SUPERINTENDENT   CONFIDENTIAL – FOR POLICE USE ONLY

WANTED FOR MURDER

RICHARD B. SPECK
Alias: Richard Franklin Lindberg and
Richard Benjamin Speck.

M/W, 25, 6-1, 160, brown blonde hair, slightly longer than crewcut; blue eyes; Tattoos: "Born to Raise Hell" upper left arm- a hat and goggles; on right forearm - a dagger and sickle. Has Acne scars on face. Wanted on warrant for murder of eight nurses at 2319 E. 100th St. R.D. E208706 – Homicide-Sex, Area 2.

WANTED ON BURGLARY WARRANT

JOHN WESLEY MYRICK – I.R. 137545
815 So. Independence Blvd.

M/N, 17, 5-9, 131, slender build, medium brn comp. brn eyes, black hair, clean shaven, wore dark green ¾ length leather coat, brn and cream knitted shirt, gray dress pants, black shoes. Warrant for burglary on file. R.D. E164922 – Burglary Section, Area 4.

MISSING PERSON

KAREN L. HORN
2731 W. Lawrence Avenue

F/W, 15, 5-2, 115, medium build, light comp, blue eyes, blonde hair. May be in company of Cecelia Taylor (See Bulletin Vol. 7, No. 196). Subject frequents 17th and 20th Dist. Missing since 8 July 1966. R.D. E2033113- Youth Section, Area 6.

SEE and HEAR • • •

"Kup Show" on ABC-TV, Channel 7, Sat., 16 July 12 Midnite. Featuring Dir. Patrick V. Needham, Planning Division.

THREE North Side youths were charged with resisting arrest and illegal possession of a shotgun Sunday. Det. Sgt. John DiMaggio (below, at right) said he subdued them at gunpoint after he spotted them handling a sawed-off shotgun in a car parked at Pensacola and Milwaukee. Above, Sgt. James Castellano holds one of the arrested youths, Timothy Cresewski, 17, of 4602 N. Hoyne. The others were Ronald Arisnedi, 20, of 4355 N. Milwaukee, and John Brennan, 19, of 3441 N. Troy. The gun they allegedly possessed is examined (below) by Det. George Lenai and DiMaggio.

(*above*) Sarge (*back row, third from the right*).
(*below*) Richard Riccio, John DiMaggio and August Locallo (*from left to right*).

CHICAGO SUN-TIMES

★ ★ ★ ★
FINAL

©1969 by Field Enterprises Inc.

3000   FRIDAY, DECEMBER 26, 1969   112 Pages—10 Cents

CLYDE WEDGWOOD

Musician with symphony slain; North Side man, woman arrested

Clyde Wedgwood, 57, French horn player in the Chicago Symphony Orchestra, was found murdered Thursday in his North Side apartment.

Police said Wedgwood had been strangled with a piece of twine in the Brinwood Apartment Hotel, 5441 N. Kenmore.

A man and woman have been arrested and charged with robbery and murder.

The prisoners, Gerald King, 21, of 5025 N. Winthrop, and Michelle Myers, 20, of 5036 N. Winthrop, were scheduled to appear Friday in Felony Court.

Wedgwood's naked body was discovered by detectives following up a tip that rifles had been stolen from the musician's apartment.

An informant had notified the police that four high-powered rifles with telescopic sights were taken from the victim's flat Wednesday night and could be found at King's apartment.

Apparently, the informant was not aware that the musician had been slain, police said.

Sgt. John DiMaggio and Det. Charles Green of Damen Av. Robbery Division, arrested King and Miss Myers in King's apartment Thursday morning. The stolen weapons also were found there, police said.

DiMaggio and Green then went to Wedgwood's apartment, intending to ask him whether he could identify the rifles and found his body.

According to a statement Miss Myers gave

Turn to Page 26

(*above, from left to right*) August Locallo, Larry Evans and John DiMaggio at the Pugwash Conference of the World in 1970. (*below*) August Locallo and John DiMaggio with Governor Ogilvie at the Governor's Awards.

10

ROBBERS AND THE MAD BOMBER

The King marches and sporadic race riots woke up the department to the need for more African-American recruiting. No one had a tougher job in the city than those new black officers. They were sneered at by fellow blacks as "Uncle Toms," and they were singled out by snipers during the West Side riot after King was assassinated. At the same time, many white officers were hostile to them. If a black officer refused to treat a black suspect roughly, some whites would say that "they favor their own." Just because the department was modernizing didn't mean the officers could change their habits overnight. We honestly didn't realize how white-centered we were.

You have to remember that in the 1960s, police still spoke as if they were on the streets. Not so much during the daytime, but around midnight you might hear a dispatcher say, "They got the bastard..." and sometimes a lot worse. We had to learn a new dictionary. "Son of a bitch," for example, needed to be translated to "offender." Now, I didn't swear much except in certain moments when vernacular oratory seemed suitable, but that way of talking just naturally slipped into my conversations with other policemen.

Our Robbery Unit was not an office. It was a small cubicle about ten feet square alongside the auto theft and homicide Units. The lieutenant's desk was next to the windows, facing the small, residential Shakespeare Avenue— and by the way, we didn't get the name Shakespeare Area from the literary quality of our reports. We were just a short walk from the California

Avenue elevated train station, but the parking spots were at a premium at all hours of the day and night. In winter the radiator hissed, but with the drafty windows there never was enough heat. We were pretty crowded, especially on the day shift, with a permanent staff of a lieutenant, two sergeants, and a secretary, and we always had detectives coming and going. Phones rang with the regularity of a pulse beat, but not all the calls were emergencies. Sometimes you heard a detective say, "I can't talk right now, everyone can hear. Yes, I love you."

At the time, two black detectives were assigned to the Area Five Shakespeare Avenue Robbery Unit—Henry Pates and Fred Jones. They were complete opposites from one another, as most close partners were. Pates was muscular, adorned himself with jewelry, and always joked and grinned. Jones was slim but well-built, and he took everything mindfully, especially police work. Until then they had worked in the black South Side areas, and their transfer to the predominantly white Northwest Side was part of the department's policy of gradual integration. They walked in on their first night and saw me at my casual best, with my feet up on the desk and talking on the phone about an exceptionally brutal robbery. A black man had pistol-whipped a tavern owner, blinding him in one eye. I faced the window after learning the attacker had been identified and blurted out, "Call for backup and get that nigger motherfucker!" I slammed down the receiver, happy the robber had been named and would soon be in custody. Then I turned toward the front of the office and found myself staring into the eyes of Jones and Pates. They were not smiling. Oh, God, sometimes you wish you could take a big eraser and rub out certain moments of your life. I had not meant anything derogatory; I was just using the language of the streets, like most officers at the time. You have to talk tough to get some suspects to pay attention to you and sometimes you tried to impress your fellow officers. But then again, I could tell what was on the minds of the two detectives who were staring at me.

Well, if I'd made a bad impression, shame on me, and it was my job to correct it. I put my feet on the floor, introduced myself as the acting unit commander, and said to them, "I want to have a word with you, all right?" I led them to an interview room, and I could tell they didn't know what to expect. Was I one of those fanatic racists their mothers had always warned them about?

"Look," I began, "you probably heard what I said, right? It's a bad word, and I'm sorry. Now, I'm not going to cop a plea and promise you I won't use it again, it's just one of those words that pop up occasionally. But I'll make you a deal. Whenever you arrest Italians for robbery, you have my permission as an Italian to call them Dagos, because that's what I call them."

That broke the tension. We all had a good laugh and shook hands on the way out of the interview room.

Just two days later, Pates and Jones came in with a few bruises, their usually neat suits torn, and they had with them two mean-looking Caucasians with them.

"Hey, Sarge," the usually serious Jones said, "we just arrested these two Dago motherfuckers!" The detectives had broad smirks on their faces. Obviously, the robbers Jones and Pates had nabbed didn't like being called Dagos. They wrenched their battered heads in a snarl, but right now that was the least of their problems.

Jones and Pates became friends of mine and sometimes took me to their South Side "social joints," which I thought was a different world, and they mixed equally well in the cop bars that sprang up near stations like puppies follow little boys.

It's been said that only a cop can understand a cop. They act tough, but many of them need love more than accountants. On the other hand, officers tend to compensate by bonding with counterparts in restaurants and bars such as the infamous and filthy Buck-Eighty next door to our station. The neighborhood locals remained at the front and tried not to mix with the policemen who had just finished their tours of duty. There was always more talking than drinking, unlike the factory worker patrons who just came there to drink and intentionally ignore us. We hung around the pool table near the washroom but the smell was abominable. You would think that policemen would get used to it, but we never did.

Police wives worried enough about their husbands, and it

was worse when the men came home hours after their shift ended. One of my former partners, Detective Kurt Bartall, a genuinely nice guy, arrived home one morning at four or five o'clock and saw on the door a note stating, "Don't Come In." So naturally he opened the door. The next day, he came to work and explained how a rolling pin caused the large bump on his forehead—just like in an old-fashioned cartoon!

An officer I occasionally worked with, Jimmy O'Toole, made it a habit of coming home late until his wife, hearing him turn the knob, fired three shots through the door. The shots missed, but from then on O'Toole went straight home every night. These same officers, by the way, were not afraid of anything on the streets.

Under O.W. Wilson, detectives across the city were being assigned to specialized units for auto thefts, burglaries, robberies, and homicides and sex crimes, clustering detectives who were the best in each field. Although I liked the specialization, the system put blinders on us. A detective who developed more street contacts for robbers lost touch with burglars. Sometimes investigations were stalled until officers were coincidentally transferred from one unit to another.

As an example, one case covered two time periods—when I was at Area Five Robbery and later at Area Six Homicide.

We at Robbery had at least fifteen pins in a map for a robber who always showed a knife instead of a gun. The detectives finally arrested Leon Poliquin while responding to a holdup-in-progress call at a cleaning store. Poliquin was a sad sight sitting handcuffed in a chair next to my desk. He was a short and squat white man with thinning hair and gaps between his teeth, poorly educated and shabbily dressed. I always tried to talk to prisoners; I thought of it as my job, but the real reason was that I was fascinated by the criminal mind. Poliquin was receptive to questioning, but his answers always had the hostile edge of someone who grew up angry at the world.

"Leon," I said, "you gave us a little problem for the last couple of months, but you can consider yourself lucky."

"Lucky? Shit, I'm going back to the pen."

"Yeah, that's true, but if the officers had found you with a gun instead of a knife, they might have shot you. They would have been heroes, and the state wouldn't have to pay your room and board for ten years, you mope."

"Thanks for the tip," Poliquin said flippantly. "I'll use a gun when I get out and then we'll see what happens."

"And maybe some cop will have the opportunity to blow you away. Why are you so dumb?"

"You're the guys who are dumb. After every hit, I stayed across the street and watched the cop cars come, just to see how long it took. No one caught on, but I was laughing my ass off."

Well, I was the one who was laughing his ass off now, to myself of course, because Poliquin never noticed all the pins stuck in a map tracing his career, and I didn't want to give away any trade secrets. He even gave me a lead for any robberies he might commit when he got out of prison—he'd be found among the neighbors watching the police. A similar habit helped arrest arsonists.

Eventually I was assigned as a detective sergeant to the Area Six Homicide/Sex Unit, and the pace was much quicker. I had been there for just a few days when the phone rang shortly after the morning roll call. A beat officer said a homicide had occurred in a coin operated laundry along a row of small shops on Lincoln Avenue.

Our dapper commander, Lieutenant Jules Gallet, worked side-by-side with his supervisors and detectives on any sort of assignment. He tried to keep a low profile, but sometimes his daring and temper showed.

Gallet, a graduate of the FBI long course for police officers, followed Bureau methods such as assigning a single "lead" detective to go over all the reports coming in on a single case. On this one, that detective was Edward Adorjan.

Gallet and I raced to the laundry, where three women were talking to uniformed officers while detectives made routine inspections. The first few minutes of a homicide investigation are usually chaotic. You enter the building and don't have the slightest idea what has happened until you sort out the—usually conflicting—details from the witnesses. All the while, you have to stay skeptical because anyone and everyone could be lying.

An employee named Gladys led Adorjan to the owner's body, which was slumped in a worn leather chair in a rear office. Gladys, the only eyewitness, said there were no customers around during the shooting because the gunman had come in while she and the owner were opening for business. The employee gave us a clear description of the gunman: He was black, about thirty- years-old, tall, had curly black hair, and he wore a wrinkled, gray, short-sleeved shirt and black pants. The district officers thought that knowing the robber was black should help since the neighborhood was white.

"McCoy, McDonough," Gallet called out, "make the neighborhood, hit the taverns and any other businesses. Look for the guy and conduct interviews. Tranckitello, Stachula, check buses and the El station, see if someone saw a vehicle that might belong to the offender."

In minutes, an all-call message was broadcast over the police radio, supplying a description of the killer to all squads in the city. Gallet then calmed down our witness and had her go over exactly what had happened, while Adorjan took copious notes.

"After the black man told us it was a stick-up," Gladys said, "he started shaking the gun at us and told us to go to the back of the store. That's where Mr. Poulos has his office and safe. When we got there, Mr. Poulos ran inside and locked the door. The robber got real mad and tried to knock the door down. He was swearing and yelling, and then he shot the gun a lot of times through the door and then he pointed it at me and just stared. Then he ran out the front door. Oh, my God, I'm still shaking!"

"He didn't take any money?" Gallet asked.

"He wanted to, but he couldn't. I tried to open the office door, but it was still locked. I called for Mr. Poulos, but he didn't answer. I thought, "Oh my God, he's dead. Then I ran to the phone and called the police. They pried open the office door and found Mr. Poulos dead. That's all I know." She started to sob.

The crime lab technicians came in and dug three slugs out of the wall and found six holes in the door. An autopsy performed the next day traced the paths of the bullets. One went through Poulos' chest, another lodged in his heart, and a third one struck his shoulder.

Gladys went with us to the Area station to give a formal statement and agreed to help the police artist sketch the killer. I was doing paperwork on another case at my desk nearby as Adorjan typed the routine info onto a form.

"This statement is being given by ...?" he asked.

"Gladys Poliquin," the witness answered.

I shot up from my desk and went over to her as she spelled her name.

"Excuse me," I said, "but is your husband's name Leon?" I didn't know if she even had a husband, but the name was uncommon enough to stick in my mind.

She glared at me. "Yes," she answered, lowering her head.

"Stop typing, Eddie," I told Adorjan. "I have to talk to you and your partner."

Adorjan wasn't the sort who appreciated intervention, especially from a newly assigned sergeant. He gave me an annoyed look as I motioned for all of us to go into another room for a private conference. When I'd heard the name Poliquin, everything came together for me, including why the robber was supposed to be a black man. Cross-race blame was sometimes the first tip that a crime never occurred or that the supposed witness was involved.

I closed the door and said, "This lady's *husband* killed her boss, and with her cooperation. That's why they made up the story of a black guy. Leon Poliquin's a career robber, only he used to use a knife when he committed fifteen cleaning store robberies before we caught him and sent him to the penitentiary. He told me that when he got out, he'd try a gun."

"Interesting," Adorjan said, and Gallet just shook his head.

Adorjan returned to Gladys and a change came over him. He was always a gentleman until he thought a prisoner or witness was lying to him, and then he became a screamer and put the fear of God into him or her. We always looked gravely concerned to avoid breaking the mood, but we rather enjoyed his ranting and the way he'd ask rapid fire questions as if he were poking a finger repeatedly in a subject's ribs.

"Was your husband in the penitentiary for robbery?" he asked, spitting his words.

"Yes, he got out last month," she mumbled.

"Why didn't you tell me that?"

"Because you didn't ask!" I had to smile a little because police officers often fell into that trap. "I know exactly what you're thinking," Gladys continued, "but he didn't do it. He's a good man, he's reformed. It was a black robber, just like I told you."

"Your husband, is he home now?"

"Yes. I talked to him on the phone right after I called the police and told him what happened. He's waiting for me to come home."

"You called your husband after you called police?" Adorjan exploded. He didn't expect an answer, and Gladys just sat there.

Lieutenant Gallet had a detective make sure the woman didn't make any calls in the office, and then he, Adorjan, his partner, and I drove over to Poliquin's home, a red brick two-flat four blocks from where the murder occurred. We walked up the front steps and knocked on the second floor door. Leon answered, and I could see that prison hadn't changed him much.

"Hi, Leon," I greeted, "remember me?" He looked as if he might faint. "It's been a long time, Leon, and maybe you don't remember me. I'm that stupid sergeant who talked to you after you were arrested for committing all those cleaning store robberies. You should have stayed with a knife, Leon."

The four of us handcuffed and held him, confident we had the killer.

"Can we look in your apartment for the gun?" Adorjan asked.

"Like hell you will," Poliquin answered cockily. "Do you have a warrant?"

It would have been easy to search the place anyway, but we didn't want to risk having any evidence thrown out of court. In the old days, detectives would have trashed the place. Instead, Gallet verbally jumped all over him.

"We have plenty of time for a warrant, Leon. We have your wife at the station, and now you're under arrest. Do you understand that?" He nodded at us. "Lock this place up, boys, we're taking him in."

At the Area Six station, Poliquin vehemently denied killing the laundry owner, but he was very nervous. Not only was he suspected of a felony murder, a homicide committed as part of another crime, the killing was done while he was still on parole. Then, surprising us all, he and his wife agreed to take polygraph examinations, and my confidence in the case started eroding. Why was he adamant in his denial when he had readily admitted the earlier robberies? And why were they volunteering to take polygraphs when he could have simply refused? Could it be just coincidental that the only witness to the killing was the wife of a career criminal?

I had been on the day shift and would have gone home at 4:30 p.m., but I stuck around to learn the results of the lie test given at the downtown headquarters. Adorjan called at seven and said, "I got news for you, Sarge. Gladys flunked the poly! The examiner says she has guilty knowledge of the crime but did not commit it. Now she's in hysterics, weeping and all that shit. She won't talk to us. But guess what? Leon won't talk to us either, and he won't take the test. He says he'll make a statement later, but only to you, face-to-face, and in private, because he has something to tell you." After a pause, Adorjan added, "Only to you." I could tell that he was extremely curious.

"Bring him back," I said. The skin-tingling I felt told me there might be some twists in this case.

Lieutenant Gallet was also working overtime, as he did quite often, to see how the case would shake out. Leon and Gladys were brought back to our creaky station and separated for questioning. I sat knee-to-knee with Poliquin in a private interview room and asked what he wanted to tell me.

The career criminal's arrogance disappeared as he spoke. "If I tell you something, you have to promise me something first."

"Leon, how can I make you a promise when I don't know what you're going to tell me?"

"I just don't want my wife involved in this," he said as tears made tracks down his face. "I want to keep her out of it. She don't know nothing, and she didn't do nothing. Your guys are going to find a gun in our closet. *He* dropped it off after he killed

Mr. Poulos and I hid it. I should've gotten rid of it."

"He? Who is *he*?"

"My nephew, Frank Reyna. He's just a kid. All he had to do was scare Mr. Poulos with the gun. I told him how to do it, but my wife said on the phone that something went wrong and he killed him."

You can't always tell if someone is lying, but I believed Poliquin this time.

The department's new computer system gave us Reyna's address—an apartment above a tavern—but after we raided it and couldn't find him there, the bar owner told us that he had moved out that afternoon. Within hours the 270 pound young man was found at his mother's home and brought in. He glanced at his uncle eating a hamburger and let us lead him into an interview room. Within an hour, we had a full confession that perfectly matched what Poliquin had told us.

Reyna was a big man with a low IQ, and he had followed his uncle's instructions in committing the holdup as if he were a marionette. He'd departed from the game plan in just one fatal detail. He never expected Mr. Poulos to run away from him and lock himself in the office. That was when the nephew panicked and started shooting through the door.

"He didn't even know that he'd hurt anybody," Poliquin said, attempting to minimize his nephew's actions.

Reyna was sentenced to twenty years for murder and attempted robbery, but the case against Poliquin was not as clear. Police, being human, never asked all the right questions all the time because so much went on when clearing up a case. The other detectives and I had neglected to have Poliquin specifically state that he intended to split the proceeds of the robbery with his nephew. Naturally, we just assumed this, so it was never mentioned in the report. Actually, we thought we had an excellent case, considering the fact that Poliquin admitted that he was a conspirator in planning the robbery, and he was on parole.

The female assistant state's attorney who prosecuted at the trial made a big deal of the question that wasn't asked, and suggested that I bend the truth a little and say on the stand that

5

162 JOHN A. DIMAGGIO

Poliquin "did make mention" that he would take a split with the nephew.

"Like hell I will," I said. "That's perjury. I forgot to ask, and it's not in any of the police reports, and that's that."

"Well," she said, surprised at my adamancy, "we'll probably lose the case, then."

"So we lose the case. I never lied before to put someone away, and I don't intend to start now." My reply carried into the hallway and was heard by Adorjan, who until then thought he had the loudest voice in the police department. Even so, the prosecutor was sure I'd change my mind rather than let an accomplice in a fatal robbery go free.

When I was called to the stand, she asked me with a leading smile, "Sergeant DiMaggio, did Leon Poliquin tell you that he planned to share the proceeds of the robbery with his nephew?"

"No," I replied with suppressed anger and watched her smile shrivel as she quickly went on to other questions.

The jury found Poliquin guilty anyway and he was given the maximum sentence for robbery conspiracy. That was satisfying, but somewhat scary in a way. What about the officers who decided to shore up cases here and there with little adjustments of the truth? Some prosecutors made it too easy for them ... all in the name of building a career. However, raising a red flag with this issue would be unfair to the many dedicated, underpaid assistant state's attorneys, because this was the only time in my career that someone suggested that I alter my testimony.

As long as I'm relating some of the cases I worked on in Homicide/Sex, I might mention a sexual assault that became part of police lore. This occurred while I was still at the old 33rd, the Derelict District.

A man abducted a nurse and forced her to give him oral sex, then raped her. She identified the mugshot of a narcotics addict with a history of sex offenses. My partner and I, just district officers but in plain clothes, staked out the rear of his house while two detectives stayed in the front. We saw the addict return home through the alleyway and stopped him, handcuffed him, and turned him over to the detectives. A couple of hours later the highly educated registered nurse identified him in a showup. The addict kept saying he was innocent and pleaded with me through the lockup's iron bars.

As I drank my coffee, confident that he was guilty, I asked him if he had an alibi or if there were any people who might have seen him at the time of the attack, and, because I had run out of other ideas, if he had any identifying marks or was circumcised. When I got back to the nurse, while everyone else was typing up the paperwork, I was uncharacteristically reluctant to get around to what I had to say. The woman had been through enough, and I didn't want to ask her if she had noticed if the attacker had a foreskin. Since she was a nurse, I decided to go ahead. She was presumably less shy about such things than big, tough policemen.

"No," she told me, "he definitely did not."

"Well, this man does," I said.

"If he's not circumcised," the nurse yelled in panic, "then he's not the one who raped me!" She bent over in her chair and cried.

My partner and the two detectives came back into the room. They practically dragged me out and one of the detectives asked, "What the fuck did you say to her?"

I told them the story, and we walked fast to the lockup and told the prisoner to drop his pants and shorts. We then went to the nurse and told her he had not been "cut." She refused to accept that she had made a wrong identification and insisted on seeing for herself. The lieutenant on duty reluctantly approved the request, apparently thinking we were breaking some sort of law. We took her down to the short row of cells. Once again, the man dropped his pants.

The nurse glanced down, turned to us, and said, "That is not the man who raped me."

We all knew the proper procedure. The man should have been charged in that he was originally identified, and then have the facts of the one-man genital-lineup brought out in a preliminary hearing. But could you in clear conscience make that man stay up to two weeks or more behind bars? Neither could we, so we let him go after filling out the release papers.

The detectives on the case drew me aside afterward and said they thought they'd seen it all until then.

The story became a classic and was told by police around the city for a couple of years.

Cops need such memorable moments to keep up with the daily uncertainties of their lives.

For example, I was working the Area Five Robbery desk on April 14, 1969, when my close friend Jerry Stubig dropped by. Everybody liked Stubig. He was a man's man, a six foot tall swimming instructor, former steeplejack, and a daring driver. He always kept his blond hair in a crew cut, and nearly all of his 190 pounds was muscle. With a wife and six children, Stubig could always use money, but he turned in a man who'd offered him a $1000 bribe. He was just that kind of guy.

Stubig and I had recently joined a stock club, but actually the club was an excuse to play poker in his home with more than a dozen other policemen and some lawyers. He was also an ardent non-smoker, but I'm sure that had nothing to do with why he transferred to the arson unit after a long career as a robbery detective. He wanted the public to know that smoking is deadly, one way or another.

As we chatted, Stubig smashed the cigarettes lying on my desk with an animated karate chop and said, "John, don't you know these things can kill you?"

In a few hours, Stubig and another officer lay dead on the porch of Chicago's "Mad Bomber."

Over the course of several years, a number of bombs had exploded on the Southwest Side. At first they were set to cause only property damage, but lately they were placed to harm people. Such a blast killed a woman in a department store. On the day that Stubig smashed my cigarettes, someone had placed a tip bomb on a toy shelf in Goldblatt at 91st Street and Commercial Avenue. If a tip bomb was tipped or titled at any angle, it exploded. The manager discovered the device and called the police. The Bomb and Arson Unit was called in, and my friend and his partner joined the investigation. They deduced that the tip bomb could not have been driven to the store because the motion would have detonated the device. That meant the bomb maker must have carefully walked to the store.

They started to canvass the neighborhood with house-to-house interviews, presuming that the person who had planted the bomb could possibly live nearby. Not too long after their canvass began, they interviewed a woman who told them that a person next door was eccentric and sometimes threw exploding objects out of his third floor apartment.

Not known to them at the time, they were closing in on Frank Kulak, a middle-aged nobody. Kulak became an instant suspect, and he fit the profile a psychiatrist had made for New York City's "Mad Bomber" a few years before. That is, he was a middle-aged man living with a sister, came from a middle-European background, was conservatively dressed, neat, probably Roman Catholic, heavy, and was showing increased paranoia.

During World War II, Kulak had been pinned down by Japanese snipers in Okinawa, and his mind sometimes made him think he was back on the island. In the last week, neighborhood teenagers had seen him walking home with bags of assorted hardware. "Kooky Kulak," they taunted. He yelled back at them as if he thought they were Japanese soldiers.

Stubig and his partner, William McInerney, didn't know the man's background, but they did call for backup. Uniformed district sergeant James Schaffer promptly arrived. When they knocked on the back door of the third floor apartment at 95th and Exchange, Kulak answered by firing through the door, wounding McInerney in the arm and chest.

McInerney told the other men he had to go down the stairs for medical attention. Stubig and Schaffer stayed without a thought of retreating, apparently to get at Kulak and take him into custody. Instead, Kulak fired through the door and Sergeant Schaffer was killed.

Stubig broke through a kitchen window and fired all five shots from his snub-nosed revolver, each one missing its moving target.

Kulak then lobbed a hand grenade onto the porch, and the blast threw my friend onto his back. Kulak went to the porch and saw him trying to get up. He shot both officers in their heads. The bomber then threw a grenade that destroyed the rear stairs down past the second floor, keeping any other policemen from reaching him through the back way.

While dozens of police surrounded the building, Kulak booby-trapped his seven room apartment with a dozen explosive devices. The police kept coming and saturated the neighborhood. Everyone at the scene knew that one policeman had been badly wounded and that they'd lost contact with two other officers.

As dusk came, 150 officers fired at any movement across a window, not knowing if Stubig and Schaffer were alive or dead.

The back steps had been demolished and there was no safe way to reach the third floor rear porch. Thirty or forty squad cars and squadrols—large police vans—were parked every which way on all of the streets, surrounding the building. A funeral home down the street was used as a command post. Tenants of the building were so scared that they huddled in the basement for hours rather than risk escaping.

The police gunfire was marked by sporadic rifle flashes in the night. Fire trucks aimed their spotlights at the building, turning it into a bright island. Occasionally Kulak fired back or threw a pipe bomb or grenade, making craters in the front lawn. The concussions shattered windows along the block.

As one police official on the street said, "It's a war zone out here." In Kulak's mind, it *was* a war.

The number two man in the department, Deputy Superintendent James Rochford, arrived in his blue uniform to take command. Rochford was a trim, no-nonsense man with a ruddy complexion. He knew that someone would have to reach Kulak by working through his delusion. Rochford, a veteran of the war in the South Pacific, ordered a halt to all firing. Officers from patrolman on up to lieutenant thought he was crazy.

Even Kulak couldn't understand the silence. He presented himself as a clear target at a couple of windows, sometimes shouting, "Kill me, kill me, I want to die!" No one took advantage of the opportunity because of the order.

Accompanied by Kulak's brother and sister, Rochford

inched up the front stairs. The siblings pleaded with Kulak to give himself up. Instead, the man called down to Rochford, "You don't have to worry about your men—I emptied my rifle into their heads, they're not suffering anymore."

Whatever hate and fear the deputy superintendent felt, he didn't let it show as he crouched on the front stairs. Rochford started talking about the Japanese snipers, almost as if this were an ordinary conversation.

"We're not the enemy, Frank," the top cop said.

Kulak stayed at the door, ready to fire a 9mm automatic pistol if Rochford made an attempt to rush him, but neither could see the other because of a bend in the stairwell. At last, reality began to break through Kulak's thoughts of jungle warfare, and Rochford's soothing voice made him remember where he was.

Kulak put the gun on the banister and surrendered. The six hour siege was over.

Thankfully, Rochford kept Kulak alive, much to the dismay of the officers who were on the scene.

Kulak revealed that his entire apartment was "rigged" and "the whole block would blow up," if officers entered and tripped one device. Kulak issued a full statement once he was taken to a police station, and he detailed killing the police officers and the exact placement of the explosives in the apartment.

There were quite a few heroes on that fateful day, and Rochford most certainly was at the top of the list. Rochford had shown where the department was heading, using psychology and courage rather than wasting lives. The two officers who were killed stayed in our minds as reminders of what could happen to us any time we stopped a car, made an arrest, or knocked on a door.

Stubig's death was more than just a personal loss to me, but I'm not sure how I can explain what I felt.

He was laid to rest with honors in his favorite black and white sport coat on April 19, my birthday, which had been scheduled for our stock club meeting.

After the funeral, I had a short talk with Rosemary about how I needed to get away for awhile. She didn't ask where I was going or how long I'd be gone. She simply trusted me, as she always did. I cleared it with my boss, packed a small bag, and started driving south with no particular route in mind. After eight or ten hours on the road, I registered at a small motel. I didn't go away to drink or drown my sorrows, I just didn't want to talk with others about Stubig. I didn't want to think that but for the grace of God, that could have been me lying on the back porch of a crazed bomber.

I returned home within two days and went back to work—always trying to keep Stubig out of my mind.

11

SURPRISES

Some officers relied on the drug addicts and other professional informants who came out of the old Area Five building, but I couldn't trust them. Anyone who lived simultaneously
on both sides of the law was bound to be playing a lot of people
for suckers. They often stole from their families and also commonly perjured themselves on the witness stand, for or against
arresting officers, depending on who was paying them off in
money or drugs. They hung around police stations like flies on
garbage cans.

These were generally sleazy people who dressed carelessly
and looked as if they had no idea of what was happening
anywhere outside their own neighborhoods. They knew their
neighborhoods, all right, and what they didn't know they
made up. A few of these men and women dropped by my desk
after delivering their latest gossip to another detective, or they
reached me outside. They'd talk about all the cases I could clear
up with their help. They got only hostile silence from me, and
yet they kept trying. There were some criminals that I liked, but
never these hangers-on, and you never knew where they would
pop up.

One time I really didn't want to go to work was Christmas
Day the following year. Our children were now thirteen, eleven,
and eight, and I wanted to spend the holiday with them. After
all, even crooks usually took Christmas off. Nevertheless, I
dutifully went in.

The holiday quiet was broken by a telephone call, though,

and I heard a distinctive voice stutter out, "Hello, Sergeant DiMaggio, do you remember me?"

How could I forget *Ronnie Byrd, one of the first arrests I ever made as a detective? Byrd had made my job easy. He dropped his wallet and identification during a burglary. There were no hard feelings about the arrest, and he sometimes called in tips to me after he served his time. Byrd wasn't like the drug addicted stool pigeons; he wasn't expecting anything in return except maybe the feeling of being helpful.

Byrd didn't stutter before he went to prison, but he surely did when he came out. He was also easy to confuse, and since I didn't really like him, I enjoyed befuddling him when work was slow … like now.

Eventually he stammered that he had seen two people taking rifles with "scopes" out of a red car, walk past his window, and go into an apartment across from his. Byrd lived in the deteriorating Uptown neighborhood, where anything could happen and usually did.

The only detective I had in the office that day was short, paunchy, highly talented Chuckie Green. Intrigued by what he'd overheard, Chuckie stopped typing a report and swiveled my way. He sat with his arms folded and head bent toward the phone.

"It was after two in the morning," Byrd said, "and then they kept me awake all night, arguing and screaming at each other."

"You have to be more specific," I told him. "Who's 'they'?"

"A man and a girl, he's a big, tall black guy, and she's white, short, and on the heavy side. All they ever do is argue, but, but they took a lot of rifles out of the car." Stuttering, he gave me the apartment number.

"Ronnie," I said, "stay home today, all right? We might want to get hold of you for a warrant."

I gave Byrd's address to Chuckie, a place I knew pretty well, and we arrived there before long. The slumlords who bought the building had subdivided the apartments into little more than cubicles and had numerous housing code violations filed against them. We walked to the third floor, knocked on the door, and stood back with our guns drawn. A heavy young woman answered; she was unimaginably sloppy and wore a filthy see-through blue nightgown. She backed up, scared. Our first hint that we were really onto something was that she kept silent and didn't ask, "Who are you and want do you want?"

We flashed our star cases and walked across the messy, grimy apartment to where her boyfriend lay under a blanket.

"Don't move," we said. Chuckie, who didn't even look like a policeman, kept his revolver pointed at the man's head and slid the blanket back, showing that our nude suspect was hiding a small revolver in his armpit. He might have wanted to shoot us until he saw that we were coming in with guns already drawn. If we had overlooked that precaution, we both could be dead.

There had to be some way to make sure the man didn't reach for the gun or have him or his girlfriend go for one of the rifles that we saw piled on the couch. Chuckie hit him on the side of the head, more of a tap than a whack, and grabbed the pistol away from him. Then he ordered, "Get up, slowly."

"Who belongs to these weapons?" I asked.

"Ain't mine, man," the guy answered. "I never saw them before."

Next to the couch were two open cardboard boxes. We could see they contained a variety of porcelain figurines and other expensive knickknacks, not the sort of interior decorating one expected in this ten-by-ten foot apartment.

"Ain't mine, man," the boyfriend repeated, "they sure ain't mine!"

I had Chuckie guard the two suspects while I went down the hall to use Byrd's phone. He already had his head out, sputtering, "Was I right? Was I right?"

"You were right, Ronnie. Thanks, and Merry Christmas."

I called gun registration downtown, surprised that someone was there on Christmas, and learned that the long weapons were registered to a Clyde Wedgwood on Kenmore Street, not far away, and that the revolver taken from the boyfriend's armpit had been stolen in a burglary elsewhere in the neighborhood in November. Then I called for a wagon to haul the prisoners to Area Six.

As we drove to Wedgwood's home, we wondered if he

would be home on the holiday. He lived in a once fairly decent building, the Briar Apartment Hotel, but the white marble facing was starting to crack. We went through the large double doors and noticed there were no individual doorbells or names of tenants. We found the manager's office but got no response. We started knocking on doors, asking if anyone knew Wedgwood. The residents clammed up as soon as they heard we were police officers.

After about five tries on the second floor, a woman said she believed that Wedgwood was the gentleman who lived one flight above. We thanked her and wished her a Merry Christmas. On the third floor, we met a woman who knew Wedgwood and said she thought he was a musician, and that he lived in Apartment 303 at the end of the hall. All we wanted to do was verify that a burglary had been committed, but that door looked clean, with no sign that it had been tampered with.

"Could the lock have been slipped with a credit card?" Chuckie asked.

"No way, it's a dead-bolt lock, and the molding strip is metal. Let's see if he's home."

We knocked and waited a couple of times. After no answer, we talked to a few tenants about getting a pass key. They said the manager could help, but he was in the hospital.

We returned to 303, and I brought out my lockpicks. Deadbolts were hard to bypass because of eccentric keyways that block the positioning of the tension bar, leaving little room for the pick to work.

Chuck, who didn't know about my training, said, "I bet you lunch you don't open that lock."

"You're on."

The department didn't sanction using lock picks for investigations, and I would be against routinely teaching the techniques to rookies, but certain cases warranted their use. I felt justified this time.

I placed the tension bar inside the lock, applied the necessary pressure, and then raked the pins with a single-diamond head pick. In less than a minute, the pins met evenly at the shear line and the lock opened. I glanced at Chuckie to enjoy his surprised expression.

"Turn the knob," I said. He followed my instruction, still not understanding what I had in mind. "Now you can say in our report that you found the door unlocked and you opened the door, lawfully entering the apartment." Bear in mind that we were only trying to contact an apparent victim. We had no intention of violating the rights of a suspect.

We walked into the meticulously clean apartment and stopped immediately. Ten feet from us was the naked body of a small middle-aged man, ashen as if drained of blood, his sightless eyes wide open. He sat on an Oriental rug, his neck and back against couch cushions. A chill shot through me. His head was tilted as if staring at us for our intrusion. We came closer and saw twine wrapped tightly around his neck, causing folds of his skin to overlap the string.

"Holy shit," Chuckie said.

Clyde Wedgwood had died as he had lived, amid a double life. The fifty-seven-year-old French horn player for the renowned Chicago Symphony Orchestra kept a tidy home of crocheted doilies and Victorian-style furnishings, but he also collected guns and hired a woman for weekly sex acts. As Chuck noted, there were "little dew drops" on his penis.

"I'll call Joe D and surprise him," I said. I had asked Sergeant Joseph DiLeonardi to answer the Robbery Unit calls when Chuckie and I left the office. I'd already called him once from Byrd's apartment, so I gave him another ring. "Hi, Sergeant D," I said cordially, "this is DiMaggio. We're in Clyde Wedgwood's apartment; he's the owner of the rifles. We found him dead, strangled, with twine around his neck."

"How did you get into the apartment?" DiLeonardi asked, always suspicious about everything and everyone.

"Chuckie Green found the door unlocked and we simply walked in, found the body."

"I'll send my homicide guys over there right away. Stay there until they arrive."

As we waited, we left the crime scene intact, but we looked around to make sure there was no other body. We then helped the homicide detectives and the crime lab technicians thoroughly search the small apartment and go through Wedgwood's mail for leads. The lab personnel took photos of the corpse and dusted the place for fingerprints, and the homicide detectives received a file number.

Once we were back at the Area station, we carried the weapons and boxes of figurines from the robbery side of the office to the homicide section, passing by the heavy-set young woman as she talked to detectives. The girl told DiLeonardi's men that she went to Wedgewood's apartment by herself to burglarize it, believing that he was out of town, but he heard her at the door and let her in. She said she gave him some sex, then her boyfriend forced his way in as she was leaving and that she knew nothing about the killing.

"Sergeant," I said, upset, "if you told that story to a donkey he would kick you right in the ass. Let's have a private conference after things cool down and talk it over."

When I had my talk with Joe D a little later, I went over the woman's story with a touch of sarcasm, and he defended it by saying, "That's what she told me, and her boyfriend confirms the story."

"Well, let me tell you this, sergeant. Chuckie and I have an informant who will be willing to testify that the woman, who says she doesn't know what happened after her boyfriend forced his way into the apartment, helped unload a car trunk and carry rifles and two boxes into their apartment. If she doesn't know more than what she told you, I'll kiss your ass at high noon at State and Madison Streets." I added, "Green and I will leave a copy of our report with you before we leave. I think you should read it carefully before you make any decision about the guilt or innocence of that woman."

As we left the office, Chuck said, "You never actually worked with Joe D, did you, John? Let me tell you that this case will go down on paper exactly the way he tells his men to report it. That's his nature, he calls the shots the way he wants. We're wasting our time."

The next day, the murder was splashed on the front page of the papers, and the story was almost exactly what the woman had told DiLeonardi. He also had leaked the news that Wedgewood had been strangled with twine, something no officer under my command would have volunteered to the press. I was angry as hell. Chuckie and I drove to the Criminal Courts Building to testify and ran into Joe D in the hallway. We raised our voices at one another, and Chuckie later said he could have charged a fee for all the people gathered around to listen. DiLeonardi denied talking to reporters about the twine, but I was sure he did.

At last, he said, "I'll tell you this right now, we're going to drop the murder charges against the woman and use her for a witness against the boyfriend."

"And I'll tell you this, Sergeant DiLeonardi: Chuckie Green and myself will testify at the trial and try our best to convince the judge or jury that, at the very least, she was involved in a conspiracy to kill Clyde Wedgwood."

We won, we lost. The woman was used as a material witness against her boyfriend, but the case never went to a jury. The boyfriend pleaded guilty and was sentenced to serve twenty to thirty-three years in prison. As for the young woman, she got away with murder.

No one ever questioned the integrity or intensity of DiLeonardi, who was eventually called "Mr. Homicide" by reporters and had an early true-crime book written about some of his cases. After his retirement from the force, Joe D became the U.S. Marshal for Northern Illinois and is responsible for guarding high profile criminals in federal custody.

I always thought he was a reallllly niiiiice guy.

I spent many years growing up on the North Side of the city and, as a police officer, I watched in awe as the Cabrini-Green public housing complex sprouted like weeds. Soon after completion of these high rises of steel, cement, and building blocks, city officials admitted that they might have made a mistake. Generally, single-parent families were packed in with a minimum of playground facilities, and the complex was destined to become a breeding ground for gangs. Residents said there were fifteen to thirty sniper incidences a month there, and the shooting could be indiscriminate.

Once, detectives John Eshoo, Robert McCracken, and I were investigating a rash of robberies at grocery and drug stores in the Cabrini-Green neighborhood. Most of the terrorized victims were elderly. We brought a young man named Willie Smith to an interrogation space we called "the trick room" because we sometimes tried every trick in the book to get information out of suspects. Smith had been arrested numerous times for violent crimes, but he was always let off because the witnesses were too afraid to appear in court. We didn't doubt he was guilty because the information we received was considered to be reliable.

Smith just glared at us during the interrogation and didn't say a word, so he was released from custody, but he was still considered the prime suspect.

Soon afterwards, another pharmacy was held up. The owner, also an elderly man, just wouldn't tell us anything. I tried to warm up to him by talking about the neighborhood as my father had told us about it. I drew the pharmacist aside and was both friendly and hard with him, maybe a little cruel.

"You better go out of business," I said. "You know the neighborhood has changed, and this same guy will be back to rob you because you're an easy mark, and he might even kill you." As I kept it up, I felt sorry for the old man, but we had a rash of crimes to stop.

"All right, his name is Willie Smith," the pharmacist finally said. "He lives somewhere in the projects. He wears a long black raincoat and he hides the shotgun under it."

McCracken promised that we wouldn't use his name, and the owner gave us all the information he could. We re-interviewed other victims, and they admitted knowing all along that Smith was the man who robbed

them. That was enough for a judge to sign an arrest warrant when all of the victims banded together.

Rather than grab him in his apartment, we thought we could arrest him outside, before anyone could get to him and warn him.

While Eshoo and McCracken questioned a man who resembled Smith, I saw above me someone entering Smith's apartment off the fifth floor walkway. While the detectives waited for a squad to pick up their suspect, my eyes never left the door of dead center apartment 516. I told my colleagues, and then stayed behind while they ran upstairs to wait by the door. That meant we could be sure that the person—possibly Smith— was still inside. These homes had no rear exits.

I went up the stairs, and then we knocked on the door. When no one responded, we pounded and shouted, "Open the door, Smith, or we'll break it down!" Still no answer.

McCracken, a large man who could have played guard for the Chicago Bears, threw his weight against the door and it wouldn't budge. We should have gone to the management office for a duplicate key, but we felt it was too late now—we'd already disclosed our intentions.

Eshoo went to our car for a tire iron. Wanting to take sole responsibility if there were any objections afterward, I grabbed the bar and dug in near the lock, applying a steady force for a few minutes. Finally the lock loosened and we surged inside with guns drawn. Smith, or the person who had entered the place, was gone. All the windows were locked from the inside. What could have happened? People didn't vanish.

I reported the incident to the female manager of the projects. She was accustomed to taking damaged lock reports. After routinely questioning the man that Eshoo and McCracken had shackled to the squad car, we let him go. My crack robbery team respectfully wondered if I really did see someone resembling Smith enter the apartment. You know the tone—" Was it possible you saw someone go in a *different* apartment, Sarge?" I hated being wrong, that went without saying, and it was worse when you were the supervisor.

We returned to Area Six headquarters, and my feet felt encased in cement as I walked up the steps to write the report.

"Hey, John," Sergeant Sam "Slats" Cirone said, "come and sit down and have a cup of fresh coffee in a dirty cup."

I slid into a chair next to Sam and was glad the coffee was strong. Sam was a great cop and a good friend. I told him my problem and was surprised to see that he wasn't quizzical.

"Sam," I said at the end of my story, "I hate to admit it, but I just fucked up."

"You didn't do your homework, Johnny boy." He had his hands folded in his lap as he leaned back comfortably in his swivel chair. "Ever hear about the Medicine Cabinet Trick in those projects? Those apartments have medicine cabinets next to each other, back to back. You pull out one, push out the other, crawl through, and then you're in someone else's apartment. We found this out when we had a couple of warrants out on people, gave the place a good search, and found the loose cabinets."

I'll be damned, I thought. "Hey, Slats, want to take a ride?"

The four of us went directly to vacant apartment 516. I eagerly pulled out the medicine cabinet and found myself facing the backside of another one. Slats had us push on it, which was surprisingly easy, and I lowered it to the sink in the other flat. Then Slats pointed out the footprints on the two sinks. They led to the apartment of Smith's friends, also gangbangers.

Hoping to find Willie, we searched the apartment while Eshoo guarded the front door in case he was there and tried to run out. The place was empty. As we put the two metal cabinets back, Slats said, "Never let them know you discovered any of their tricks. Let them think they fooled you, and the knowledge might come in handy some day."

In a few days, Smith realized he couldn't escape a manhunt forever and surrendered to Officer Renault Robinson, later to be the founder of the African-American Police League. Robinson assured him he would be safer in the hands of a black officer than with us. To me it seemed the start of a new racism, inventing a white bogeyman to encourage black solidarity or personal ambitions. But what the hell ... all I cared about was that Smith was off the streets. He pleaded guilty and received a sentence of three to ten years.

Maybe I shouldn't have said "a *new* racism." It was already shown during the fireplug riot, and we were about to see some of its deadly consequences.

12

NIGHTMARES

We had become targets.

Any officer parking near the sprawling Cabrini-Green complex, just a twenty minute walk from the richest part of the city, could expect to find his car punctured by bullet holes or his tires flattened. For fun, teenagers robbed insurance men who entered the building in suits and carried telltale attaché cases; sometimes their clothes were stolen so they would have to run in their underwear for blocks before a squad car caught up with them. None of us fully realized how dangerous the situation had become.

Cabrini-Green, ironically named partly for a saint who had died in Chicago—Francesca Cabrini—did not yet have its own police unit. Instead, a special task force of personable officers was chosen to keep the peace as best they could. Without saying so, the department, for reasons of its own, had a general hands-off policy toward the housing complex.

Conditions were festering. We in Robbery could tell that the gangs were becoming more organized because we kept confiscating ever more sophisticated weapons. The gang leaders, once rather ordinary, were now wearing expensive clothes and driving distinctive autos. It was harder than ever to get information about them, and the good people of the projects were terrified.

In no other neighborhood were criminals so protected by the interwoven motives of greed, hate, a need to belong, racism, fear, and loyalty. Mothers wouldn't tell on gangs because of the heroin money they brought in. Young women wouldn't tell because they were either involved or in fear. Boys, eight to ten years old, most living without fathers, were being recruited as lookouts by gang members offering them friendship and adventure. The more these children bad-assed, the sooner they could be absorbed into the gang.

Officers frequently responding to calls at Cabrini-Green knew that at any moment they could be under attack. The department instituted a "walk and talk" program in which patrolmen carried walkie-talkies in order to communicate with each other and call for backup at a moment's notice. During the "walk and talk" period, I got to know two pretty good cops, Sergeant James Severin and Officer Anthony Rizzato. Like most of the officers assigned to the program, they had volunteered— whether because it meant less paperwork or because they just liked people. In fact, Rizzato's brother, Nick, also signed up for the program.

It failed, as all the programs did, but the idea was that tenants would get to meet men in uniform personally and say to themselves that the police were not so bad after all. Then all of them would go to the police with their problems and turn away gang members, who would see the error of their ways and become governors or advertising executives. It didn't happen that way.

Not all of the officers fell for it and they expressed their feelings. District Sergeant Tom McGady wrote a report stating that, in his opinion, "someone was going to get killed."

Severin and Rizzato came up to the Robbery Unit daily, and I signed out shotguns to them. They had never needed them, but they were locked in the trunks of their unmarked cars as a precaution. Their shift started at six p.m., but I always counted on them to arrive half an hour early. I looked forward to seeing their unusually smiling faces; they helped keep away the cynicism.

If we weren't busy, Severin and Rizzato told me some of the interesting recent experiences they had at Cabrini-Green, and I informed them of any arrests we made or investigations we had going on there that might concern them. The two men hated the gangs but liked most of the people. Hundreds of families were trying to keep their children off drugs and were hoping to get jobs or *better* jobs so they could move to a nicer place far removed from Cabrini-Green. Some of them felt sorrier for the officers than for themselves.

Severin was tall, slim, soft-spoken, and fairly good-looking. There was something about him that encouraged people to talk to him, maybe because he seemed more like a priest than a policeman.

Rizzato was a short, quiet guy who kept a low profile. You couldn't expect two nicer officers to represent the police to a hostile neighborhood of multiple human warehouses.

"We're doing the job, or at least trying," Severin once said, "but it really doesn't show, does it, John?"

On July 17, 1970, the eight-man walk and talk team had flipped a coin to see which ones would start work and who would go to a restaurant first. Severin and Rizzato lost the toss, so they started walking across the outfield of the seldom-used baseball diamond outside of Cabrini-Green. At the same time, several teenagers crowded around a window, keeping the two men in the telescopic sights of a rifle. A minister who happened to be near the field heard shots and simultaneously saw both officers fall without having a chance to draw their guns. Rizzato tumbled facefirst to the grass, and Severin dropped to his knees, pitched forward, tried to crawl away, and then stopped with a walkie-talkie in his hand.

In minutes, police cars raced to the complex and halted with a lurch. One of the other men from the unit, Officer Jarrett Yedlinski, saw the bodies in the field. He jumped his police car over the curb and screeched the brakes once he was on the field near the bodies. Sniper fire came down, and he couldn't tell if it was from a single window or not. There were loud cracking sounds and the dirt kicked up all around him. He ran with two other walk and talk officers and three district patrolmen, weaving and ducking as they approached their fallen comrades.

In sheer anger, Yedlinski hauled out his revolver and emptied it at the rooftop, not really aiming at anyone.

He reached Severin, saw a bullet wound in his bicep, and

thought the fallen man was only wounded. Turning him over, he discovered that the bullet had mushroomed as it tore through the bones and sinew, ripping nearly four inches from his chest.

This was not going to be like the Kulak shootout, when the bodies of two policemen had lain for hours on the back porch. Even under fire, the officers picked up Severin—leaving Rizzato to be carried off by other men—and brought him to an unmarked car.

The driver raced to nearby Henrotin Hospital. On the way, officers in the front seat kept asking, "Is he alive? Is he alive?"

"I don't know," he answered, but he knew the truth.

The car reached the hospital in no more than two minutes. The officers jumped out and thought only of getting some help. Yedlinski was sure Severin was dead and yet was hoping that somehow he could be revived. In his rush, Yedlinski forgot that the emergency room doors opened outward rather than inward. He hit them with his arms thrust forward at the elbow, like wings, and broke the glass in both doors. Behind him, the other officer carried Sergeant Severin by the armpits and legs. Ten feet away, a district officer brought Rizzato's body in a fireman's carry all by himself.

Yedlinski told me all these details as I made notes for this book.

The day after the sniper murders, Police Superintendent James Conlisk asked that the officers involved in reclaiming the bodies show up at the crime lab auditorium for a recognition speech. At the ceremony, he called them heroes.

"After he started talking, we just walked off the stage and left the building," Yedlinski said, "not really out of disrespect. We just didn't want to hear anything about what happened that day. You know what we got out of it? An Honorable Mention—a piece of paper—and you know what? We ripped it up. We didn't want anything."

Those ambush shots were like clubbing a hornet's nest with a baseball bat. Immediately after the double killing, there was an invasion of Cabrini-Green by scores of police officers—black, white, and Hispanic, in uniform and plainclothes. They just ignored their regular assignments and rushed in. I'd never seen so many officers in so confined a space, their faces showing such rage. It's not just that two of their own were killed. It was also because two good cops were slain for no other reason than that they had volunteered to help the people in the projects.

Most of the officers banged on the doors to ask the tenants what they saw and heard about the sniper murders, or anything that might be related to the killings. A few officers rushed to the site just to stare at the buildings—*just stare*—with who knows what on their minds.

When the assigned team from the Homicide Unit arrived, there was no way to protect the crime scene for evidence. An army of officers had trampled the field and been through the room from where the shots were apparently fired.

The doors of known gang leaders were sledge-hammered open. The officers wanted information fast, and they wanted to get even for all they and the Cabrini-Green residents had to endure. Gang leaders were hauled out and pushed around, because now, that was the only common language between them and the police. Some of the tenants even cheered when cops pulled gang members to their feet and demanded to know about the hiding places of guns and drugs.

"No bullshit this time!" The questioning was improper and the searches were illegal, but this wasn't police work in the truest sense. In their minds, a housing project had declared war on the Chicago Police Department.

I couldn't approve what was going on, and yet I was proud of the intensity these officers showed. The police invasion of the buildings turned up a lot of guns, and numerous arrests were made for weapons and drug violations. In the long run, though, the house cleaning time at Cabrini did more harm than good because everyone from gang members to pastors now had examples of police misconduct for their lessons about resisting the establishment. They quickly forgot about the massacre of the two police officers and dwelled on the subject of police brutality.

The methodical work of the Homicide team—not the swarm of angry policemen—solved the killings. Two young men, Johnny Veal and George Knights, were convicted and sentenced to serve from 100 to 199 years in prison. The state chose not to prosecute a mentally-disabled teenager, who was encouraged by gang members to take part in the shooting so he would earn points and join the gang.

An uneasy cease fire settled in between police and the housing project. Still, the tension was always there whenever we had to return to look for a suspect, and Cabrini-Green was in the back of our minds as a permanent reminder of the hazards of police work.

You have to keep in mind that these Cabrini-Green nightmares were just part of the paranoid atmosphere of the early 1970s. There were political assassinations across the country: the Black Panthers had snipers on rooftops around their West Side headquarters; street gang coalitions called the Blackstone Nation and the Disciples were vying with one another for the most gang killings; and Chicago police were still on edge from the rioting of peace demonstrators and misfit yippies at the 1968 Democratic National Convention.

Officers were beginning to show what the military would call battle fatigue. Efforts to professionalize the department at a time of what seemed like the collapse of law and order caught many officers between two gears meshing. That led to some hasty judgment calls in life or death situations.

All of the Cabrini-Green projects were torn down by 2011.

13

THE MYSTERIOUS TAPES

A rash of tavern robberies was occurring throughout the busy North Side. Our Area was understaffed, the overtime was staggering, and our once-proud rate of solved cases was dropping. As I worked the desk on a rare slow night, I yanked out some files to look for similarities. The robbers, invariably described as hillbillies, sometimes ordered the customers to shut their eyes and place their hands on the bar while their wallets were lifted. At times the men wore wigs as disguises, and they occasionally beat some of the victims for no particular reason.

The assigned evidence technicians couldn't find fingerprints, even though the robbers sometimes ordered drinks and left the glasses behind. Even so, we guessed at some things because every type of crime has its own mentality. Tavern robbers tended to be men who already had served time and had the nerve to hold up places where the bartender could pull out a gun and start shooting, and on many occasions did. There was also a chance that customers, sometimes off duty policemen in their favorite hangouts, might try to stop them, and several times a year either the robbers or the policemen lost their lives.

Another link to the holdups was that the robberies became more vicious. Some customers were whacked over the head with some sort of metal cylinder. The facts of the similar cases led me to tell my lieutenant that I thought I'd worked out a crime pattern.

"So what else is new?" Lieutenant *Ross Lonello asked.

"We're getting hit with everything. Notify the Crime Analysis Unit and find out why they didn't pick up on your so-called pattern."

Lonello was a great guy when things were going well and he was receiving accolades from his downtown bosses, but in slumps like this he would holler at detectives in front of everyone, using the worst sort of vulgarities. We had worked as sergeants together in the old Area Five Robbery Unit, and he was fine then. When he was promoted to lieutenant and became the unit commanding officer of the Area Six Robbery Unit, he persuaded me to transfer there. Off duty, was as pleasant as could be, but a change came over him as soon as he was at work. He became, as would be said today, "the boss from hell," and none of us could figure him out.

The lieutenant worked off his personal frustrations by zeroing in on one detective or sergeant at a time and eventually forced him to transfer out of the unit. If he wouldn't transfer out on his own, Lonello found a reason to have the bosses downtown demote the detective to uniform. In four years, he forced the replacement of fifteen sergeants and an astounding number of detectives. The survivors spent their time wondering if they were next. Through it all, Lonello sat in his office cubicle and rolled steel balls in his hand like Captain Queen of *The Caine Mutiny.*

One Friday evening after work, I opened my mail at home and was surprised to find a sixty minute audio tape in a plain envelope without a return address. There was also no message inside, and no markings on the tape. I played it on my tape recorder and heard a conversation by two southern men. The sound quality was poor, and sometimes their drawls turned into the Donald Duck quacking you heard when a portion of a tape was recorded at a higher speed.

While I listened the thought occurred to me that someone wanted to put me on a trail and yet apparently tampered with the tape to avoid my hearing—what? I couldn't even imagine, but I was curious.

From my experience in the Intelligence Unit, I assumed an FM transmitter had been used in a phone tapping. There was no mention of a crime, just a forty minute conversation between two southerners. *Okay, it's a joke*, I thought, and my buddies at Area Six were known to play pranks on numerous occasions. As I told my wife, one of them must have heard I was looking for hillbillies regarding a crime pattern and decided to see if I could get excited over a bogus taped clue. I put the cassette in my drawer, had dinner, and thought no more about it.

A second tape arrived in the mail exactly one week later. I came home at about five p.m., had a fast dinner, then opened the envelope and found another unmarked Sony tape.

I was startled when this one started out clearly and with the same two voices. Their southern accents made it a little difficult for my Chicago ears, and there was some static, so I raised the volume to the highest level and heard:

"I sawed off the barrel and now you can use the shotgun and I can use the barrel to hit the sons of bitches."

The barrel—so that was the cylinder!

I eagerly flipped over the tape but the sound was worse, and the Donald Duck voices returned. I played the tape again, taking notes, excited to learn they were similar to the notes I took from the robbery case reports I had reviewed a couple of weeks earlier.

"You know, I gotta come up with thirty-one hundred for that guy by next month, that's my next court date and with the places we been hitting, that means we gotta hit at least ten."

"Ten, shit," the other voice said, *"more than that, we only been getting two-, three-hundred between the three of us ... and we have to get more guns ... we lost that one, and we been sharing the money with Herbie."*

"Yeah, I been thinking about that."

I was starting to know one voice from the other, but I really wanted them to mention each other's name.

"We really don't need him, and there would be more for us if we cut him out. I reckon we should get rid of him anyway, and if we did, the fucking police wouldn't even start looking for the ones who did it ... not with his record and all."

"Remember when Dickie Kay was hit? Shit, the police didn't do diddly to find out who did it."

Names were being mentioned and I took pages of notes, still hoping that their names would come up.

"Well, I tell you, I'm tired of having a starved stomach, and I think that we're going to have to start a-choosing better places to hit."

"I still got this parole thing hanging over my head, so we gotta be extra careful. You know, that snake-eyed Herbie is too cautious, and sometimes when you're over-cautious it's worse than being careless. He bends down and sneaks around trying to be cautious and that draws attention, 'cause people start to look at him and it's a helluva thing, and he thinks he's a smart ass."

"I'll tell you, I ain't going to help him none if he gets us in trouble."

"All I worry about is coming up with the thirty-one-hundred for the fucking lawyer. I counted up and I still need about seven hundred dollars, and when I get my car from down south, we can use it, but I want to be cool with it and not let it be seen."

"If we get lucky, we can pick up three G's for the receipts in there. We might get three, maybe four hundred off the customers, and I imagine that payday's on Friday up there just like it is here ... and I was thinking about the storeroom. We may lock the motherfuckers in. We'll lock 'em in and that'll give us time to get back to Chicago."

One of the men said, "Let 'em freeze to death," and there was a laugh. Then the tape became inaudible and I sighed with discontent.

I was hoping for something more definite but decided there might be enough to go on after I played the tape over. I also thought that my detective powers of deduction would help me reason why someone had sent me the two tapes—it didn't. I listed all the possible reasons why I was selected to receive them and then crossed off each one that was contradicted by the circumstances, and not one was left. I thought about the most reasonable explanation—or half an explanation. Maybe someone was involved in an unauthorized wiretapping on an intersecting investigation. But why send *me* the tapes? Maybe the source was paying back a favor but he didn't know how to go about it. Surely the source must have known the name or phone number of one of the men, so why not pass it along? And why send the first tape, containing only idle conversation?

That was as far as my thinking got that night, and ever! To this day, I never learned who sent the tapes, and no one ever came up with a plausible explanation. Whoever that someone was, a lot of people should be thankful to him. He may have even saved some lives.

After repeatedly listening to the second tape, I called Lieutenant Lonello at nine o'clock that night. He asked me to come to his house immediately to discuss what to do. As he intently listened to the tapes, his clenched hands moved up and down in a throbbing pattern that must have been part of his nature, since I constantly saw the same rhythm when he threw his office tantrums.

We discussed what we had and didn't have, and then he asked me to start work a little earlier in the morning for a staff meeting. I went home but couldn't sleep that night, constantly tossing and turning. There was just too much to think about.

I went to the office early, finished my paperwork, and was in the lieutenant's office at nine a.m. along with eight daytime detectives and five people from the midnight crew. Lonello told me to play the second tape and yelled to Dario Larcher, an old-timer detective in the outer office, "Take the phones and don't interrupt us!"

We heard clues and small talk, some fascinating and infuriating at the same time. I even picked up some comments I'd failed to hear the previous evening. When it was over, Lonello looked at all the faces in the room and said, "I want these guys, and I want them as soon as possible. I also want everyone in this unit to work together and try your best to get these voices identified. Everyone here has contacts."

He then made assignments. "Eshoo and McCracken, make a determination who Herbie is and what taverns he might frequent; Fornelli and Kurth, find out everything you can about Dickie Kay. Check with the Homicide Unit and the Records section."

Lonello then turned to one of the most reliable supervisors in the unit and my first partner on the job. "Sergeant Coughlin, pick up two men and work closely with them to find out about the person mentioned on the tape who said he has a court date next month. Get right on it, he might have had a court date last Monday or coming up, we don't know because we don't know when these conversations were recorded. I want you to obtain all the court appearances for robbery cases starting last Monday and then type up a daily list. Then we'll check them out, do you understand?"

I said, "The tapes appear to be spliced or tampered with. There is no phone ringing at the beginning, which is usually common with a complete phone tap recording, and at certain sections did you notice repeated sentences like, 'You know what I told you?' That would indicate splicing. Whoever is sending me the tapes might be trying to help us, but they're going about it in the wrong way. The delay might get somebody killed. You heard the tape, now read the packets on robbery cases I put together that form a crime pattern, and see if you can pick out additional connections between the reports and the tape you just heard."

Lonello was back in his element, and I must admit he was a very good administrator. "I have a hunch that another unit, a specialized unit like Narcotics or Gambling, or even Intelligence, might have been working on these guys. When they started mentioning planning robberies they figured they should bring it to our attention and then sent the tapes to Sergeant DiMaggio. What do you think about that, John?"

"Lieutenant, I was going to mention that possibility and also that the tapes could have been sent to me by someone in our own Area. But I don't think there is anyone in our Area that would be stupid enough to tap a phone, receive valuable and sensitive information, and then not disclose it immediately. I can't give you an answer."

The meeting was over, and then Lieutenant Lonello asked if I could stay a little after my day shift hours so I could play the tape for the night watch. In my free time, I made copies with blank tapes and distributed some of them to homicide detectives for work on the Dickie Kay murder.

All Fornelli and Kurth had to do was mention Kay's name to the homicide men and they instantly knew who he was.

Kay had been bound, gagged, and dumped in Lake Michigan, Chicago's largest graveyard. When the body surfaced a week before my first tape arrived, it was so bloated and fish-eaten that the officers were lucky to get him identified.

Sergeant John Coughlin and his two favorite robbery detectives set out to check on people who had court dates for holdups, which averaged close to five hundred per month, and all of the other detectives were attempting to identify the voices on the tape and who Herbie might be.

At the end of the week, my wife called me—another tape had arrived. In the beginning, this one was like the two others, just idle conversation. The sound quality was bad, but then the tape cleared up to a professional quality level and the shockers began:

"You know, Billy Joe, I really enjoyed that last tavern we hit. That barrel I sawed off the shotgun makes a good tool to bonk people over the head. You know, it's like when we're drinking and I play music by tapping beer bottles, and you get a different sound from each bottle."

Billy Joe—whoever he was—had the stronger voice on the tape. Both men laughed, but more than thirty police officers were listening with grim faces.

The voices started talking about a score they were planning—could that be the heist somewhere north of Chicago, with the cooler? The softer voice asked, *"Do you think we should bring some wire along to tie up the people?"*

"Yeah, that's a good idea," Billy Joe said.

"Well, I'll let you handle that. I was thinking 'bout throwing a bunch of cigarettes in that bag, but they would have Wisconsin [tax] stamps on 'em."

"I didn't think about that."

"You know, Billy Joe, those cops up there, if they stop us and if we can get the drop on them when they walk up to the car—if you're sitting on one side and me on the other, or if I get in the back seat— that's what we gotta do, and then we got the drop on 'em, you know what I mean?"

"I know what you mean. But then we'd have to take some

precaution to stop 'em from getting our plate number." The way the word "precaution" was spoken—it was hard, knowing, and dangerous.

"If we get the drop on 'em and they see us," Billy Joe continued, *"we're just going to have to kill 'em. I want to avoid violence as much as possible, but we gotta do what we gotta do. We can stuff them in the trunk if we have to."*

There were all kinds of silences. Police officers hearing plans to kill other cops—it was the kind of quiet that wound up so tightly that your mouth went dry. Some of the detectives simply lit cigarettes while others glanced at one another and looked away. Scattered vulgarities were muttered around me like steam escaping from cracks as the tape continued its run.

"If we stop fucking with Dugan"—who was he?—*"and Herb, well, we need Herbie right now,"* Billy Joe continued, *"well, we gotta get ourselves some more guns. Herb lost your sawed-off jamming it up the drainpipe when you had him outside and he saw that squad car coming down the street. I know a place in Zion* (Illinois, near Wisconsin) *where there's a hardware store run by an old man. I used to visit a guy up there … and this hardware store sells guns. And he's got lots of guns 'cause all the people up there go hunting and such. If we can burgle the store we can get us some guns, some shotguns, pumps, and saw 'em off, put 'em in a tote sack and keep the extras in Junior's attic."* Who was Junior? *"And we gotta get a lot of bullets, and if there's money in the cash register, we'll take it and then when we come back maybe we'll get a hold of Elmer."* Who was Elmer? *"Then we'll start making some good scores because we ain't making shit right now."*

A few sentences more, and there was an obvious splice. Whoever our source was, he took out a passage that probably concerned what he was investigating.

"You know," Billy Joe said, *"there's this friend of mine by the name of Frank. I used to go out to his house and drink all night, sometimes starting at midnight—so we can stay overnight at his house if we have to. He was in the joint with me and we can sure trust him."*

"Where are you talking about?"

"Itasca, it's a west suburb of Chicago."

The conversation continued about their plans to hit numerous places in the Chicago area and elsewhere. When the tape ran out, burglary detective Dennis Farina—who became a familiar Hollywood actor—said, "So these motherfuckers want to stuff police officers in the trunk." He spoke so sternly that he foamed at the corners of his mouth.

"We might have a problem," Lonello said. "I checked with Judge Doherty about the two other tapes. He gave me his unofficial opinion that we can listen to these tapes but we can't use any of the information as evidence in court."

Not even if they mentioned in some later tape that they killed Dickie Kay or even Herbie, who might be running around unaware that Billy Joe and his partner had plans to get rid of him?

"That doesn't make any sense to me whatsoever," I put in. "I think we better start getting legal advice from someone other than Judge Doherty."

"Sergeant," Lonello said, his fingertips digging into a desk, "we'll talk about it after we get these men in custody."

"Lieutenant, I think we better talk about it now. We still don't know who's sending the tapes. It could even be Herbie, who might suspect he's on a hit list. I think we should start researching the ramifications immediately, and then we can go with alternate plans."

Glaring at me, Lonello told all the men, "I will run this investigation and you will take your orders from me. Is that understood?" His voice bounced off the walls, but he calmed down almost immediately. Strangely enough, he asked for the cooperation of everyone. "Keep those names that you heard on the tape in your minds, and try and develop information to make a determination who these robbers are. We need your help." Then he walked back to his office and slammed the door.

After the meeting, I tapped Detective Larry Evans on the shoulder and told him to check with the parole office regarding any Billy Joes that could be on their lists, and advised him to talk to some of our favorite people there because we didn't always receive complete cooperation from the parole office. Some of our investigations were compromised because of that.

Before I went home that night, I called the police in Zion, which was about fifty miles north of Chicago, explained the situation, and asked a Sergeant Halas if his town had a hardware store that sold guns.

"We certainly do," he said. "Old Man Webster runs it. We get a lot of hunters here, pheasants and rabbits, and he does a pretty good business selling licenses, ammunition—and guns."

"Sergeant Halas, I would appreciate it if your department put a watch on Mr. Webster's store, and at your discretion you can tell him that you received information from our department." That's what I said, but if you had asked me then, I would have told you the possibility that the store would be hit was remote. This was just a courtesy call.

The weekend dragged on because we all expected the Billy Joe gang to pull off a robbery, but nothing happened. Then, on Monday, we hit the proverbial jackpot. Larry Evans came into the office with a smile and said loud enough for everyone to hear that he knew Billy Joe's last name. Lieutenant Lonello came flying out of his office.

"The parole office came through—his name is Billy Joe Wiley," Evans said. "He's an ex-con who lives on Roscoe Street. He got out of the joint last September after serving five to ten for robbery, and now he's on parole." Evans pulled out a three page rap sheet and put it on the desk. "He's supposed to be a badass. He's spent ten years in the joint, mostly for robbery, but he has a lot of burglaries on his sheet and also a few pinches from Little Rock, Arkansas. He had a couple of attempted murder indictments, but they were either discharged or the victims didn't follow through."

"Are you sure that's our guy?" one of the detectives asked.

"He has to be, Wiley's the only Billy Joe on parole, and his address is around where we've had several robberies. Those were robberies where they used disguises."

Even cops love a good mystery, and we were ecstatic that the tapes had led us to the threshold of nailing the gang. Our investigation could not have gone any better or faster, and it was obvious that we were receiving the complete cooperation of the other units.

Until the lieutenant took over, that is!

"This case has gotten completely out of hand," he barked, interrupting Evans and startling me. Lonello was always full of surprises, and most of them went against his own men. He kept us playing the game of anticipating his next move, mainly to stay out of trouble.

"I talked to my boss over the weekend," he continued. "He says that due to the increasing violent nature of these men, it would be difficult to have them identified in a showup once their identities become known to us."

What about the robberies where they didn't wear disguises? I thought to myself.

"Therefore, we need to catch them in the act."

Oh shit, I thought. We'd had similar cases in the past and just went out and pinched the bastards without going through the bullshit that always seemed to come when the "bosses" became personally involved. In police vernacular, there was a fine line between a leader and a fool, and now Lonello—who we thought we knew so well—had stepped over it. A few lives were going to be endangered to turn what otherwise would be a page six newspaper story into a chance for a front page bulletin.

As Lieutenant Lonello was telling us how the investigation should and would be conducted, detectives from other units came into our office, interrupting him, to give us information that they had picked up on their own.

One team from Burglary informed us that the accomplice possibly marked for death was called "Herbie the Cat." Although they had not yet learned his last name, they received reliable information that he hung out with Billy Joe Wiley and a guy named Davey Lee Williams in Uptown, then the city's Appalachian haven.

"Sergeant DiMaggio," Lonello said coldly, "record all the information and clear out this place, and then come to my office." He was directing his anger at me instead of thanking the men for the work they'd done.

When I went to his office and sat down in front of him, Lonello, who had the steel balls in his hand, said, "I just got off the phone with the boss, and he wants to be included in everything that will eventually culminate in the arrests of these individuals. In fact, he's on the way from headquarters right now. He'll direct all future operations from this point on, which means I don't want you to take a team out and make any arrests. Do you understand?"

"Absoluuuuutely, lieutenant."

I returned to my desk and didn't say a word to anyone. I didn't have to describe what happened—Lonello's office was just a three-sided cubicle with an open top in a corner of the room. It was obvious that my mood could have boiled water.

The headquarters boss showed up within half an hour, and a private meeting was held in the first floor roll-call room. The boss had already made up a list of detectives that he wanted on the detail, and when he spoke of the investigation he didn't say "our case" or "this case." He said "our mission." *Uh oh*, I thought. Trouble ahead.

His first mistake was to assign too many officers, and when he read off the list of names I was somewhat surprised by his explanation that the "mission" would be in operation around the clock. I felt that the excessive number of men entailed additional planning, and each step offered another possibility for something to go wrong.

I took orders from the boss because he was the boss, but I also thought that I should remind him of details he may have overlooked. The boss thought there was no time to issue photos of the robbers, so I told him I'd already sent two detectives to the graphic arts office for multiple mug shots.

"The guys you selected are excellent detectives and supervisors," I said, "but I can tell you this—hunters never go after bears if they don't know what a bear looks like. They might shoot a deer." That statement was probably the dumbest thing I ever said, but it just flowed out of me like honey.

The boss should have terminated me from the "mission" then and there, but he told me in front of the others that he appreciated my candor. Before the meeting was over, I also mentioned that the tapes had suggested that the gang apparently scouted several taverns before robbing one. Our men should know this so we wouldn't jump the gun and try to take them before they make their move.

"I know that you don't intend to apprehend them in the course of the robbery," I said, intending to plant a seed, "but intend to capture them as they're leaving *after* committing the robbery, correct?"

"Yes, exactly," the boss answered, "and I want you to supply all the men on this mission with copies of those tapes so they can listen to them while they're at home or on stakeout duty."

It had been a high stress day, but I felt somewhat relieved, believing that the investigation was heading in a good direction. Only time would tell if I was right or wrong.

While we were on stakeout, one of the teams radioed when they saw Billy Joe leave his home and enter a car with license plates that had been changed since the previous stakeout. Almost immediately, we verified that the plates were stolen, which gave us a pretty good idea that Billy Joe might be heading out to commit a robbery. Larry Evans and I were working together. We joined other squads in a moving surveillance and formed a virtual box around our subject. Lieutenant Lonello rode with the boss, with the designated call number of Car One.

The first call was from Car Four. "Car Three is sliding in front of me and will take up the Eyeball." That was the surveillance car directly behind the suspect's vehicle while on a moving tail. That team was responsible for giving directions to the other squads, and some officers were naturally better at it than others.

Next came a transmission from Car Three. "Car Four, he's stopping on Barry in the middle of the block." That was the location we now knew as Davey Lee's home. "I'm going to have to pass him and make a right on Leavitt, and cut back to Clybourn. Someone else will have to pick him up. Is that a ten-four?"

"Car Three," said Car Four, "that is *not* a ten-four, I'm out of position. Someone else will have to take up the Eyeball."

"This is Car One," came a voice from the boss' car. "We're standing by at Barry and Clybourn and we'll take the Eyeball."

A few moments passed and then came another transmission. "The suspect is still in the middle of the block and he's blowing his horn." A pause. "Another guy just got in the car. Can't tell if it's Davey Lee. The car is moving. He's going straight ahead— east, east on Barry."

In all, eight cars were following Wiley, and Car One was still the Eyeball. However, they were neglecting to call out the streets and the turns they were making. There was silence on the air for a long time. Car One finally came on and informed us that the suspect's car had been lost in traffic. Evans and I couldn't believe it, and I'm sure that the men in the two other squads were also disturbed. All of us raced, circled, and traveled in random directions, but we couldn't find Billy Joe's car.

After about half an hour, we heard a transmission, "Car One to all cars, report back to the traffic roll-call room for a briefing."

Evans uttered one of his "Oh shit" remarks, and we decided to drive by Billy Joe's house, and then take a slow ride down Roscoe on the off chance that we might locate his auto parked near a tavern.

When we walked into the roll-call room, Lonello explained the reason for losing track of Billy Joe. He said another car had blocked them, and they didn't want the suspects to catch on that they were being followed. Evans and I just glanced at each other and saw other members of the "mission" shaking their heads. The boss then took over the meeting and assigned one car to keep watch on Wiley's apartment, and Sergeant Higgins to stake out Williams' bungalow. Then he thanked the rest of us and told us to go home. I was in no mood to let go of the chase for the day. I suggested to Evans once we were outside that we check out Itasca, the suburb mentioned on one of the tapes, and look for Wiley's car along the route he gave while he was talking to Williams. It was a long shot, but it was something to do.

On the way, Evans said, "I'm glad that we weren't the Eyeball that lost the car."

Trying to be kind and sarcastic at the same time, I answered, "Well, Larry, you know it can happen—another car can block you out, and you don't want to get too close to the suspect's car and get burned, right?"

"Yeah, right."

We stayed out for a couple of hours and then checked with the surveillance teams and learned that neither Wiley nor Williams had returned home.

The boss and the lieutenant were getting impatient for a big arrest, and on Friday, payday for thousands of tavern patrons, they arranged to have a police helicopter help us follow Wiley's vehicle. When Evans and I met at our car, we had to laugh— each of us brought lunches for both of us because we'd sensed it was going to be a long night.

Wiley climbed into his auto at seven p.m., and it still had stolen plates. Helicopter pilot Allen Boehmer was in the air ten minutes later. "Chopper One to all cars," he said, "we have visual contact with the Blue One (the suspect's auto). Car One, you can tell your cars to back off and my co-pilot will give street-by-street directions."

The helicopter assistance was especially helpful because of heavy traffic and confusing slanted streets in the neighborhood. Soon after Billy Joe had picked up Williams, a heavy drizzle started coming down.

During a lull, Boehmer, a friend from Area Five, called down. "DiMaggio, why don't you do the trick we used to do?"

A short time later, when Wiley and Williams stopped for a few beers, I showed Evans what the chopper pilot meant. I removed a tire iron from our squad car trunk.

"What are you going to do with that?" Evans asked. "Hit them on the head?"

"You'll see."

Looking around to make sure no one was watching, I punched a hole near the top of the lens on each tail light of Wiley's car. That would make it easier to follow in the thick weather. When Wiley drove off after casing the second tavern of the night, Boehmer called from his transmitter. "Thanks, John, that car is lit up like a Christmas tree."

We then followed the car to the Saddle and Cycle Club, a combination restaurant and tavern. One of the detectives got out and reported to us from near the front window, hiding behind signs and plants.

"Car One to Radio Four," which was the code name for the scout, "stay there if you can but move around a bit. Don't just stare into that window. Somebody might get suspicious. Just give it a peek once in a while and let us know what's happening."

The scout was Bill Erickson, one of Sergeant Coughlin's

hand-chosen partners. Erickson was a tall, well-built blond Swede who had the ambition and common sense to handle any dangerous assignment. Nothing ever bothered this quiet, low-profile guy who could smile while pulling a trigger in a gun battle.

The boss, sitting in the command car with Lonello, then positioned everyone to be near the Wiley car in order that we could get the men before they had a chance to drive away, if they pulled a robbery. I could practically see what all the other "mission" detectives were doing—reaching for their shotguns and checking their emergency equipment. My scowl must have showed.

"*Now* I know what you were talking about!" Evans said. "This is going to get all fucked up if they come running out and head for their car. Our men will be chasing after them from all directions."

"You got it. The boss should have designated one team to be stationed by Wiley's car, and the rest of us could follow and close in on him at our convenience, eliminating the danger of crossfire. We had four surveillance cars the other night, and now we have *eight*, plus a helicopter, just to take down two robbers."

"So?"

"The boss is forgetting police instincts. If Erickson sees customers getting bonked with that pipe, that shotgun barrel, he just might forget to radio us that a robbery is going on. Instead, maybe Erickson, Green, and Coughlin might confront Wiley and Williams as soon as they come out, or maybe before. Wiley and Williams might panic and shoot somebody or take hostages. Hell, they're on parole, they're committing a robbery, they've got guns, and they're driving around with stolen plates. They also can't trust Herbie the Cat to shut up if they're picked up. We'll just wait and see, but I know what I would do if I were in Erickson's position."

"Yeah, just listening to the tapes makes me think they're going to go down the hard way."

We'll never know if such a scenario would have happened because, as it turned out, Wiley and Williams were apparently just casing the place. The suspects came out of the tavern, got in their car, and drove away. By then the boss had decided to send the chopper back because of the downpour.

As Boehmer was banking away, he said, "Goodnight, John. Best of luck to you, and thanks for the trick."

They soon learned what the helicopter message meant when we followed the blue car with the punctured tail lights to the Mainstream tavern, and by then the rain was falling without spaces between the drops. We had our heavy wipers working, and once again Erickson volunteered to be a scout, this time including his partner. It wasn't a surprise when Erickson broadcasted, "We'll hang around in front of the place and play drunk."

"Chuckie Green must feel that this place is going down for Erickson to convince him to stay out in the rain with him," I mentioned.

"It's a good joint," Evans said. I had to agree. It was an out of the way location with no houses or businesses, just a big parking lot and a popular tavern with a good escape route.

For forty-five minutes—complete radio silence. At last we heard, "They're getting up and it looks like they're coming out." Just another casing.

Each car communicated with the others as we started to follow Wiley's auto out of the lot. Car One announced that it had the Eyeball, and then just a short time later we heard an "Oh shit!" being broadcast—it was Car One notifying us that they had lost sight of Wiley's car *again*. Once more, we fanned out and drove around the streets, but all we saw were each other. Finally, the boss came on the air and asked all "mission" cars to meet him in a business parking lot.

We had a standup meeting in the pelting rain.

"We blew it," the boss said while everyone looked at Lonello. "I don't think they're going to hit any Chicago taverns now, they're too crowded and so far they appear to be just casing them. They might decide to come back at closing time. It's only eleven-thirty, and I have a hunch they might be headed to that Kenosha (a town just over the border in Wisconsin) supermarket they mentioned on the tape. We can all hustle up there and check it out, then if nothing happens up there we'll have enough time to come back and check the places they scouted tonight. We'll meet in Kenosha and make radio contact."

We scooted up the Kennedy Expressway on our way to Wisconsin, drenched and muttering to ourselves. Something was on Evans' mind as he drove, and I had an idea what he was thinking about. "John," he said, "why did the boss think they might score in *Kenosha*? The tapes mentioned something with a cooler up north, but they didn't say Kenosha, did they?"

"What do you think Lonello and the boss have been doing in the last week? I got a call from a friend at the lab, and he said some of the other guys there were clearing up parts of the tape that sounded like Donald Duck. The lab must have picked up something about Kenosha, and our fearless leaders forgot to tell us."

"I don't like it. The secrecy, I mean. I think everything should have been laid out, right at the inception, and better planned."

"Larry, I don't know what's going on and I haven't asked, but if they suspected a place in Kenosha might be hit, they should have sent a couple of cars up there earlier, and why is the whole 'mission' team going up there now, all eight cars? Why not leave some behind for the taverns? Larry, it's almost midnight. Will you go along on a hunch of mine?"

"Sure, Sarge. What have you got in mind?"

"We're so close to Zion, I'd like to have a talk with Sergeant Halas if he's still on duty. Maybe he can show us where old man Webster has his hardware store. On a night like this, a burglary is more likely than a tavern robbery." Robbers wouldn't want to make a getaway on wet pavement and in slow traffic. My idea was to do a fast side trip, then cross the state line and catch up with the other cars.

"If you say so," Evans said, "but Zion's a quiet town, it's pretty much locked up by now."

A Zion gas station attendant who was closing up shop pointed the way to the combined police and fire station, adding, "You can't miss it." We found the building and went through the glass partitioned door marked Police and saw the one-person communications center manned by a dispatcher. The uniformed sergeant sitting at the desk happened to be Halas, and he perked up when we introduced ourselves.

"We were just passing by on our way to Kenosha," I said, "and I thought we'd stop by and say hello, if you were still working."

"I get through at midnight, but I usually hang around a little while, have a cup of coffee and just relax. I just put my rookie out there to fight the elements. How did you guys get so drenched?"

"It's a long story," Evans replied.

"By the way, sergeant," I said, "could you get your rookie to show us the way to Mr. Webster's hardware store?"

"Hell, I'm off duty, I'll show you the way myself, it's on my way home. You can follow my car, and then you can take off for Kenosha because it's just north of here. Webster's a little bit on the senile side, and when I told him about your phone call he said that he was going to sleep in the back of the store every night for a while to protect his property. He's really a character, the last of the old-timers."

Halas got into his squad car and we followed in ours for a mile or two, then down a diagonal road for a mile and a half. That took us to the parking lot of a fairly large building just off the hunters' woods. The rain was so bad, Halas was feeling his way through with his headlights until he reached what we assumed was the rear of the store.

Then all hell broke loose.

There was an explosion of gunpowder, and a shotgun muzzle lit up the rear doorway of the store. Evans shoved his foot on the brake and our auto slid seven feet in the muck, ending alongside Halas' squad. Evans jumped out, and I was on my feet and splashing in the mud before I realized that we were not the targets!

Old man Webster didn't seem too senile as he let go with another blast. Wiley and Williams responded by firing back at him from near the blue car we'd been following all night, and then at us. We kept our car doors open for cover. Evans held his eyes low on the driver's side as I crouched behind the passenger door. We could hardly see anything except the night, the rain, the two robbers in our headlight beams, and the flashes from the guns.

Mr. Webster was at one side of a broad triangle of gunfire. Halas, Evans and I were firing at the other side, and the robbers were at the vertex. The headlights of the two police cars bore down on the criminals. Amid the nearly fifteen shots from us, Webster got off a third blast. Then came silence, except for the raindrops thudding on the cars and the moaning coming from the direction of the blue auto.

The shootout had lasted so long—thirty seconds—that for a moment nobody did anything until we realized it was all over. Then Evans and I grabbed our loaded secondary weapons and cautiously crossed the muddy parking lot. Each robber had crumpled face down with a gun in his hand. We didn't know which man was Billy Joe or Davey Lee, and we didn't care.

Evans put his foot on one man's gun hand, and put his own weapon against the man's head. I did the same with the guy closer to me. We picked the men up and leaned them against the car. Blood flowed from their wounds and streamed into the rainwater.

"We're hurt bad," one of them cried.

Billy Joe Wiley and Davey Lee Williams were sentenced to serve twenty to forty years for robbery and attempted murder. As for the murder of Dickie Kay, that remained unsolved—like the mystery of who sent me the tapes.

The case was satisfying, most robbery cases were, but working under Lonello, the most unappreciative person I'd ever met, was so unnerving that I eventually asked to be transferred from Robbery to Homicide.

I'd have to wait a year, though, before I could get away.

14

STRIKING BACK

I was in just the middle of my career when it nearly ended. I was assisting Summerdale District officers as they led a handcuffed robbery suspect down the back stairs of the Area Six building. He had to be transported to a district station since our antiquated Area headquarters had no processing capability. I didn't know the man's name or details of the arrest, I was just walking down the stairs in front of him to make sure he didn't decide to make a fast tour of the neighborhood. The robber had not been giving us any trouble, so I wasn't prepared when he kicked me in the back. It felt as if I was whacked with a sledgehammer. I tumbled head over feet down two landings, and then lay in pain, seeing mostly a deep black in front of me with little reality around the edges.

The detective walking behind the prisoner grabbed him before he could walk over me and get away. I don't know what happened to him, but whatever it was, it wasn't enough—and that should be enough said.

I should have gone to a hospital, but I didn't. I thought I could tough out the severe pains in my lower back, but they wouldn't go away. Maybe somewhere in the back of my mind I didn't want to admit I had an injury that might keep me out of active police work. I was trying to will it away or wish it into something that could be fixed with a few aspirin.

After six months, the pain and the worry were wearing me down. Finally, through a friend who was high-ranked in the police department, I obtained an appointment and consultation with a well-known orthopedic surgeon by the name of Louis Kolb. Kolb, at the time, worked with the chief bone mender for the Chicago Bears and they were on the sidelines for all football games to evaluate and treat the many injuries.

Kolb studied the results of my spinal taps and myelogram and bluntly told me, "John you have two lower spinal discs, L4 and 5, that have become bulbous and you most certainly will require a spinal fusion—if not now, then in a short period of time."

"How short?" was the dumb question I asked.

"You will know, when one of these days you will not be able to take the next step."

He went on to explain that the operation would necessitate the removal of the two damaged discs from my lower spine, with replacement bone shavings from my hips, creating a fusion. The doctor looked at me as if I were something broken and needed repair. At that time he couldn't see me as a police officer whose sole existence was involved in the game of cops and robbers. I felt my life submerging.

"Could I delay the operation?" I asked.

"Give it some serious thought. It will not get any better and it might get worse."

For some reason I thought I could put off the inevitable. Just a few months later, while I was working at a secondary job as a security officer for a Marriott hotel, I suddenly felt as if I were being knifed in the lower back and it was difficult for me, as Kolb had warned, to "take the next step."

Feeling that I had no real choice, I signed the waiver for surgery. I told my wife the decision I had made, not knowing what her reaction would be. For once, Rosemary didn't say something like, "Whatever you think is best." Instead, she broke down and cried.

I was a season ticket holder for the Chicago Bears, and from my hospital bed saw the great running back Gayle Sayers, wearing jersey number 30, injure his knee in a televised game just after Kolb had given me the bad news. As a regular patient at Illinois Masonic, Sayers asked for the room that I happened to be in because the way it was shaped assured that only his feet would be visible to passersby. That meant he wouldn't have people gawking at him. Since I was occupying the room, Sayers agreed to take the one next door.

At seven o'clock one morning in the fall of 1971, I was anesthetized and wheeled in for the operation. The room seemed vast as I lay groggy on my back, trying to look out the corner of my eyes, and my helplessness made me feel very alone. The surgery took six to eight hours, and when I awoke in the recovery room, I saw Sayers lying unconscious on the gurney next to mine, and then I went under again.

When I awoke in my room around seven at night, a nurse told me my wife and children had been with me all day but left just a little while before, assuming I would remain asleep. Now I was wide awake and felt no pain at all, but recalling Dr. Kolb's words, I remained perfectly still.

The drugs kept me constantly in a daze.

Three or four days passed. Dr. Kolb dropped by as often as he could and sometimes he swapped experiences. He was genuinely interested in police work and felt that if my back healed properly, I could return to duty in about five months—as long as I followed his advice and the recommended therapy.

My room became my prison for weeks, and I tried not to think about the future. Sometimes Sayers rolled his wheelchair into my room for long talks to cheer me up, and he jokingly reminded me that I had *his* room. I suspected that one reason I had so many visitors was that my friends kept dropping by in hopes that I would introduce them to him. Sayers was always accommodating, giving autographs and little souvenirs.

That night, quite a few Bears players gathered in Sayers' room to watch *Brian's Song*, the television movie about his friendship with the late Brian Piccolo. A few policemen friends came to watch the film with me, and having Sayers in the room next to mine made the movie all the sadder.

By mid-December, my muscles had lost their tone and I was still in a great deal of pain, but the staff had me up and around with the aid of a walker and a back brace. I was discharged two days before Christmas and was picked up by a good friend, Officer John Coughlin.

I had visions of soon throwing my brace and walker away,

but almost immediately my arms and hands felt numb as I tried to make it through the house. When I touched my face, there was no feeling—my hands seemed like balsa wood. I hopefully assumed nothing was seriously wrong and that the numbness was caused by my back brace.

My wife called Dr. Kolb, and he told me to come back to the hospital as soon as possible and meet him in the emergency room. Knowing that I would be re-admitted, I asked Rosemary to stay home and take care of the kids, and I had my father drive me to the hospital. My dad helped me in. Sick and injured people sitting in the emergency room all offered me a seat—I looked that bad—but I declined and slid my feet toward the desk where I'd spotted the doctor.

Kolb and the neurosurgeon from my operation were quarreling about me.

"He will require ulna transplants," the neurosurgeon said. *Ulna, ulna… that meant elbow,* I realized.

"He will not have to go through transplants," Dr. Kolb insisted. "We will keep him off his elbows and place him in special therapy and on a restricted diet." Off my elbows? They had been my only relief when I was confined to my bed—could I have used them too much?

Kolb said to me, "John, you're going to be all right. I promise you, the feelings will return to your arms and hands." I had faith in him. He didn't say so at the time, but he was trying to save me for police work. From our many conversations, he knew how I loved the job, and only after my slow recovery could I appreciate what his intervention had meant for me.

All I knew was that I couldn't stand or walk for more than a few minutes at a time and I was relying on strong medication and sleeping pills to get me through my pain—and feeling sorry for myself. Until Dr. Kolb stopped that by the cold-turkey method with a goal of self-sufficiency.

Every kind of treatment he prescribed worked, and that included occupational therapy, diet, and elbow pads. Feeling gradually returned to my arms and hands, and now it was up to me to exercise and recover my strength so I could hit the streets again.

In May of 1972, seven months after the robber kicked me down the stairs, I was walking up to my floor of Area Six again. I was a little slower, but the climb was part of my exercise. The detectives seemed glad to see me, and no one made fun of my back brace because injuries in this business were a badge of honor. As a sergeant I was considered "inside personnel," but I kept looking for a chance to be out with the field detectives. That is what led me to help disarm Robert Nelson after the long standoff in his home by jumping on his back and holding his shotgun until help rushed in, and most thankfully, Dr. Kolb's work proved to be a complete success.

Afterward, I was transferred to the Homicide/Sex Unit of Area Six, and that required a whole new type of thinking. There's an old saying in the department: Put a door in front of a robbery detective and he'll break it down. Place a door in front of a homicide detective and he'll knock on it.

When I was a robbery sergeant I believed in that philosophy, but when I was transferred to Homicide, my thinking changed a great deal and so did my respect for the detectives.

A lot of eager men wanted to be assigned to Homicide, but they were turned down because they were *too* eager, did not possess the multiple talents required to do the job, or could not cope with the assignments. Disregard what you see on television and in the movies. Homicide detectives are low profile investigators because they're required to speak to grieving families and have the patience and intelligence to handle a mound of paperwork that often lasts for years.

Homicide detectives are also best at holding back their feelings. They see so much that could sicken the average person. They know, for example, that some little children that die, supposedly from accidental falls, are actually victims of rapes—as indicated by the symptoms of a swollen abdomen and ruptured internal organs. There are some babies less than a year old that die as a result of attacks. The repulsive men who do this invariably show no remorse, and detectives who arrest them show the restraint necessary to treat them no worse than pickpockets.

With burglars and robbers, the motive is usually something

you can understand.. With murders and sex cases, what you are told is usually not what really happened.

We once investigated a case regarding a four-year-old girl who had been scalded by a pail of water hot enough to cook instant oatmeal. What concerned us was that both her legs had one-foot ring lines. The little girl could have put in one leg without knowing the water was so hot, but she wouldn't have put in the other leg, too. As we learned, part of her mother's violent sexual abuse involved dipping the little girl's legs into the scalding water.

Such cases, and many much worse, always amazed Assistant State's Attorney Joseph Urso, chief of the Felony Review Office. We often called him at home in the middle of the night and asked him to come down to mediate disputes between us and lawyers under his supervision.

Urso, a rotund, good-natured, sensible man who later became a judge, once said that if we ever wrote about our experiences, no one would believe them because they'd read like fiction.

Homicide detectives commonly mature while assigned to other units, as I did in robbery. By the time I was transferred, I thought I'd seen it all and knew it all. Then came a hot summer day when we received a call regarding a homicide at a flophouse. As I approached the decrepit building, I saw some officers puking and others smoking cigars to mask the reeking odors of what they'd seen. I thanked my deviated septum, a product of a few broken noses, for reducing my power of smell.

One of the detectives in the hallway really disliked me—he hated *all* new officers and supervisors who, he believed, didn't possess his capabilities. The large man wore a perpetual scowl. Even though I knew his general attitude and dislikes, I gave him the highest mark in the unit during his six-month evaluation because he was one of the most talented homicide investigators. As I walked into the hallway, though, he snubbed me as just a robbery cop transplanted to homicide and invading his personal turf—that of the prestigious Homicide Unit.

Other detectives told me he thought I didn't examine the bodies, watch the autopsies, or cope with the assignments, and I kept this information in the back of my mind. When I approached him directly and asked him what was going on, he replied in his usual way.

"The responding patrol officers went directly to Room 132, which is right behind us, and when they opened the unlocked door they discovered the body and called for us. We're presently awaiting the arrival of the mobile crime lab."

"Okay, I'll have a look," I said, and he followed me into the room.

A mummy—a 20th Century mummy—lay on a cot in a cubicle measuring six by eight feet. One of the beat officers thankfully had opened the window, but the stench was so overpowering that some of it was bound to linger until the aging place was demolished. The tiny room was cluttered with garbage and empty wine bottles. I expected maggots, but there were none. Just lots of cockroaches having a picnic, and some other unidentifiable creatures.

"Don't touch anything," I told the officers behind me—not that they wanted to. I turned to the guy who disliked me and said, "Let's make a determination of how this guy died."

"I hope you don't intend to unwrap this person."

"That is exactly what I have in mind." I knew it would have been wiser to wait until the body was taken to the morgue, but I felt it was the perfect opportunity to prove something to this pompous individual. Observing a raggedy end of the cloth strip, I lifted it carefully and slowly from the top of the victim's head and worked my way down.

What had happened, we learned later, was that this man's drinking partner had quarreled with him and waited until he fell into a drunken sleep. The buddy then took the time to tear up the two sheets into strips about four inches wide, then suffocated the victim by wrapping them around him from head to foot. Whoever did this was drunk and irate, so he was less than meticulous. He might have started with the nose and mouth to keep his victim from struggling, but why did he continue?

The cloth became soggier as I lifted it from the eye sockets, then the sunken nose, and then from the goo around his teeth.

Next came the maggots, crawling from eye holes and the nostrils and the mouth. The big, experienced detective looked uneasy, and I casually stopped the unwrapping.

"Until the autopsy, I'd say this man died by suffocation," I said. "Let's wait for the morgue to take all this off." I rewrapped the cloth around the decaying face as if my stomach and sense of humanity were unperturbed.

The detective and his partner went out and made an arrest before the day was out.

During all the time I spent in Homicide, he always avoided me and was never friendly. I had impressed him all right—he probably thought I was mad or completely without feelings, but with this particular individual I couldn't care less.

The most rewarding part of the Homicide Unit was working with the truly great partnership of methodical Paul Roppel and fun-loving, handsome Jimmy Nolan. They weren't partners by coincidence. A mutual friend, Detective John Philbin, worked with Nolan in the Intelligence Division, and when he learned that Nolan was being transferred to the Homicide Unit he suggested that he hook up with Paul Roppel.

Most people assume that partners must think alike, but Philbin knew that a good working relationship needs two people who have the same goals but use different approaches. Although Paul and Jimmy were in their late twenties, about five-feet-eight or nine, good-looking, and trim, they were completely different.

Roppel was the methodical and serious one, and nothing could upset him. He had begun as a police cadet and was permitted to take the detective's examination shortly after becoming an officer. He posted so high that he had the distinction of becoming the youngest homicide detective in Chicago. He was a quiet, friendly, homebody-type of guy, and extremely knowledgeable. He handled difficult situations and problems with other officers with the talents possessed by trained psychologists. Paul went out with the guys occasionally but he always kept in total control of himself and made it a point to help detectives who were going in the wrong direction in a variety of ways.

Nolan, whom everyone called "the Kid," still had a few

rough edges but threw himself into police work with intensity. He pretended to be upset with prisoners, raised his voice, and went into mock outbursts. That was to keep them in line and also part of a running joke with the other detectives. It was always fun to watch him in action. That was one reason I was surprised to learn that Nolan always carried a secret sadness around with him. He was living in an upstairs apartment of his parents' bungalow because he was separated from his wife, and that kept him away from his little daughter. He saw her as often as he could, but he had the feeling that she was growing up without him. He realized that she needed a father. I think one of the reasons why Nolan pulled so many pranks was to keep his mind off his personal problems.

Nolan was sent to the Intelligence Unit for a while but didn't show his true flair for police work until he was transferred to Homicide and teamed with Roppel.

In contrast to their tough act with prisoners, they were considerate with crime victims. The partners knew they had already been through enough, and there was no point in making their ordeal worse. They worked out a way in which just one of them, usually the personable Nolan, would talk to victims of sexual assault conversationally while the other stood off to the side and took notes. That avoided the constant alternating questioning by two detectives in a way that unintentionally seemed like the third degree. The method was so successful that they carried it over to most of their interrogations.

When I arrived in the unit, I immediately liked these dissimilar detectives with their well-scrubbed faces. I was about ten years their senior, but in many ways felt old enough to be their father. Sometimes I treated them as if I were. I found myself looking for interesting cases for them to work on whenever they could spare the time from their routine assignments, and then I would ask to ride along with them.

I could see at first they weren't happy with my company. They thought that as their sergeant, I should remain in the office, as most sergeants did, and they later admitted that as a supervisor they suspected I might impede their individual styles of investigation. Instead, something clicked. Our three personalities, so different in some ways and very similar in others, seemed to form a single thought and one path of direction.

"Leave the paperwork, Sarge," Roppel would say. "Put someone else on the desk, we're going out on a case and we might need your help."

"You gotta go with us," Nolan might add, "we got something to show you." That might be a bizarre development, an intriguing mystery, a different restaurant, or maybe nothing at all.

To my knowledge, we were the only informal team of a supervisor and two detectives in the city, or at least in Homicide. Maybe ever. We weren't even supposed to be a team; my listed duties would have tied me to a desk most of the time, but no one would think of breaking us up. Before long, we were called the Three Musketeers, and I wasn't sure if the nickname was complimentary or the source of some type of jealousy.

When some rapes on the North Side showed a vaguely familiar pattern, I compared the circumstances with the files we had on other sexual attacks. Not only for the last few weeks, but for the dated files going back for two years. Then I started talking to Homicide/Sex detectives in other parts of the city as well. If my hunch was right, the same man was using the tricks of a rather sophisticated con man to attack perhaps more than a hundred young women over a five year period, and that included models, secretaries, and stewardesses. He was able to elude investigators because he didn't confine himself to a single neighborhood. He spaced the attacks and used various M.O.s to avoid calling our attention to him. All of this showed the cunning of a pathological criminal, someone who played a game with his victims and with the police, yet with the ultimate goal of avoiding detection.

I found it difficult to convince my supervisors and other sergeants that the same man might be responsible for many of the attacks in Areas Five and Six and the western suburbs. In an effort to substantiate my beliefs, I started riding with Nolan and Roppel as they were assigned to every rape that occurred on the North Side.

To help confirm there was a pattern, we asked the victims to fill out a questionnaire I had made. From this we learned that some victims had recently placed an ad in the newspapers seeking to sublet their apartment. Occasionally a man called without mentioning the ad. He sounded friendly, even flirtatious, and, already knowing her address through a previous call to sublet the apartment, claimed that the two of them had met at a business or at a singles bar near the apartment and that she had given him her number.

Other times he apparently made random calls from the telephone book, saying he was an insurance agent, an employee from the credit department of a major department store, or a surveyor from the American Bootery Association. When that was his ruse, he promised a free pair of boots if the woman would let him interview her in her home.

The link in all these cases, the element separating this attacker from all the others over the previous few years, had to be the telephone call. That was his signature, and the questionnaire proved without a doubt that a crime pattern had been in existence for a long period of time.

Whether posing as a casual acquaintance, a credit investigator, or a salesman, the man showed up acting very cordial, even charming—he was a little heavy, but not bad looking in a dark, masculine way, and had a thick, well-groomed mustache.

Once he lulled the women into trusting him, he pulled out a knife or gun and bound them with string from his pocket. Sometimes he wore surgical gloves and placed boots on the victims before assaulting them. He was one sick puppy, and the entire unit took an interest in him.

With *Leona Nockman, he called as a salesman and got details about her shoe size and clothing preferences. He waited an entire year until she forgot the call, then dialed again, this time pretending to be a friend she had met at a trendy bar near her home. In their conversation, he used the information he had kept in his notes to convince her that the two of them had really met.

"Tomorrow's my birthday," he said. "How about you and

me going out for a nice dinner and champagne to help me celebrate?"

The next evening, the man, claiming to be John Morris, picked her up outside her home, kissed her chastely on the cheek, and drove her to a small but nice restaurant. During the drive, Leona tested her memory on when and how she'd met this stranger. He was a perfect gentleman during the course of the evening and she genuinely liked him.

Dropping her off later, he said, "I really need to go to the washroom and hate to impose, but would you mind?"

Without a thought, she let him.

Once inside her third floor apartment, he pulled out a gun and ordered, "Go to your closet and get a pair of boots." She complied, terrified at what would happen next. "Take your clothes off and lie on your stomach." Then he tied her hands behind her with twine and struggled to put the boots on her. "Keep quiet and keep your legs still."

Then he violently raped her, hogtied her arms and legs, and ran down the stairs. She screamed so loudly that her neighbors called the police. The officers found her battered, tied, and hysterical.

Now, of course, everyone realized the pattern. All detectives in Area Six were effectively working on the case in addition to their regular homicide assignments.

Lieutenant Julien Gallet assigned this case to Roppel and Nolan, and I was with them when they interviewed Nockman. Seeing the terror on her face and knowing that this kind of attack was being committed repeatedly, the partners went on a personal crusade to stop the man.

When Leona mentioned that she wanted to change her phone number, they asked her in a persuasive manner not to do so. Seducing victims by phone was part of the excitement "Morris" derived from his crimes. The two detectives said that if he ever called again, she should string him along and then contact the police—but they advised her that at no time was she to place herself in danger.

This didn't mean we were going to wait around for the rapist to call her or any of his other victims. Since the attacker stuck to a pattern, we felt that we could use the same one to trap him. We went through newspapers and dialed women advertising to sublet their apartments, asking if they had received any calls from a man claiming to be a bootery salesman. Several had. We told them to contact us immediately if he phoned again. Then we placed our own ad in the sublet column. A woman officer assigned to that number received an initial call, possibly from the suspect, but for some reason the man never called back. Perhaps her tone lacked the naiveté he sought in his victims, and maybe he sensed a trap.

Whatever the reason, he went back to his list of victims. Like many rapists, he had the arrogance to think that the women enjoyed what he had put them through.

In late October, thirteen months after Leona was raped, he called her again.

"Hi Leona, this is John Morris, remember me?"

"Yes, I do, and I think of you constantly," she said, trying to sound calm and replying as Roppel and Nolan had asked her to do. That took a lot of courage.

"Say, how did you like it?"

"I really did, it was good. Please call me again, and we can talk about it. Maybe we can do it again, but the right way next time."

The man said he might call back later and hung up.

Lieutenant Gallet asked for volunteers for a night stakeout at the building. We Three Musketeers did so along with detectives John Toenings and John Philbin.

Detective James Phelan from Area Five and a police woman, Sherri Martin, were already with Leona at the entrance of her building on Lake Shore Drive when we parked on a side street some distance away to avoid any suspicion.

I get along with most people, but Phelan was not one of my favorites. He once worked for me when I was at Area Five and our relationship was like oil and water. He was in his thirties, short, prematurely gray, highly educated, and thought at the time that he knew everything about police work. When a person was like that, there was a great temptation to make him realize how much he had to learn.

Phelan spoke first, as if he were in charge of the details. "Roppel, Officer Martin, and I will cover the victim in her apartment," he said with authority. I was flabbergasted that he would think of breaking up the successful partnership of Roppel and Nolan, and that he should be making assignments without consulting us. "Toenings, Nolan, Philbin, and *you*"—he said to me—"will take up a fixed surveillance in the lobby. I have three radios, one for us in the apartment, one for the lobby people, and one in case you want to put someone outside as a roamer lookout."

I'm sure that Phelan, who was single, was trying to impress the attractive victim, and I wasn't alone in my thinking. I was also fairly sure that my friend Lieutenant Gallet had instigated this series of events as a joke or to test my reactions. The two other Musketeers were surprised that I was letting him dictate the assignments, and I suspect that even Phelan was bewildered that he was getting away with it. He had worked with me long enough to know I was never submissive to abrasive or strong-headed bosses or let a subordinate do my work. My madness had a method, though. Letting Phelan think he was in charge put him upstairs and out of our way. That gave us a free hand if Morris showed up, and we most certainly had the advantage of intercepting the rapist before he got to the upper floors.

Phelan's idea of dividing eight people into two equal groups was made more on the basis of mathematics than on sound police judgment, and there was no point in having us lounge around in the lobby. Suppose you were a rapist and saw four men who looked like cops, would you go in? After all, the attacker had been eluding the police for a number of years largely because he'd developed animal instincts for what was safe.

Nolan, Toenings, Philbin, and I decided to wait behind a door in an alcove that led to the front stairwell. The door had a window that allowed us to see everyone coming and going. The neighborhood was fairly nice, but no one had mopped this neglected hallway in months. Heat poured from a fixed vent and we quickly blocked it with some cardboard. We made ourselves as comfortable as possible with a table and a few chairs we borrowed from the foyer and posted a continual watch on the door window.

The apartment detail called down to us on the radio.

"Are you boys comfy?" Roppel asked. He was being a comedian and possibly rubbing it in that Phelan had taken charge.

"We're fine," said the tall, muscular Toenings.

After the communication terminated, Nolan chanted in singsong, "No, we're not fine, DiMaggio's pissed, DiMaggio's pissed!"

I scowled a little.

"Hey, Sarge," Nolan asked, "when are you going to get back at that guy?"

I felt my face stretch into a grin. Nolan knew me so well that he sometimes read my mind.

Detective Philbin—a friend who chose me to be the godfather of his child—looked over his shoulder and asked, "Yeah, how could you let that pipsqueak get away with calling the shots?"

"It's not so bad," I answered. "I'd rather be down here than upstairs with him."

"Apartment to First Floor," squeaked Phelan a little later. "Leona just received a phone call from the offender and she convinced him to come right over. Be on your toes down there!"

Toenings thought the message was a prank, but Phelan was not known for his jokes. Then two and a half hours passed without another transmission, and I felt pretty sure the attacker wouldn't be coming that night. I decided to look around the building while Nolan and Toenings kept watch on the front entrance and Philbin roamed and furtively looked for anyone suspicious. I checked all the doors leading to fire escapes to make sure no one could get in from the outside, and then I found a locked utility room near Leona's apartment. Out of curiosity, I used my Intelligence Unit training and picked the lock in fifteen seconds. Inside was an electrical cabinet with circuit breakers identifying each apartment on the third floor, and one was marked "Hallway." A devious thought instantly came to mind. What if I used this opportunity as a training exercise? Common sense dictated that all three officers should remain in the apartment if the lights went out so they could protect the victim and guard the door and windows. I flipped off the power to Leona's apartment and the hallway. Then I felt my way in total darkness to the stairs and hurried down, arriving just in time to hear Phelan's voice over the radio.

"He's here! He's here! All the power is shut off, the lights are out, the hallway's out, too!"

How did he know that except by opening the door, which should have remained secured?

Nolan stared at me and asked, "What did you do?" It was the tone one uses when a dog misbehaves.

"He could have got in through the fire escape doors," Phelan's voice gasped into the radio. "I'm going to check it out."

I grabbed the radio and said, "Who has the victim and where is she?"

"She's with me, and I'm protecting her."

"In the hallway? In the darkened hallway?"

"Yeah, in the hallway."

"Where are Roppel and Martin?"

"They're in the apartment."

"Well, Phelan, get back in the apartment with them and lock the door! We'll take care of the electrical problems. Do you understand?"

My God, the highly educated Phelan had taken Leona out of a locked apartment, where there was nothing to fear, to a completely darkened corridor where, for all he knew, an attacker could be waiting. Boy Scouts would have known better, but as I mentioned before, Phelan thought he knew it all.

"We will contact building management and determine the nature of the power failure. Is that a ten-four, Phelan?"

"Ten-four," he responded, apparently dejected that I was taking over command after letting him play around at being in charge.

The stakeout for us continued to six a.m., when we from Area Six all went to breakfast while Phelan stayed with Leona. As we ate, Roppel complained that there had been nothing to do in the apartment but watch television, and the victim had very little food. "She opened up tuna fish cans and we had sandwiches with dry bread and no mayonnaise," he lamented.

"What did Phelan do?" Nolan asked.

"He sat on the couch with his arm around the victim to console her."

That made us laugh uncomfortably.

"Hey, Sarge," Roppel said, looking at me seriously, "I know you won't admit it—"

"Here it comes," Nolan interjected.

"—but I think you had something to do with the lights going off. You know, that was the best test anyone could give Phelan. He really panicked. We told him not to go out in the hall, be he insisted and took the girl with him."

I just sat back, pleased with my little revenge.

Phelan got his come-uppance when he told Lieutenant Gallet the next day about the power outage and his course of action. Gallet chewed him out for going into the hallway and leaving the victim exposed. For years afterward, Phelan suspected that I was involved with the lights going out, but he never could figure out how I did it. Nolan and I never told him.

Since phone calls were the attacker's trademark, that was the only sure way he could be caught. Leona went on a two week vacation, and the man resumed his calls when she returned. We obtained a court order to tap her phone and arranged to have police officers riding the streets at all hours to spot anyone at a phone booth who looked like the composite sketch. We also kept a woman police officer standing by at the Area Six phone listed in ads about subletting an apartment, but there were no more calls to that line.

The rapist made more than thirty calls to Leona, and each time she had to seem eager, when in reality just the sound of his voice made her sick. After a few failed attempts at tracing his calls, the telephone company notified us that our man was in a phone booth on Clybourn Avenue. Three Area Six detectives rushed over and found him calling Leona for what would be the last time.

"Police!" they shouted, and that was the last thing she heard before "Morris" hung up. As he was put into the squad car, one of the detectives called Leona back. He identified himself and asked, "Can you identify the man you just heard over the phone as the man who had attacked you?"

"Yes, oh God, I've talked to him so many times."

Within hours, Leona and five other victims identified the suspect. The monster turned out to be a seemingly happy married electronics salesman named *John Michael Morgan. The follow up investigation and physical evidence in his apartment in suburban Woodridge linked him to many more victims. His notebook and phone directory was a dossier to his past and future victims. Astounding revelations were copiously recorded.

He turned out to be an extremely cooperative degenerate while he was in custody and being processed, trying to impress everyone with his friendliness. Morgan, a man with fifteen aliases, pleaded guilty to five of his rapes, an attempted rape, and eight counts of deviate sexual assault. When he was sentenced to serve from five to twenty years in prison, he wiped away his tears and shook the hand of the judge and female prosecutor.

Seventeen officers who had worked on the case were cited for the coveted Unit Meritorious Award, and at a special ceremony we were presented with a ribbon bar to be worn on our uniforms. The real satisfaction, though, was knowing that Morgan was off the streets.

15

THE THREE MUSKETEERS

A long nightmare began half an hour before dawn on Saturday, November 8, 1975.

Under a pair of eyes hidden in the shadows, *Carrie Barns stepped out of her car in a school lot and crossed the street to her North Side apartment. The nineteen-year-old bank employee was wearing black slacks and a black jacket over a white blouse so that she would fit in with her former high school classmates at a yuppie bar called "Mother's." Carrie was a pleasant, quiet girl who needed the company of friends to become fully alive, which then made her open to jokes and dares.

Carrie practiced some dance steps with them after knee surgery that had put her out of the singles action for nearly a year. Normally she'd have a couple of beers, but not on this night because she was on medication. She just ordered orange juice and ran into a casual acquaintance, *Mike "Butch" Brooks, and talked to him for a while. Two weeks earlier, they were involved in a drinking contest at Mother's and the young man slugged down scotches while she guzzled Michelob's. She won.

As Carrie walked closer to her home, a strange looking man in an imitation leather coat appeared before her with something in a paper bag.

"Say, can you tell me how to get to Newgard Avenue?" he asked.

She tried to ignore him, thinking he was drunk, even

though he didn't seem intoxicated. His eyes were like glass.

"Hey, you want to be nice to me?" he asked as she continued to walk away. "How about a blow job?"

"Go pay for it on Howard Street," she snapped.

"I want a blow job or I want to get fucked, that's all I want."

"If you don't leave I'll call the police."

"It's just a blow job."

"I'll scream—"

"Go ahead. Do you know what can happen to you if you don't give me what I want?"

"You're going to find out what's going to happen to you if you don't leave me alone!"

Carrie tried to walk quickly out of the man's way, but she noticed a blue handle protruding from the paper bag.

"I'm going to kill you," he said calmly.

He drew a hatchet out of the bag. The young woman panicked and ran to the two-flat building where she lived with her family, but before she could slam the hallway door behind her, the man stopped it with his leg, struck her a few times, and then stretched his arm and removed both light bulbs in the vestibule. It was then completely dark. Next, the small axe came crashing down on her head and face. Carrie screamed but the blade sliced her repeatedly. She thudded against the wall, the door, the wall, and the door again …

"Joanne!" she shrieked, hoping to wake her sister, who was sleeping in a bedroom directly above the hallway. No one could hear her. She stopped thinking, stopped seeing. All she could feel was the pain as he hacked once more. A swipe of the blade cost her the sight of one eye. Another whack ripped out part of her cheek and cut through her palate. Still the man kept pounding. When her face was destroyed to something resembling raw meat, he reached down and pulled her legs forward. As she slid back, she felt her dislocated jaw go into her chest.

"Stop, please, stop," she attempted to say.

He struck her again and the hatchet embedded in her skull. The attacker had to put his foot on her shoulder for leverage to pull out the weapon. Then he raped her, his eyes smoky from alcohol and drugs. After penetration, the man appeared as if his thoughts had drifted elsewhere, as if this was not what he had intended to do. He climbed off and started to leave.

Carrie felt relieved that at last her ordeal had ended, but on impulse he turned back. She felt him removing her shoes and slacks, but left her underpants hanging on one leg. One of the two light bulbs dropped to the floor and shattered with the sound of a gunshot, and Carrie's head felt as if it would explode. The attacker then walked out with her clothes as trophies or anything that might have his fingerprints.

Lying helpless in the silence, unaware of the time, Carrie inched her hand to her face and felt her left eye dangling. The young woman also felt that two upper teeth were shattered. When she went to remove them, her hand went through her gashed-open cheek instead of her mouth. She clutched the teeth and tried to ring the doorbell for help, but she slipped in her own blood. She weakly tried again, ringing repeatedly, not realizing she was pressing the button of the vacant apartment on the second floor. At last her bloody fingers moved a fraction and she reached the right bell.

Carrie's mother thought she heard something and opened the door. The stairway curved and she couldn't see anything in the dim light of dawn.

Her daughter said in a weak, trembling voice, "I need help."

When the fire ambulance arrived, one of the paramedics putting a stretcher board under Carrie asked, "Where does it hurt?"

My God, she thought, *where does it hurt!*

She had just survived thirteen blows of an axe by an enraged human animal. Her head pounded, every one of her bruises and wounds were on fire, and the rest of her body was cold from the late autumn air and loss of blood. She couldn't answer him.

Naked from the waist down, she trembled and had only partial awareness of what was happening. Carrie was unaware that her father rode in the ambulance with her. Mr. Barns persuaded the crew to bypass the closest Chicago hospital and take his daughter to the trauma unit at St. Francis Hospital in neighboring Evanston. Every pothole and depression in the street made her body wrack with pain.

Carrie drifted in and out of consciousness, yet she still held her shattered teeth tightly as she was carried out of the ambulance. The hospital staff rushed to her. A doctor unclenched her fist and found her pulse racing. As she lay in a hallway gurney, two officers asked if she knew who did this.

"Yes," she said, "it's Butch."

"Do you know his last name?"

"My girlfriends do. We were with him at a bar ..."

"Are you positive that this is the same man who attacked you?"

"Yes, with an axe," she said, and then she was wheeled away to rooms where her injuries were measured, X-rayed, EEG'd, and catalogued. Her vital signs were 70/0.

Seeing her parents crying, she made a conscious decision not to die.

Her parents told police they didn't know anyone called Butch, but friends of Carrie identified him as Brooks. Since the twenty-seven-year-old telemarketing salesman lived in an apartment by himself, there was no one to verify if he was home at the time of the attack. He was taken into custody and the case was closed as far as the police were concerned.

When I questioned Brooks at Area Six headquarters, he said, "Sergeant, I know you won't believe me, but I didn't do it."

How many times had I heard that—hundreds? This time, though, I really sensed it was the truth. He was a smart young man with a good job, and he looked terrified at being trapped in something he didn't understand. I could imagine him being capable of a "date rape," but not anything as horrific as this. Yet there was nothing I could do. An assistant state's attorney from the felony review section approved the charges of rape and attempted murder, and Brooks was taken to Cook County Jail.

Part of Carrie's hair was shaved so the surgeons could examine her scalp. She had been struck eight times on the top of her head and five times in the face. The doctors determined that fortunately none of the bone fragments from her bashed skull had penetrated her brain. She would possibly recover fully but remain disfigured for life.

When she arrived in the emergency room, her left eye had been hanging out onto her cheek. The staff simply put it back in the socket and taped it up. She was in a coma for several days, and after she regained consciousness the doctors gave her a choice of keeping her dead eye in place or having it replaced with an artificial one.

Working as a supervisor in the Homicide/Sex Unit, I had an uneasy feeling after reviewing the report and talking to one of the arresting officers. The viciousness of the attack seemed to me that it was committed virtually at random. The broken glass bulb and the removal of the other one suggested that this was part of a ritual. I decided to bring up my findings and my feelings to the unit commander, Lieutenant Gallet.

Until Gallet arrived, the Homicide Unit generally did not make its own arrests. Once the detectives solved a case, they turned their information over to other units, which received credit for making arrests, and then the Homicide personnel would have more time to investigate the next murder or rape.

Gallet had hardcore experience in Robbery, and he knew that the detectives who built the case would be better able to question the suspect. Not all of the men in the unit liked Gallet's new procedures, but before long they were clearing up cases that had been unsolved for years. We were on a high and felt that nothing could go wrong.

The felony review system was just a year and a half old, and some officers throughout the department was still fighting it. Before felony review came into existence we could charge anyone just because he looked guilty. Now an attorney from the prosecutor's office needed to authorize major charges by determining how the evidence would appear to a judge. I was one of the officers who supported the concept because it helped in presenting good cases and weeding out the ones that never should have been brought to court. Every once in a while, a detective's instincts were stronger than those of the prosecutor's office ... such as now.

Today was a Saturday, and Gallet should have been relaxing

at home, but he had shown up at Area Six to look over reports. He was a handsome man who was meticulously well-groomed. The detectives swore that even if he were to be involved in some slam bang chase and arrest, he'd come out of it with every hair in place.

"The girl named Brooks in front of reliable witnesses," he told me, "and the charges were approved by a state's attorney."

"I don't think the girl really knows what she told the cops. Look, she was traumatized after being viciously attacked. Maybe she was unconsciously trying to remember what the guy looked like by thinking of similarities to this Brooks, and she got all mixed up—"

"But you have no basis for saying that."

"I hate to say it, lieutenant, but we'll probably find out the hard way in a few days."

"You mean like a slasher—the start of a crime pattern?" This was when there were relatively few serial killers around, at least to our knowledge, and most of the time such men involved in vicious murders were just called maniacs. The term "serial killer" had not actually been coined yet.

"I'll bet this is just the beginning of something, and I have a strong premonition to go on. Why would Brooks, who's educated and has a good job, attack and rape his friend in a hallway on a cold day, when he could have used his auto or some convenient place, and why would he use a hatchet as a weapon? It just doesn't make sense."

"So what's your suggestion?"

"Put me on nights and let me start a little later, say six to two," I said. "I'll work later whenever I have to. And I want Nolan and Roppel assigned to me exclusively for two weeks, unless something unusual comes up, and then they can stay with me until we track it down."

"Just what I had in mind," Gallet grinned. "John, I had the same feelings after I read the reports. The attack was unusual and I don't think Brooks had anything to do with it. Talk to Jimmy and Paul, but I'm sure you'll have no problem recruiting them. Get a detail going, notify the timekeeper of the changes, and keep me posted."

From the office I called Nolan to come in at six o'clock that night and he said, "Okay" without asking why. Roppel said he would but did ask, "Why?" That was typical of them. Nolan was always eager but never curious, he just rolled with the punches. Roppel was skeptical and inquisitive, and sometimes he asked as many questions as a six-year-old. I had worked with detectives who were as good as Roppel and Nolan, and even a little better, but none had their special combination of astuteness and dedication. They were my own private task force. I wouldn't want a Hollywood hero on my team. I needed someone who could build up a case over long hours so that chases and shootouts weren't necessary. Some of the other officers accused me of favoritism in certain special assignments—and they were damn right!

One reason I wanted our hours to begin at six p.m. was because that was the quietest time in any station. Many detectives were on their assignments after the 4:30 roll call, and others were out to dinner. The old building was so still you could hear the clackety-clack of a one-fingered typist finishing a report in another part of the building.

I told my men to get their usual start-of-the-shift coffee and meet me in the interview room, where I outlined what we knew so far and what we did not know, since the victim was still in critical condition.

"What have we got?" Roppel asked as he sat up straight.

"We've got nothing," Nolan answered. As usual, Jimmy spoke and listened while staring at the floor in a slouch while he recharged his batteries. He paid attention by picking at his fingernails and cracking his knuckles. "But I agree with Sarge that the real guy could still be out there."

We laid the ground rules for working together. That I outranked them meant nothing, we Three Musketeers were just equals talking over ideas. The men had the common sense to call me "sergeant" in front of other officers rather than make it look as if we were lazy about discipline.

The detective autos were always taken on a first come, first served basis. Since we started later than anyone else on the shift, we got the clunker nobody wanted. Our priority, we decided, was to learn if there would be any more victims, assuming, of course, that Brooks was not the person who attacked Carrie Barns. I told the night sergeant to send us on all aggravated battery cases in which any kind of weapon was used on a female. That was Mistake Number One. We and our beat-up car were sent out on family quarrels, tavern fights, street disturbances, and a variety of other incidents.

My little team that night must have been working four times more than anyone else on the shift. "What the hell are we doing?" Roppel asked as we drove back from a minor case. "We're just spinning our wheels and wasting time."

We didn't make much conversation, but Nolan turned and stared at me in the back seat. A silent stare from him cut like a knife. The Kid loved action, and in times of just driving around and waiting for something that might not happen, he must have thought about his young daughter and how his marriage broke up. The long hours and the special emotional demands of police work could be devastating.

To ease our disappointment, when our shift ended, we went to a bar near the station. Because we needed to talk over our feelings, each of us ordered one drink, maybe two, and made them last from two a.m. until the four o'clock closing time. I assured Jimmy and Paul that I would narrow down the types of cases we'd investigate, and I asked if they wanted to be put back on their regular assignments. They looked at me as if to say, *Are you kidding?*

The next day was a slow Sunday, giving detectives throughout the rickety station time to catch up on writing reports. On Monday, I put my two man team in a good mood by offering to buy dinner. Afterward we cruised the general area of the Barns attack. We still didn't know what our man looked like. Besides, he might be lurking in the shadows or slouched in a car, so we kept an eye out for potential victims. We saw more of them than we thought we would, walking alone every few minutes to their homes on otherwise deserted streets.

"There's one," Nolan pointed out as a woman left a bus stop and headed down a dark street.

We certainly weren't going to use her as bait. We pulled up, identified ourselves, and offered to drive her home, which bent department rules a bit. She was grateful and along the way told us how she had been attacked by a robber the previous year. She was always afraid of another mugger, but what could she do?—she worked nights. We knew her story only too well. There probably were more women out by themselves than ever before, feeding some twisted person's fantasies.

We felt that our stalker didn't like daylight. Night and surprise made him feel more powerful. He didn't strike that night or the next, although we stayed on the streets in that squad car until five a.m. to be ready for him.

I had already asked the other units to look for cases in which young women were attacked with an axe, but we didn't have enough to establish a crime pattern. These sheets were usually prepared by the Crime Analysis Section, giving details of the incidents and similar offenses in the same general neighborhood.

Crime pattern sheets were considered valuable reading for all officers since even a rookie might notice something suspicious that fit the sequence. Criminals, after all, were not the most imaginative of beings. They tended to stick to one pattern, even though it might lead to their undoing, like the "Fudge Bandit" I helped arrest when I was in Robbery. He was called that because he only held up candy stores, and at precisely the same time. For now, though, all I had was one vicious attack and nothing to prove that anything like it would ever occur again.

I had told Paul and Jimmy that when they made calls to other units they shouldn't mention we thought the wrong man might have been charged, but I let James Phelan of Area Five Homicide know of my concerns. Although Phelan and I weren't the best of friends, I had to admit he was a talented, tenacious investigator, and I felt that disclosing my suspicions to him could be beneficial.

However, I soon caught a little hell from the other Musketeers.

"Oh, sure, John, you tell us not to disclose the nature of our calls," Nolan said, "and then you tell Phelan everything."

They were right. Policemen are unpredictable. There is no way you can follow your mental outline for an investigation or detail, no matter how hard you try. There are too many unexpected circumstances and too many emotions that get in the way.

On Tuesday I called Lieutenant Gallet and briefed him on what we were doing and what we had accomplished, which at that time seemed to be nothing.

"Do you think you're on to something?" he asked.

"I really do, but it's still only a premonition." I hated to use the word "hunch." "There were too many ritual tags in that attack. We can't let this guy on the loose, especially since someone else has been charged."

"Well, I just got off the phone with the chief," Gallet said, "and I let him know we had a detail in place, just in case something surfaces, and he was apparently pleased. The chief also thinks we might have the wrong person in jail, although there isn't much we can do about it yet. Keep on it, and maybe we can get him out."

When Wednesday and Thursday came around, Nolan and Roppel volunteered to work on their days off, although they were skeptical. By now everyone at Homicide/Sex knew there was a team working on the possibility that the Barns attack was a pattern crime, and several detectives did whatever they could to help us, including looking out for women walking alone on dark streets and alleys in the Foster Avenue District. It was called the Summerdale District until the "Babbling Burglar" scandal of a few years before.

We certainly didn't want the news people to catch on; the publicity could scare off our man, and at this stage there was actually nothing worthwhile we could give them anyway. Thanks to the Brooks arrest, reporters had stopped asking questions about the case.

Things began well that Thursday, November 13. Out of pity, the sergeant on the desk reserved a brand new squad car for us. With all of our paperwork taken care of, we left the station at seven p.m. and stopped for a quick sandwich. This was Nolan's night to drive, and he took the assignment as if he had been asked to break in a wild horse. The handsome Irishman was called "the Kid" because he was a good-natured prankster at heart, in contrast to most other homicide investigators. He was barely more than a joyriding adolescent behind the wheel of the new squad.

After what appeared to be another slow night, the dispatcher announced, "Eighty-six-ten!" That was our call number. "Go to Edgewater Hospital on a woman stabbed. It came from your desk."

Nolan flicked on the switches for our flashing headlights and activated the siren as we tore through traffic. We were tense, and we didn't say anything to one another. You'd think that all the cars in our way would pull over. Well, maybe in heaven, but not in Chicago. Nolan cowboyed us through traffic and halted with a lurch outside the emergency room.

We ran through the doors, twisting this way and that with our elbows up to keep from colliding with staff members and an unusually large number of friends of the latest victim. Most of them were from nearby Loyola University. Clusters of young people, sobbing and talking in low voices, were everywhere. Even before we found out what had happened, we needed to calm them and say the police would do everything they could.

Nolan and Roppel went over to the nurses and doctors while I sought out the district officers on the case.

I learned that twenty-year-old *Maggie Flynn had been stabbed repeatedly in an alley near campus, and that she was already in the operating room. When Jimmy and Paul got back to me, we took the district officers to a private section near the emergency room for a briefing.

Maggie was a pretty third-year student with dark blonde hair and blue eyes. She had just made a final payment on a woolen coat she bought at the upscale I. Magnin's downtown, with tips she had squirreled away from working at a fancy restaurant. All she had wanted to do was show off the coat at dinner with friends half a block away.

As she took a shortcut down a well-lit alley, she noticed a man changing his path and coming toward her from the parking area under a large apartment building.

"Hey," he said in a way that frightened her. This wasn't the tone of a total stranger—it was as if he felt a personal connection with her. The man, who wore an imitation leather jacket, followed her to the middle of the alley and said, "You have to do me a favor, you have to give me a blow job."

"No!" she snapped.

"I'll kill you if you don't."

"Leave me alone!"

She tried to run but he grabbed her by the new coat, spun her around, and pushed her. Maggie started moving backwards, ready to fight him off if he came closer. The man overtook the college student and started beating her under the dusky orange glow of the alley lights. Maggie thought this would end soon, and that her friends would have trouble believing that a stranger would hit her for no reason. But he didn't stop.

Crouching and with her arms guarding her head, Maggie didn't see him pull out a hunting knife. He stabbed her on the head, repeatedly in the chest, and once, as she fell, in the back. Although both her lungs were punctured, all she felt was a relentless pounding. The attacker might have kept stabbing her but he fled at the sight of headlight beams when an auto entered the alley.

Maggie realized the seriousness of her injuries only when she felt blood running down her legs and filling her shoes. Her immediate concern was her expensive new coat. She tried to remove it, but couldn't. She stumbled down the alley to her friends' building and still had the strength to open the heavy steel door. Her bloody hands fumbled on the bell. She was buzzed in, but Maggie crumpled in the elevator and was barely conscious when the doors opened on the third floor.

"Oh my God!" her friend Cathy cried. She helped Maggie into the apartment. Her breathing became more difficult every couple of steps until she fell on the floor. A bearded friend, Fred, held towels to her punctured sides and kept exhaling air into her flattened lungs as they filled with blood.

While officers were taking Maggie out on a stretcher, her friend Susie arrived, saw her, and screamed at the horror. The police cars drew dozens of neighbors from their homes. Maggie tried to think but she couldn't, everything was in a fog that came and went. Not until she was riding in a squadrol did she say her first clear sentence since collapsing—"Am I going to die?"

"We're doing our best, hon," said an officer at her side. If he'd simply said "No," even if he had to lie, she might have calmed down and let the healing begin. Now her system was going into a panic.

"Go faster," the officer told the driver.

While an emergency room nurse cut through her clothes, Maggie kept calling for her father and was unaware of what was happening except for the background voices speaking with urgency. As the student lay on a gurney in a cubicle, though, she was able to give district police a description of her attacker before she was wheeled into an elevator, headed for the operating room.

This young woman, who had her whole life ahead of her, felt she had taken her final journey. As she told us later, she seemed to lift away from her body, leaving all the doctors and her sobbing friends behind. "At the point where my clothes were being removed, I was no longer on that table. I was no longer in my body. I was, instead, viewing a scene from a corner on the ceiling, watching a team of lab-coated professionals working on my bloody body. I saw the scissors moving up the middle of my chest as it cut through my blue sweater. I saw my very white skin smeared in very red blood. Shortly thereafter I saw a very bright white light. It was soothing, and my fear and panic went away."

All her anxiety disappeared as she seemed to merge with eternity, and yet something called her back. She felt she was making a decision between life and death, and began to think about how much she would miss her family.

Doctors struggled with Maggie's life, and I knew we would have to fight against time in our own way. I hadn't mentioned it yet to Jimmy and Paul, but I was sure that the man who had done this was the same guy who had attacked Carrie Barns. There was nothing I could point to as evidence except perhaps the way he had approached the victim and the sheer savagery of the attack. One was hacked with an axe, and the other was stabbed with a knife, but these differences were just variations of the same pattern.

I was sure that the man would be hunting down another victim in just a few days.

16

VICTIM TO VICTIM

Maggie's friend Cathy told us at the hospital that she knew who the attacker might be—a neighbor who was always making obscene remarks to women passing by. "You should investigate him," she said.

We also wrote down the names of all the friends and university students who were crowding into the emergency room. Then I asked one of the nurses to show us where Maggie had been treated before she was taken into surgery. The nurse took us to a curtained cubicle. I slowly picked up Maggie's brand new woolen coat, now sodden with blood.

"Holy Christ," Nolan said.

We saw at least a half dozen knife rips. Not just puncture marks; these were at least an inch and a half long, appeared to be the width of a hunting knife, and some were still filled with her blood.

"I'm going to call for the mobile crime lab to assist," I said.

"They only come out for homicides," Roppel told me.

"I know, Paul, but this might turn out that way."

It took a few minutes of talking, but the crime lab downtown agreed to assign the mobile lab technicians to process the scene as if it were a homicide. In my own mind, I was being logical and reasonable, but Jimmy and Paul later said the entire emergency room vibrated with my shouting.

Maggie's burly, good-looking brother came to the hospital and took his anger out on us. "What the hell are you guys doing just standing here?" he yelled. "How do you expect to find the man who did this? You should have every man on the street looking for this maniac."

"We have to get the information first," I said, trying to pacify the distraught young man. "A flash message has already been sent on the description of the offender, we'll do the best we can."

When the brother settled down, we took him to a waiting room where his parents were nervously awaiting word from the operating room. The gentlemanly father was a doctor, but none of his medical experience had prepared him for this wait. His emotional wife was so upset that I told her, "Don't worry, Mrs. Flynn, I am making you a promise. We are going to get the man who did this."

Something in my voice or eyes must have shown how sincere I was. She was so relieved that she practically fell into my arms, and I hugged her like I would hug my mother. I could almost feel her grow a little stronger. By now I was used to comforting people in grief. The rioters who shot at us at random and the young people who called us "pigs" didn't know what police meant to those who really needed us. Those embraces were rewards of the jobs.

The district officers found the weird, ogling neighbor that Cathy had told us about, and he ranted about his innocence and denied making obscene remarks to women. He was advised of his rights and taken to the hospital for identification. Nolan and Roppel learned it could be days before Maggie would be able to talk to us, so we decided to have the man taken to the district station, photographed, and released for the time being.

Although the "suspect" gave us permission to search his two-room apartment, he kept insisting in his Mid-Eastern accent, "It's agin' the law, it's agin' the law!" We found rooms filled with old greasy motor parts, and both of his closets had used automobile batteries stacked to the ceiling. On paper the guy looked as if he could be guilty, but there was absolutely no evidence. We all agreed that he was probably just a harmless eccentric.

At around midnight, we retraced Maggie's steps from her apartment on Sheridan Road through the alley to Winthrop

Avenue, but we couldn't find anything with our long flashlights. There was no evidence on the stairwell or near the parking area where she first saw the man. We spoke to a woman who had heard screams and footsteps, but for some reason she didn't look out her window or call the police.

At two a.m., we returned to the hospital and learned that Maggie had been brought into intensive care. Her family looked as if they were on a death watch. As we drove back to Area Six to finish up our paperwork, we heard an all-call broadcast about the attacker over the police radio. We were pleased his description was still being repeated more than four hours after the crime. Usually it was sent only once or twice and then terminated.

Jimmy, Paul, and I hardly said a word. At last I broke the dejected silence. "The man who did this is the same guy who attacked Carrie Barns."

"Jim and I knew you were going to say that," Roppel shot back, "but it just can't be. The M.O. is all wrong. This guy used a knife, the other guy had a hatchet."

Nolan continued Paul's thought while he kept driving. "The hours are even different, John. This girl was attacked at about nine-fifteen at night, and the other girl was attacked at five-thirty in the morning."

So-called psychiatric experts at the time were saying that pattern criminals never changed their methods, that they followed a set routine as if programmed. We now know this wasn't always true, and that some people derived excitement from adding a variation to each attack. I wasn't thinking about psychology, I concentrated on what these cases had in common.

"The viciousness, the short distance away for both attacks, the mention of a blowjob," I said. "Think about it."

We reached the station and wrote up our reports and finished at 3:30 a.m. I was bleary-eyed but told Jimmy and Paul that I intended to come back to the office at 8:00 a.m. to talk to Lieutenant Gallet about how the investigation was progressing and fill him in on the most recent attack.

"How about if I come in at eight, too?" Nolan asked.

"Me, too," Roppel added.

"You guys are special, you really are," I told them. "You don't even agree with me!"

"That's okay, Sarge," Nolan said, "I know you'll convince us."

"But I have to level with you," I said. "I told you at the start that I wanted you guys for just two weeks unless something unusual came up, and now I think it has. This thing might last longer than what you were expecting, is that all right?"

"Sure," Nolan answered, and Roppel nodded approval.

We met back at Area Six at eight while Gallet was still going over our reports. He was supposed to start at nine, but sometime he came in at seven to review cases with the midnight crew. During his tour of duty, he made sure he was in contact with all three shifts.

We had conveniently left out mentioning the ogling neighbor, not wanting to muddy the waters in an official report. We learned that when Detective Wally Klein was nearing the finish of his midnight tour of duty, he obtained permission from Maggie's father to interview his daughter, even though the hospital staff thought it would be too soon. Shortly after Maggie described the man for Klein and said a few words about the attack, she relapsed and had to be sedated. Klein then made out his report. I was surprised at the approval to question the victim of such a savage attack that early, but at least we learned that the height, weight, race, and general facial information of the man fell within the range of the description we had in Carrie's attack.

When Gallet finished going over the reports, he called us in and asked what we had. I'm sure Nolan wanted to say, "Zilch," but instead he told Gallet, "Let the sergeant tell you."

"We got a pretty good description of the offender," I said. "That alley was well lit. It most likely is the same man who attacked the Barnes girl, and if I'm right you can expect another attack on the seventeenth or eighteenth, figuring five or six days in-between."

Gallet looked skeptical, and he could see that my two-man task force didn't entirely agree with me. Nevertheless, we weren't going to put the investigation up for a vote.

"John," Gallet said, "I really don't know if the same guy

might be responsible, but it is possible. Let's go ahead as if it is."

We went directly to Edgewater Hospital with the station photo of the leering neighbor, but Maggie's father informed us about her relapse. We offered our apologies and decided to prepare a special mug book for Maggie to look through when her condition improved, narrowing the selection of photos to suspects of the same general description and age.

In the movies, officers seem to have just one mug book, but that wouldn't do in a high crime city. After reviewing a certain number of pictures, they all start to blur. A few years before, a high-ranking officer at headquarters came up with the bright idea of putting the photos on film to make it easier for the victims. The film would run through a specially designed projector. After each session, the detective in charge had to put something down on the "Remarks" line of the pilot program survey report. The brass no doubt expected comments such as "Wonderful! The victim picked out the offender from the second photo and made a positive identification." Instead, the detective usually wrote that the victim fell asleep. The project was a total flop and was abandoned after one year. I was surprised it lasted that long.

We accumulated stacks of photographs from detectives in other Areas in addition to the ones we had on file in our Area. Then on Saturday, November 15, Maggie's father escorted us to his daughter in the ICU. The young woman had tubes in her nose and mouth, and she appeared to be in extreme pain. She wasn't ready to speak to all three of us, so Jimmy Nolan stepped up and gently explained to her that we were doing everything possible and that, even more importantly, we wanted her to get well and return to her family. It was as if I were hearing a kindly old priest who knew just the right things to say.

While Jimmy spoke, he gradually introduced information that we had someone in mind and that his photo was among several we wanted to show her. He held each successive picture up to her, including a shot of the "ogler." Each time she moved her head to the side, as if to say, "No." We thanked her and left.

The three of us returned the next day, Sunday. With her father's permission we showed her stacks of other pictures.

Some victims just flipped through the thick pages of a mug book, not really expecting to identify their assailant, but Maggie Flynn studied every photo carefully. Then she laid her head back against the pillow with a sad look in her eyes. The concentration had fatigued her. We left her alone to continue her physical and psychological recovery.

We talked to her father—who happened to be a physician—about the advisability of having Maggie help the police make a composite sketch. Dr. Flynn agreed but said the artist should contact the hospital in the morning to see if she was up to it.

I called the department's artist, Otis Rathel, at his home. Otis, a friend of mine, was a tall, slim, slightly-balding black man with a light complexion. He said he had several appointments Monday that he couldn't break, but that he could come over right then. Not only was Otis on his day off, he lived on the Far South Side, at the other end of the city.

After receiving Dr. Flynn's permission, Otis met us in the hospital lobby at six p.m. We went to the ICU and introduced him to Maggie. As Otis was going through his excellent sketching techniques on the information Maggie supplied, we had a casual conversation with the doctor about our families and a variety of other subjects. When Otis was finished, he thanked Maggie for being a very good witness and came out with a picture of a long-faced, average-looking Caucasian with straight hair and enlarged round eyes. We would never see those eyes like that, for those were the eyes of someone letting his private demons take over.

Otis stayed with us for coffee at a restaurant near the Area Six station. We needed his sketch for the daily police bulletin, but we also wanted copies of our own. That was all right, but Otis said they shouldn't be circulated until he cleared the assignment with his commander. In other words, he needed to explain to his boss that he had traveled across the city on his day off because the case was important, not to rack up overtime.

Before we split up and went home, well over twelve hours since we began that morning, we worked out an agenda for what we'd be doing the next day, Monday the 17th. I had predicted our man might strike then, but that was just a gut feeling. I was as surprised as everyone else when he did, just like clockwork.

This time he chose not the Loyola University area of the North Side but an equally quiet, bungalow neighborhood several miles across the river, on the Northwest Side. This was where the Ravenswood elevated line ended after making a loop around downtown.

A twenty-three-year-old married woman, *Christine Piecher, was returning on one of the trains after attending a meeting of the Theosophical Society. She came down the wooden stairs of the old station with several packages and crossed wide Lawrence Avenue a little before ten p.m.

After a block or so she felt she was being followed. She discreetly looked behind her, but didn't see anyone. Christine fumbled with her packages and dismissed her fears as childish. A few minutes later, she reached the lobby of her apartment building on Carmen Avenue. She was checking her mailbox and had her key ready to unlock the safety door when a man with greasy hair and a beige jacket entered. He carried a black attaché case. He started looking over the row of brass mailboxes with an odd disinterest as if he really didn't care who lived in the building. Christine had no way of knowing that in the case was a change of clothes to replace ones that would soon be covered in her blood.

No words were spoken, but when she turned to open the safety door the man pulled a small axe from under his jacket. He lunged at her and she raised an arm to stop him. The axe bit into her arm and a second blow dug into her head, knocking her to the floor against the wall. Then she surprised the man by reaching out and grabbing the hatchet as it fumbled out of his hands. She gripped the handle as tightly as she could and kicked at the man's legs and knees until he wrenched the axe from her. Next he put the hatchet in the briefcase amid her wordless screams, and then left the lobby calmly and slowly.

Christine walked in a daze of pain up the stairs to her apartment. Her husband wasn't home, but a Hispanic neighbor helped her until the police arrived.

Since the Northwest Side was covered by Area Five, the case was coincidentally assigned just after midnight to James Phelan and his partner, Cindy Pontoriero, who, three years before, became the department's first female detective.

At Swedish Covenant Hospital, they learned that Christine was in critical condition with a compound skull fracture in the back of her head and deep defensive wounds on her hands and wrists. X-rays showed that the blade had missed her brain by only a few centimeters and had removed an inch and a half circle of her skull.

The two detectives spent their shift interviewing neighbors and other people who might have seen the attacker.

When the doctors reported that Christine was able to talk to the police, the detectives showed her the composite sketch of Maggie's attacker, which we recently had supplied to them.

"Yes, it's close," she said as she cringed.

At eleven a.m. on Tuesday, Phelan and Pontoriero drove to Area Six for an immediate conference with Lieutenant Gallet and my team. This was the first time I wasn't alone in thinking we might have what today would be called a serial slasher and, but for the grace of God, could have been a serial killer.

Our session was a lot like panning for gold in the way we kept throwing out dissimilarities in the three cases and concentrated on the similarities—intelligent young women walking alone in the dark, usually crude talk of sex as a prelude, hallways, weapons with blades, and the victims left for dead. In each attack, the description of the man was approximately the same, from his reddish blond hair to his wild eyes. The sex talk may have been some sort of pretext since he had raped only the first woman, and even then it seemed to be an afterthought.

There was still one similarity we had not realized yet— the primary target in each assault had been the victim's face, although Christine had covered hers as she crouched under the blows. That was probably the only reason why the women had lived. The man for some reason was mainly concerned with striking their faces, but as they wiggled and turned he hit them any place he could.

The five of us kept throwing out the names of sex offenders who might have been capable of such attacks. Police kept track of "deviates" as well as they did with professional burglars and robbers. Their arrests were discussed at roll-call, and cops remembered them in their own ways. My memory was good but not photographic, so I kept a binder that eventually included more than a thousand repeat offenders, all cross-indexed with their associates.

One of the names brought up was that of Robert Scott Dominique. He had been arrested a few years earlier for sexual assault. He was not listed in the binder.

"Isn't he still doing time?" Nolan asked.

We decided to check immediately, and prison officials told us that Dominique had been released in October after serving a one-to-three-year sentence for burglary. Sex offenders with a strain of voyeurism often dabbled in burglary as well. Dominique became a possibility.

Nolan and Roppel drove to the Bureau of Identification downtown for copies of Dominique's photos and record sheets, as well as those of a handful of other potential suspects we had mentioned in our meeting. I stayed in the office when Jimmy and Paul returned to the hospital. Dominique's side and frontal mug shots were dark and grainy, and the profile shot had a rip through it—but Maggie tapped the picture and said, "This could be the man if he didn't have a mustache."

My men called me, still sounding a little dubious. I told them to come back and we could follow up this lead after talking it over.

Going over Dominique's record sheet more carefully, we saw that he was arrested by Mass Transit Unit officers on November 13. They had found him drinking beer on a Chicago Transit Authority train just half an hour after Maggie Flynn was savaged. The officers had searched him and discovered a hunting knife in a scabbard tucked behind the small of his back. My team and I talked about how the attacker might have used the elevated trains to get to and from the neighborhoods. In a silence that fell between us, I thought, *This is it*. For some reason, Paul and Jimmy weren't as optimistic, and that was unusual.

I called Lieutenant Gallet at home about the tentative information, and in our conversation his tone became more excited than his measured words. Roppel put in a call to the

State's Attorney's Office, and an assistant prosecutor assured us we had probable cause to take Dominique into custody. That meant we were authorized to haul Dominique in for questioning and lineups because of Maggie's photo identification. That was never as easy as it sounded.

When Dominique was picked up on the city train, he gave his address as 12 West Van Buren Street. That didn't mean he really lived there. A few hours earlier, we could have checked his latest address with the parole office. Maybe it being closed wasn't such a bad thing, for we had been double-crossed a few times when parole officers on the take notified suspects that we were looking for them.

We drove downtown to the State and Van Buren area. The song may call State Street "that great street," but after a few blocks in those days it became pretty seedy with pawn shops, girlie shows, and transient hotels. The aging flophouses around the corner looked even more dismal because the elevated tracks ran right alongside them at the second floor level.

We had to walk up a flight of stairs to reach the desk clerk. We hadn't cleared the last couple of steps when the fat, slovenly man called out, "What do you want?"

Apparently the three of us didn't look like customers, especially for a man who'd had run-ins with the law. Experience had taught us never to disclose the name of the person we were looking for, especially to desk clerks. Instead, we asked for the registry book they're required to keep and show to the police on demand.

There were a few John Joneses and John Does, a lot of Foreign Legion-sounding names, but eventually we found Robert Dominique listed for room 512 on the third floor.

I raised my eyebrow as a signal, and Nolan went into his Humphrey Bogart act. He glared at the desk clerk and said, "Don't you have a Robert Billingsworth living here? Don't lie to me. We know he's here even if he's not listed!" Jimmy whipped out a generic mug shot and pushed the photo in front of the slob at the desk. "This is the guy, do you recognize him?"

While they barked at each other, Paul and I looked at the keys behind the counter. Flophouse guests were usually required to turn in their keys when they went out to make sure they didn't lose them. The key for 512 hung on its hook. That meant Dominique was most probably out, and we'd have to conduct a stakeout for him.

When Nolan was through harassing the desk clerk, we parted on unfriendly terms and went to our car parked a half block down on Van Buren. It was now about 9:40 p.m. We did a lot of talking as we waited, mostly about the case and the unfortunate victims. It would be easy to say they were lucky to be alive, but victims were never lucky when they were left permanently disfigured and their entire lives altered.

"What if he's still got a mustache?" Paul asked. "Maggie Flynn said Dominique would be him if it wasn't for the mustache."

"He isn't going to have a mustache," I said, as if I knew.

"That was a pretty bad picture we showed to Maggie," Nolan commented, and now I suspected why they weren't hopeful.

"He's probably still at work," Paul mentioned. The arrest sheet indicated he was a cook at a nearby Pixley & Ehler's, one of a chain of small, cheap restaurants.

"Or maybe he's celebrating his birthday," Nolan suggested.

"November 20th, that's his birthday?" I asked.

"It's on the sheet."

"Funny, I didn't think about that," I said. "I hope we get him before midnight. We'll give him a birthday present—metal bracelets."

By eleven p.m. we were starting to wonder if Dominique might have skipped town or was possibly looking for another victim. That was our worst fear.

We drove to the restaurant and saw that it matched the transient hotel. There was a floor of white ceramic tiles that indicated whoever cleaned up at night never rinsed the mop. A large cockroach walked along the counter, and the coffee came in huge paper cups that appeared to have been already used. One taste and we thought we knew what the cleanup crew did with the mop water.

Three pairs of eyes looked in all directions, but there was no sign of Dominique. What we did see were a handful of stubbly customers who were not so much eating as lost in thought, probably of better days.

We told the manager we were health inspectors and searched the place thoroughly. Our man definitely wasn't there. We returned to our stakeout at the hotel, and Nolan volunteered to check whether key 512 was still in the slot. A few minutes later he came out and motioned to us at the front door. Roppel and I jumped out of the car and ran toward him.

"He must have come in while we were at the restaurant," Jimmy said.

We ignored the desk clerk and ran up two flights of stairs to meet this animal face to face.

17

TWISTED

Dominique's room was at the end of the hall. Nolan opened the door of the adjacent fire escape and whispered that he would cover from there in case our man tried to escape out a window. Paul and I knocked, ready for anything. Dominique opened the door—and what a sight to behold. Even before we noticed that he was without a mustache, what caught our eyes were his blue Baby Doll pajamas. He was dressed as if he were a teenage girl.

We flashed our stars and stepped in, followed by Nolan. The four of us made a crowd in that room, which was only about eight feet square. The walls were haphazardly covered with pictures of nude and nearly nude women carelessly torn from magazines. A basket of soiled panties was next to the door. I informed Dominique that he was under arrest and recited the Miranda warning about his right to have a lawyer. He didn't ask why we were taking him into custody. Criminals should know that's a guaranteed tip-off.

"May we search your room?" I asked.

"Go ahead, I have nothing to hide."

I asked him to open his dresser drawers one at a time. He complied, stepped aside, and then closed each drawer when I was through. We hoped to find the knife, the hatchet, or some bloody clothing, but nothing incriminating came up.

"Well, let's go," I said. Dominique, who wasn't a bad-looking man in a twerpy sort of way, changed into his street clothes and headed for the door. "Why don't you put on your jacket, it's cold outside." I didn't let on that the jacket could be useful for evidence because it matched the description supplied by the victims.

The four of us headed for the Area station with Roppel at the wheel. Paul drove the way he was thinking—slowly and safely. I was sure he and Nolan were still a little skeptical about our suspect. A burglar, yes. A peeper, maybe. A man who went around slashing women? He looked a little strange, but harmless—he was absolutely meek as he rode next to me.

"Do you have anything to say to us?" I asked.

"No," he answered flatly.

"Oh, by the way," I added without meaning it, "happy birthday." He was thirty years old that day.

"Everything that happens to me, good or bad, seems to happen around my birthday."

While Roppel typed up the arrest slip at headquarters, I went through the work record notebook we had confiscated from the top of Dominique's dresser. I checked the dates and saw he was off that day and on each day an assault took place. Since most detective headquarters didn't have lockups yet, we called for a squadrol to take Dominique to Foster Avenue Station for processing, which would take a couple of hours.

"Let's go home and get some sleep," I said, "and then come back early."

We left at two a.m. and were supposed to meet at seven, but I was there by six-thirty. On some days, it's easier to get up early than fight to fall asleep. I called the district station and asked the uniformed officers to bring our man back now that they were through processing him.

The squadrol arrived just as Jimmy and Paul were coming in. They took custody of our prisoner, brought him to an interview room, and went for coffee. I reminded Dominique again of his rights and added, "You really don't have to tell us anything, because we have people who can identify you in a series of serious attacks."

Nonchalantly, without a blink of those passive eyes, Dominique remarked, "I would like to talk to you about my problems."

I'll be damned, I thought. "Go ahead, Robert."

"I want to talk about several attacks on white women." Since he was white, that seemed like an odd thing to say.

"You attacked them?" I asked, coaxing him to say more without leading him on.

"With a knife and hatchet."

I purposefully had not mentioned to him that women were the victims, or what weapons were used. Since the attacks had not received much play in the news media, I thought this had to be proof that he was guilty.

"Excuse me, Robert," I said, "would you mind if we take a pause for a couple of minutes so we can talk in front of my partners?"

"Sure, anything you want." He sat comfortably on a bench although he was manacled with a through-the-wall handcuff sleeve.

I found Jimmy and Paul and playfully said that Dominique "wants to tell us something."

Roppel and I sat on each side of the prisoner in the interview room while Nolan stood against the wall with his arms crossed.

"Robert, if you don't mind," I said, "would you continue to tell us about your problems? And remember that you have already been advised of the Miranda warnings."

There was no hesitation as he repeated everything and added details as if filling in the pieces of a puzzle.

We learned about the change of clothes he kept in an attaché case in the final attack and how after nearly killing Carrie Barns he had changed into clothes he'd already stolen from a laundry room. I listened to every word and at the same time watched Roppel's and Nolan's expressions of disbelief. Dominique told us everything, even about an attack we knew nothing about.

At dawn on November 6, two days before the Barns assault, he had followed a woman who was in her early forties down the street near Clark and Fullerton because he noticed she was hobbling. When he asked *Carol Jean Heintz why she limped, she told him she'd been hurt in an accident a few years earlier.

"I'm sorry to hear that," he said.

Carol turned away and Dominique kept walking, but he

told us he stopped and "something" drew him back.

The woman had gone into a foyer and was startled to see that he was behind her. He stabbed her four or five times, trying to hack at her face, until she fell screaming to the floor. He stabbed her once or twice more, and then he took her purse and ran to an underpass. Dominique kept a wallet with two dollars, and then dumped the purse and knife. It was this that made officers believe the attack had been a robbery, so the case was handled by detectives across the hall from us. Since that case involved a knife, no one made a connection when Carrie Barns was slashed with an axe.

Dominique told us that raping Barns was an afterthought, and he was not fully aroused when he committed the act. Later he went to his room on Van Buren and burned his and her bloody clothes on the fire escape.

I was exhilarated that we had stopped Dominique.

The worst part of a detective's life was putting all you have into a case and the criminal is never caught or a judge lets him off.

As for Jimmy and Paul, they were spellbound that such an ordinary man could have such evil in him, and that he could relate his crimes in detail without emotion.

"They're the only girls I attacked," he said. "Oh, except for one more, and that was a girl in Rockford." That was an industrial city about eighty miles northwest of Chicago.

"What happened there?" I asked.

"I was paroled to Rockford a year ago and I stabbed a girl a few times, but I wasn't caught. I went to Las Vegas. I was a parole violator then, and the Vegas police arrested me for being disorderly. I gave them a phony name, but when they checked my fingerprints they found out who I was. I was extradited back to Chicago and went back to jail for a year."

"Robert, how come we didn't find the hatchet in your apartment?"

"I went out yesterday about seven p.m. and I took the El up north. I was carrying the hatchet in a brown paper bag, and I walked all over looking for someone I could hit. I walked for a long time and then I decided to hide the hatchet in a garbage container and come back the next day to look for someone."

"We seized a basketful of ladies' underpants from your room," Nolan said. "Where did you get them, do they belong to the victims?"

"Oh, no. I took them from laundry rooms while I was walking around looking for people. I took them back to my room and would wear them."

"Where did you get the hatchet?" I asked.

"I did a lot of burglaries to get prescription drugs from medicine cabinets, and in one place I found a hatchet and I liked it."

"When was that?"

"The night I stabbed that crippled woman. I'd thrown my knife away because it was bent."

We broke for a huddle outside the interview room. I didn't know about Dominique's theft of prescription drugs. That meant we were lucky. As I explained to Paul and Jimmy, he had been in police custody long enough to be free of medication and liquor when he made his unexpected confession. I assured them the statement would hold up in court.

After our breather, Dominique surprised us again. "Sergeant," he said, "you told me they are living?"

"I never told you what their condition was."

"Well, you sort of did when you said you had witnesses for a lineup. That's one of the reasons I wanted to tell you about my problems."

"Yes, the women are still living, but they are in serious condition."

"I thought they were all dead."

I couldn't tell from his empty tone if he was glad or disappointed, or maybe it didn't make any difference to him.

"It felt good telling you all about it," he said.

It seemed he had absolutely no feelings of remorse. "I want to talk to you later, Robert," I said, "after the state's attorney does, and things quiet down. Will you tell me everything about yourself, going back to when you were a kid?"

"Yes, especially about my mother," he answered. "I really hate her. I think that's the reason that I try and hit women in the face, because I think that I see my mother's face when I hit those women."

Well, that gave us something to think about along with a great deal of other matters. Contrary to what some people think, an arrest does not end with police rubber-stamping a folder "case closed" and forgetting about it. Politically, the most important part of any major case is the notifications. Reporters and aldermen would either praise or damn us, and no one from the mayor to the officer who fingerprinted Dominique would want to be caught unprepared by not knowing about a major case.

We assigned Paul, the most diplomatic of the Three Musketeers, to notify police headquarters that several investigations were about to be cleared. At the time, it was department policy that big overnight arrests be reported to the detective division headquarters downtown by six a.m. That way, if the case hit the papers or morning newscasts, the bosses had access to the reports and were ready with answers to sound as if they had been on top of the investigation all along. Transfers of personnel were swift when someone neglected procedure. Knowing this, certain concerned bosses would show up at an Area station to become personally "involved." Their efforts were not always appreciated, no matter how sincere they appeared to be. Occasionally, these bosses appeared on TV and got the details wrong or, worse yet, gave out information we wanted withheld until the loose ends were tied up.

Nolan was having trouble with the State's Attorney's Office because no one wanted to come out during the change of shifts, so I told him to call supervisor Joseph Urso at home, as usual. Next, I ran across the hall to the Robbery Unit where I used to work and quickly went through the files for the Heintz report and found it easily because of the date supplied by Dominique. I photocopied the pages, notified the on-duty sergeant that we might be clearing up the case for him, and then brought the report to Jimmy and Paul, who had already started labeling a large file folder.

Lieutenant Gallet rushed to the station after I called him and said he would get the evidence technician ready for us to retrieve the hatchet. In the meantime, technicians at the microscopic analysis section processed the hunting knife that had been confiscated during Dominique's arrest on the El train. Soon afterwards, they told Gallet that the tiny splotches on it were human blood, and in their next testing they determined that the blood was the same type as Maggie Flynn's.

Dominique was as cordial as a prisoner could be. "Nice to meet you, sir," he said when we introduced him to Gallet. The man didn't seem to know that we all thought he was sickening. We removed his handcuffs and drove him around the North Side. With him giving the directions, we went to where Maggie Flynn was brutalized, and then he directed us six blocks away to point out Carrie Barns' hallway.

"We better go for the hatchet," Dominique said, "the garbage men might pick it up."

According to department policy, we should have had Dominique handcuffed at all times, but we didn't want to draw crowds by hauling out a manacled man at the different locations we intended to visit. Besides, by now we were sure Dominique could only be a terror to the unsuspecting, and I was sure that Nolan and Roppel could ran faster than him.

Our prisoner led us directly to a dumpster, and Jimmy and Paul opened the lid. Dominique pointed to where the hatchet was wrapped in a plastic bag against the side, near the bottom. Roppel stayed at the dumpster while Jimmy and I returned Dominique to the car. I called the evidence people who were waiting for our message and gave them the address. Since we had set everything up in advance, we had to wait only about five minutes for a technician instead of the usual two hours.

From the white plastic bag, the technician pulled out a paper bag containing a hatchet with a black rubber handle and steel shaft, just as Christine Piecher had described it. The technician took photos of everything, dusted the hatchet for prints—there were none—and turned it over to us. I went to a nearby phone booth to tell Gallet about our progress.

"Get your asses in here," he said. "A crowd is gathering. Joe Urso is here with the state's attorney and a court reporter and several bosses. They're impatient." "And," he added, "so am I."

"I wanted Dominique to show us where he attacked the others, I want the whole package, boss."

"Go ahead, but hurry up."

The always-methodical Roppel took extensive notes as Dominique led us to the other scenes and detailed how he'd nearly killed each of the women.

"Robert," I said as we rode back to the station, "did you attack anyone immediately before we arrested you last night?" I dreaded the thought that a body might be hidden in another dumpster.

"Sir," he answered, "I saw a lot of different girls to hit but things just didn't work out. I decided to go home because it was my birthday. Everything seems to happen to me around my birthday."

He didn't say "attack" or "cut" or "try to murder." Repeat criminals have all kinds of code words for what they do. With Dominique, it was usually "hit."

The prisoner also led us to the apartment where he'd found the hatchet while committing a burglary. The initial report made no mention of an axe, and when we checked later we learned why. The tenants didn't know their tool was gone until they heard from us. That was absolute evidence.

When we returned to the Area Six headquarters, we were surrounded by police officials and representatives from the prosecutor's office. We kept Dominique happy with a ham and cheese sandwich and chocolate milk while he talked with assistant state's attorneys for three hours, and he gave the court reporter statements regarding the four Chicago attacks. Urso was amazed at how Dominique, a man with only a little education, could have such a good memory for all the details of his crimes.

Lieutenant Gallet wanted us to clinch our arrest with special showups. The usual procedure when a victim was hospitalized was to bring the suspect to a corridor outside the patient's room. I never liked hospital lineups because they did nothing for the victim's recovery and they were not well-received during a trial.

We learned that the first woman assaulted, Carol Heintz, had just been released from the hospital, and doctors at Edgewater were speculating that Maggie Flynn might be able to travel to a police station if her father consented. Gallet and Urso saw this as an opportunity and suggested that we hold a lineup in the as-yet unopened Area Four headquarters, the new high-tech West Side station. It had double rooms built with two-way mirrors. Urso and Gallet were innovative by suggesting that a videotape be made of the lineups and shown to the two victims still in a hospital—Carrie Barns and Christine Piecher.

Gallet wanted Maggie brought to the new station in an ambulance and with an attending physician. Maggie said she would agree to view the suspect but resisted being transported in an ambulance for her own private reasons. Her father specifically asked me to escort his daughter in an ordinary squad car.

When I arrived at Edgewater Hospital, Maggie was waiting for me in a wheelchair, dressed in slacks and with a sweater over her blouse. She was sad and expressionless, but the fact that we had a suspect may have made her a little stronger. Her mother placed a heavy coat around her and buttoned the top few buttons, then she removed her own heavy-knit hat and carefully placed it over the bandages on the back of her daughter's head.

Dr. Flynn and I wheeled Maggie to the elevator and helped her into the squad car. After the well-groomed Mrs. Flynn kissed Maggie good luck, the mother unexpectedly hugged me.

"Thanks," she said. "Thanks for keeping your promise."

Maggie didn't say a word as we went halfway across the city. She obviously was in pain from the jarring of the car, even though I drove as slowly and cautiously as I could. Along the way I cursed at myself for not taking the folding wheelchair with us. Fortunately, the maintenance staff at Area Four rushed out with a wheelchair of their own when they saw us pulling up in front.

As the first of the new Area buildings, the station had district offices on the first floor and detective squad rooms on the second. There was even an elevator! The new station was impressive and smelled fresh, but it was also impersonal. The building would have to stand quite a few years before its walls would collect as many memories as the old place, Maxwell, which later was used as the exterior for *Hill Street Blues*.

Jimmy and Paul had already conducted a lineup for Heintz. She viewed a row of suspicious-looking characters that included Dominique, a felony review attorney, a district officer out of uniform, a detective, and Lieutenant Gallet. The victim couldn't be sure, and that was understandable, but the lineup took an unusual twist after it was over. When police told Dominique the victim couldn't pick him out, he volunteered to see if he could recognize her! After seeing Carol in another room, he said, "Yeah, that's her. That's the lady who limped." He went on to describe in toneless detail to her face how he'd attacked her. Carol cried, but held back what she might have been feeling, and signed complaints against him.

When it was Maggie's turn, I took her into the darkened viewing room accompanied by her father and Paul Roppel. We gently lifted Maggie by her arms from the wheelchair to be at the height for seeing through the two-way glass. Nolan had Dominique stand third in a well-lit line of the same volunteers, only now they were in a different order. As soon as I had a firm grip on the young woman's arm, I felt her body quiver and she began to sob. No one spoke a word as Nolan asked each man to step forward, turn right, turn left, and step back. He had each one speak different phrases that were used during the attacks and then told all of the men to face the wall.

When the lineup was finished, Maggie said, "The number three man is the one who stabbed me." Then she collapsed in our arms as we eased her back into the wheelchair. She cried while her father and I took her to the outer offices. Assistant State's Attorney Mike Carey quickly approached her and asked, "Are you sure you can make a positive identification?"

With just a faint smile, she looked up at the attorney and said, "You were the number five man, starting from the left. I'm positive I identified the man who stabbed me."

I began to see why Maggie's parents had so much faith in her ability to bounce back from an attempt to destroy her. She was intelligent and courageous. On the drive back to the hospital, neither Dr. Flynn nor I mentioned that we ourselves had cried a little after the identification, and there were very few words spoken.

Before we climbed out of the squad car, with the wheelchair standing by, Maggie said, "Sergeant, I'm a little tired, but I'm feeling great and I'm glad it's over. I'm sure I'll get a good night's sleep." I think she said this so I would stop worrying about her.

"Maggie, you're the one who stopped him with your identification of his photo," I told her. "If he'd kept on, someone might have been murdered. I want to thank *you*, really."

Maggie's mother, who did not want to attend the lineup, was waiting for us on the second floor. "Mom, I identified the man, it's all over!" the young woman beamed. Mrs. Flynn hugged her daughter and started to help her off with her coat, but it was stuck to the back of her blouse. Then we saw why—the blouse was saturated with blood. Dr. Flynn took over as if he were a staff physician and set everything in motion. In the intensive care ward, doctors discovered that, incredible as it seemed, one of her wounds had gone unnoticed and that its self-mending probably had ruptured during the two and a half hours she was away from the hospital.

"She'll be okay, sergeant," her father told me. "She's a gutsy girl."

I couldn't agree more. I stayed around long enough to learn that her newfound wound would not cause additional complications.

By the time I arrived back at Area Six, the office had thinned out. Assistant State's Attorney Carey was sitting in a tired slump as he awaited the results of videotape lineups at the hospitals of the two other assault victims. Dominique was still in the interview room eating ham and cheese sandwiches and drinking chocolate milk.

The lineup crew came in with such smiles that we knew the rsults immediately.

"We showed the tape to both victims and they instantaneously identified Dominique as the man who had attacked them with a hatchet," Urso said. The friendly, hefty man became excited only on major cases like this.

Ever since Maggie Flynn had identified Dominique from a bad photo, I'd been thinking about the way Mike Brooks had looked at me and said, "Sergeant, I know you won't believe me, but I didn't do it." Now, I asked, "Joe, did Barns say anything about why the hell she identified Brooks?"

"You're not going to believe it, John, but she doesn't even remember naming him in the emergency room. She told me that in the last couple of days when her family and friends asked her about it, she said Brooks never attacked her. But those people never called your office or notified my staff."

"We've got to get him out of jail."

"I can't do anything over the weekend, he'll be out on Monday."

Dominique was ordered held without bond, and Brooks was freed from the Cook County Jail. I wish I could have talked to him and assured him that all of us had been doing our best to free him from the beginning, but we would never hear from him again.

Dominique, tried only for the Maggie Flynn attack, was sentenced to serve one to two hundred years in prison, where he remains today.

Thanks to Jimmy Nolan's good humor, the grim Dominique case ended for us on a note of hilarity. To celebrate the win, we Three Musketeers parked in front of Mike's, the home away from home for most cops in the Area. To enter you had to be recognized through a small triangular window in the door and be buzzed in.

This was fairly early in the evening for Mike's and only a few people were inside. We said hello to the owner, our good friend and police buff, Mike Lucas, and drifted toward Detective John Toenings at the end of the bar.

A tall, good-looking former paratrooper, John was a tough guy, but not all the way through. One night while working with him, we were sent to Weiss Memorial Hospital to investigate a drowning. A nine-year-old boy had fallen into Lake Michigan while playing on the rocks. We asked a nurse where the body was, and she showed us a small area next to the emergency room where it lay uncovered on the floor. "Get this boy's body off the floor and do it now," Toenings commanded in a voice that resonated. "The family lives close by and will probably be here shortly. Do you know how seeing this would make them feel?" Hospital employees bumped into one another as they ran in, picked up the boy, placed him on a gurney, and covered him with a clean white sheet.

Toenings had thundered partly because he was so upset at how young the victim was. People don't become cops if they don't care.

At the bar and after one drink, Jimmy Nolan said quietly into my ear, "Hit me."

"Are you drunk or just nuts?" I asked.

"No, no, no, no," Jimmy said in his way of repeating certain words when he was excited or planning something. "Just clap your hands and I'll go down and they'll think you really hit me."

"Jimmy," I said in admiration, "you are a real work of art." Before I could finish the sentence, he slammed a fist into his hand and dropped to the floor like a sack of potatoes. Any friend of Jimmy's always went along with his spontaneous gags because you never knew what else he had in mind. So I stood over him and scowled, "I told you to lay off me. Did you have enough or do you want some more?"

Toenings was agape as he and Paul sincerely thought I'd whacked Jimmy. Toenings, a good friend of Jimmy's, looked ready for vengeance. The bar owner pulled away from us, not wanting any part of a donnybrook because all of us were friends and he didn't want to take sides.

"I'm all right," Jimmy said, acting dazed as Toenings and Paul helped him up. "Let me go, I got a few words to say to John. Don't worry, everything'll be okay." Once on his feet, he whispered to me, "Do it again, only really swing at me this time."

Again, before I could do anything, Jimmy clapped his hands in secret and went staggering back—downward, sideways, then all the way down—knocking over two or three bar stools in his path. I shouted at him and pretended to kick him as he lay on the floor.

Toenings and Paul were just about to send me halfway to the morgue when Jimmy couldn't hold back anymore. He laughed himself red in the face while rolling on the floor.

"John didn't lay a hand on me!" he said, through the

chuckling, chortling, and guffawing. "You should have seen your faces! Oh God, oh God, I can't take it anymore!"

Jimmy and I were amused as hell, but not Paul and Toenings. They were extremely angry, and for once I thought Jimmy had gone too far, and the gag could have presented some unforeseen problems.

A few months later I would learn that gags could go much further, when Paul and Toenings staged their own event to shock us. But that, you will see, is another story.

Our investigation into the Dominique attacks had filled all the gaps but one: How could a man, so docile and polite in custody, be one of the cruelest attackers this often cruel city had ever seen? Over the years, I couldn't get him out of my mind. Sixteen years after we put him in handcuffs, I met him once more. This time, it was in the old Stateville Correctional Center, a rundown, paint-peeling, dilapidated building about forty miles southwest of Chicago. I was preparing this book and was hoping Robert would help me understand the twisted workings of his mind.

Paul Roppel volunteered to go with me. We had special permission to conduct the interview from the warden himself since Dominique had never been a disciplinary problem. He had aged well. He'd put on a little weight but it was well distributed, and he'd apparently been exercising.

He greeted us formally in his much-washed prison uniform with C-71009 in faded print above his shirt pocket. There was no attempt made to shake hands. I explained I had recently retired and wanted to understand him better with the possibility that I might write a book. The dirty room was uncomfortable with steamy, musty heat, so we opened a small window to help us think. The room was not soundproof, and every type of noise constantly filtered in while our interview was in progress.

What Dominique told me was the story of an average boy who couldn't cope with everything thrown at him. If what he said was not entirely the truth, it was the truth as he no doubt believed it in the stories such people tell themselves to justify what they do.

Robert never knew his real father because his parents

had split up early. Robert's stepfather was a clam digger and plumber in Babylon, Long Island. The boy's conservative Catholic relatives looked down on him because his mother was divorced, and they often called her a whore and him "the brat." For someone who claimed he was driven almost to murder by hatred for his mother, Dominique spoke rather fondly of the times she stood up to her relatives for him, telling them, "He's my son and I love him."

Robert was befriended when he was around seven by a young man who lived down the block. The man would dress him up in girls' clothes and put makeup on him, then undress him and give him oral sex. "He would do things to me all over my body and that would make me feel good, and then I would do the same thing to him." Next the man would masturbate in a frenzy while the boy watched, but the man never attempted to sodomize him. Although the man had a wife or girlfriend, he sometimes put on panties and women's stockings and pranced around.

Robert said he had his first sexual experience with a girl when he was eleven and went into a closet with the coach's daughter. When he later tried doing "sex things" with the girls at school, his parents were notified and that brought more beatings. Once, he said, he came home and surprised one of his aunts as she was in bed with a man. She yelled at him.

The boy developed a fondness for the feeling of silk. After Robert's man-friend moved away, the boy would put on his mother's panties. One time he was wearing not only her panties but also her stockings and brassiere while lying in bed with his blind younger brother. Dominique said his mother was "very cold about sex" and that when she found out he was wearing her undergarments, she "freaked out and beat the hell out of me" with a heavy belt buckle. He told me he never felt any special attraction for any one particular sex in his early years.

Robert had a learning disability that was mistaken for "retardation." Although he was a little slow in reading and math, he grew up "rather more sexually knowledgeable than most people."

He said his stepfather was not a bad man but that he and

his mother ignored him because they were busy with the younger children. "Anything I could do to get their attention, I would do just to aggravate them. If they said no, I said yes." His rebelliousness made everything worse because relatives still looked down on the family at a time his stepfather was trying to get money from them.

When Robert was thirteen, his mother had him placed in a mental institution, where he stayed until he was twenty. "I felt deserted. They didn't say they were putting me away, they said they were getting rid of me." His confinement meant to him that his mother had stopped loving him. He occupied his time by thinking how much he hated her.

Whenever he attacked a woman in later years, he told me, "I was thinking of my mother, and I was aiming at their faces because I saw my mother's face when I got the urge to hurt someone."

Sometimes he was taunted by the other boys in the juvenile ward of the mental institution and had to fight back. He was bothered by recurring nightmares until the staff started giving him Thorizine. After he developed an allergic reaction, they gave him drugs and tranquilizers that he said made him "like a zombie."

Around this time, he developed a crush on a student nurse who told him he was a child "who was neglected, who needed to be a little more loved and understood." Dominique admitted the same mixture of fondness and gratitude for her as for the young man who had dressed him as a girl, and for his mother before he began to hate her.

Robert, then fourteen or fifteen, mentioned to people his feelings for the nurse, who, he claimed, had talked of adopting him. When his mother learned of this, she showed up and went into a rage.

"My mother said, 'No, you can't do that, you're not allowed to love.' I looked at the doctor and he said, 'That's right. You are not to have feelings. You are not allowed to love. And if we find out you're doing this, we're going to put you in a straitjacket.'"

The tape recorder wheels kept spinning as Paul glanced at me from his position behind Dominique and shook his head slowly to indicate that he couldn't believe something or, at most, Robert was exaggerating.

When the student nurse was transferred, Robert blamed his mother and Aunt Peg, the matriarch of the family. After he was placed in the adult ward at age sixteen, Robert was raped by one of the men, but doctors told him it "was just a hallucination"—even though attendants had to put stitches in his anus. Afterward, he told us, he consented to oral sex with other men in the ward for money, candy, cigarettes, and other things.

All the while, according to him, his parents needed him committed for life so they could get money from uppity relatives, and the sole purpose of the staff was to "keep me mentally disturbed."

His mother was allowed to take him home for one weekend, and that turned out to be a disaster. His aunt came over and said, "What's the little bastard doing here? I thought you put him away," and then he made all hell break loose. He said he broke everything in the house and beat up his aunt.

When he was returned to the institution, he said, he saw a document signed by his mother stating that they should "keep him on medication and not allow him to recover."

One night after he had taken some contraband alcohol, marijuana, and speed pills, he went on a pass to buy a straight razor and other things in town for some of the men. Then he blacked out. When he came to, he had blood all over him and was in the car with three men who were talking about how they should blow his brains out for almost killing a woman.

"My understanding was that I came up behind this woman and assaulted her with the straight razor I bought, cutting her two or three times on her face, and then I ran."

The townsmen drove him back to the mental hospital, met with the security officers and local police, and told them what he did. "And they just put me back in the hospital," Dominique said.

Before coming to Chicago, he went up to a woman going to her car in Rockford and made coarse remarks because he felt he was losing control over his life. He wanted her to "do something like push me, shove me. I needed her to aggravate me." Instead, she screamed. He chased her down and stabbed her. "Something had to be done, but I couldn't do it unless I was pushed."

In one of the Chicago assaults it was the same thing. "I was trying to get her to provoke me so I could attack her ... I needed the rage, the hate, the symbol that I wanted—I wanted her to be my mother to me. I was trying to attack my mother," he blurted. "At times when this rage was coming, I thought of all the bad things she did to me, and this gave me the courage and the opportunity to get violent. I'd go in and out of a mental block while I walked around looking for girls to hit. When all the rage was released, the wall came back and I'd feel relaxed, if you can understand what I'm saying."

He apparently started by asking the victims for a "blow job" in hopes they would go into a frenzy. "The first lady that limped really looked like my mother. That's probably why I hit her." It was as if his body went into automatic pilot. He had impressions of what was happening and knew what he was doing, but the acts remained vague to him.

He explained that always after an attack, there would be an inner peace he could find in no other way. As he spoke, I saw a memory of that calm coming to his eyes. It was scary. The long prison term he was serving only locked him up, it couldn't reform or rehabilitate him. Calling up hatred for his mother and attacking women virtually at random gave Dominique the energy to hold himself together, and prison life served the same purpose.

As Paul and I were leaving the interview room, feeling a little as if we were being let out of someone else's hell, Dominique said with a strange voice, "DiMaggio, if you write a book, make sure you tell everyone that there are a lot of lucky women out there, because I looked at a lot of them and followed a lot of them and they didn't get hit because I just didn't have the urge at the time. I know when that urge is coming."

If Robert Dominique is ever paroled, he *will* soon afterward buy a knife or axe and strike again. Sometimes hate never dies.

266

FIND
HALF MILLION IN DOPE
Chicago Tribune
THE WORLD'S GREATEST NEWSPAPER
SUNDAY, SEPTEMBER 20, 1970
30c

$500,000 Marijuana Is Found

Marijuana, reportedly valued at half a million dollars, was confiscated yesterday by two off-duty detectives who intervened in what apparently was a double-cross among suspected members of a drug smuggling team.

The arrest of 11 persons in a room in the Marriott Motor Hotel, 8535 W. Higgins Rd., resulted in the seizure of more than 120 pounds of the narcotic which was being sent from Mexico via Tucson, Ariz.

Lt. August Locallo of the Damen Avenue Robbery Unit said the action took place as he and the other arresting detective overheard what they thought was a robbery attempt.

Walking in Hall

Locallo said that he and Sgt. John DiMaggio, also of Damen Avenue robbery, were walking in a hall on the second level of a wing at the hotel, about 2:30 a. m. when they heard shouting and cries coming from one of the rooms. Locallo and Di Maggio are employed as security guards in the hotel when off duty.

A man later identified as Keith Freeman, 23, of 550 Clyde St., Calumet City, burst from the room holding a blackjack and a can of a disabling chemical spray. After capturing Freeman, the detectives entered the room.

Two men were holding blackjacks and other cans of the spray, Locallo said. They were identified as Michael R. Raney, 18, of 14716 S. Kenwood Av. Dolton, and his brother Patrick [Dix], 20, of 1944 Memorial Dr., Calumet City.

[TRIBUNE Staff Photo]

Police Lt. August Locallo [left] and Sgt. John DiMaggio of Area 6 Robbery Detail examine drug cache taken in raid at Marriott Hotel.

268

CHICAGO TRIBUNE, SUN

Police Seize $500,000 in Marijuana

[Continued from first page]

hidden under a bed was William Smith, 19, of 4548 Oriole Blvd., Norridge. Two others, Steven Thompson, 23, and Holmes Bevington, 23, both of Tucson, were handcuffed together on the floor of the room, according to Locallo.

When the hotel's night manager, John Hertzler, arrived, Bevington allegedly took him aside, saying, "I have another room with kilos of marijuana. If you go over and take care of it, I'll split it with you." Hertzler told the detectives of the offer, Locallo said.

Down the hall, the detectives found five suitcases containing 36 kilograms of marijuana formed into bricks and 52 smaller plastic bags. Locallo said that Bevington gave police the keys to the cases. Also in the room was a bottle containing about 30 pills believed to be amphetamines.

Arrested in the parking lot in Freeman's car was Thomas O'Malley, 21, of 15090 University Av., Dolton; Patrick Raney's pregnant wife, Vicki, 17; and an unidentified 17-year-old girl, Locallo said. Also arrested later in the hotel was Lawrence E. King, 22, of 4431 N. New England Av.

Under questioning, the suspects from Tucson told Locallo that the marijuana was to have been sold to the Raney brothers and Freeman for the wholesale price of $200 a brick.

When the price was to be raised another $100 a brick, King, who Locallo said was the key man in the transaction, allegedly arranged with the local men to steal the entire shipment. Locallo said police learned that King and Smith had flown to Tucson to get the shipment and came back Friday morning with the rest of the Tucson group.

The Raney brothers and Freeman were charged with armed robbery. Thompson was charged with conspiracy to commit armed robbery. Miss Bagalini, in whose purse police said they found a small quantity of marijuana, was charged with possession, as were Thompson, Bevington and Smith.

King was charged with conspiracy to commit armed robbery and possession of mari-

juana. The two young women, who also were charged with conspiracy, were released to the custody of their parents and

scheduled to appear in Family Court. The remaining suspects will appear in Holiday Court today.

Youths, arrested in Marriott Hotel room, await questioning at District Police Station.

[TRIBUNE Sta]

Walking in Hall

Locallo said that he and Sgt. John Di Maggio, also of Damen Avenue robbery, were walking in a hall on the second level of a wing at the hotel, about 2:30 a.m. when they heard shouting and cries coming from one of the rooms. Locallo and Di Maggio are employed as security guards in the hotel when off duty.

A man later identified as Keith Freeman, 23, of 550 Clyde St., Calumet City, burst from the room holding a blackjack and a can of a disabling chemical spray. After capturing Freeman, the detectives entered the room.

Two men were holding blackjacks and other cans of the spray, Locallo said. They were identified as Michael R. Raney, 18, of 1471 6S. Kenwood Av., Dolton, and his brother Patrick [Dix], 20, of 1944 Memorial Dr., Calumet City.

Girl Is Under Chair

Under a chair was Miss Mary Bagalini, 20, of Tucson. Partly hidden under a bed was William Smith, 19, of 4548 Oriole Blvd., Norridge. Two others, Steven Thompson, 23, and Holmes Bevington, 23, both of Tucson, were handcuffed together on the floor of the room, according to Locallo.

When the hotel's night manager, John Hertzler, arrived, Bevington allegedly took him aside, saying, "I have another

[Continued on page 2, col. 1]

John DiMaggio enjoying his home city.

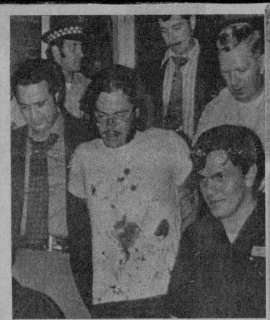

Robert Nelson is led by police from a building at 2225 W. Giddings, where he had barricaded himself for 2½ hours. (Daily News Photo/Donald Bierman)

Angry man with gun
holds off cops 2 hours

By Diane Monk

A 21-year-old man who said his cousin was killed by a policeman held scores of officers at bay with a double-barreled shotgun for 2½ hours before he was subdued and arrested.

Barricaded inside 2225 W. Giddings with Robert Nelson Monday night were his sister, her three small children, his mother and two of his friends.

Nelson stood at an open first-floor window with his finger on the trigger of the shotgun and said, "A friend of mine was killed by police and my cousin was killed by Richard Nuccio."

NUCCIO, a former Town

Hall District policeman, was convicted of the June 4, 1968, murder of Ronald Nelson, 19. Nuccio shot the youth outside a restaurant at N. Clark and W. Armitage.

"My cousin was killed... that's why I'm in my bag against police," said Nelson. "I'm holding this gun, but I

Today's chuckle

Real estate agent to young couple: "Yes, I think we have some $10,000 homes. How much would you like to pay for one?"

Wabco Core Driller

ain't gonna shoot. I don't want to hurt no one."

Nelson barricaded himself inside the brick two-flat on W. Giddings around 6:30 p.m.

It was shortly before 9 p.m. when Sgt. John Di Maggio grabbed the shotgun.

DI MAGGIO, who is assigned to the Area 6 Robbery Unit, went into the apartment when Nelson agreed to talk with a policeman inside.

The two talked in the living room for about 10 minutes.

"He kept pointing the gun at me, and it didn't look like he

Turn to Back Page, this section

Angry man holds off cops 2 hrs.

Continued from Page 1

would give up," Di Maggio said later.

"I waited for a chance to jump him, and when he took his finger off the trigger to scratch his nose, I jumped."

Di Maggio and Nelson were wrestling on the kitchen floor when dozens of other officers broke through a window and entered the apartment to assist Di Maggio.

BEFORE NELSON was subdued, scores of neighbors stood in the streets and listened while Capt. Thomas Hayes, Foster Av. District watch commander, pleaded with Nelson over a megaphone.

Inside the apartment with Nelson until he was captured were two of his friends, identified only as "Dave" and "Malcolm."

Upstairs on the second floor were Mrs. Karen Harding, Nelson's sister, and her three children — two girls aged 8 and 3 and a 1-year-old boy.

At 8:30 p.m., Mrs. Harding and the children were led down the back stairs by Sgt. Robert Westerholm of the Foster Av. District.

NELSON'S MOTHER went into the apartment at about 8 p.m. to talk with him. His father, Charles, remained outside with police.

Twenty minutes later, Mrs. Nelson came to the front window and said, "I can't reason with him." Then she left the apartment.

Nelson's father told police outside that he and his son had an argument earlier Monday.

At one point while he was barricaded inside the apartment, Nelson apparently put his hand through a window. Sounds of breaking glass came from the apartment several times.

After Nelson was led out to a waiting police wagon, he was taken to the Foster Av. District station and charged with aggravated assault.

CITY OF CHICAGO / **DEPARTMENT OF POLICE**　1121 South State Street　Chicago, Illinois 60605　744-4000

RICHARD J. DALEY, *Mayor*
JAMES B. CONLISK, JR., *Superintendent*

10 May 1973

PERSONNEL ORDER NO. 73-110

The SUPERINTENDENT'S AWARD OF VALOR is conferred upon SERGEANT JOHN DI MAGGIO, Star 1091, Area 6 - Robbery, for outstanding action on 14 August 1972 in which he demonstrated a great degree of personal courage, selflessness and devotion to duty without regard to his personal safety.

Sergeant John DiMaggio responded to 2225 W. Giddings where a citizen had barricaded himself in a bedroom and, armed with a shotgun and rifle, was threatening to kill police officers and himself.

Sergeant DiMaggio attempted to talk the young man into surrendering himself and the weapons to no avail. Sensing the serious potential of the situation, he requested and received permission from other supervisors at the scene to attempt to enter the home and talk to the belligerent and distraught young man.

Sergeant DiMaggio spoke to the man, Robert Nelson, and asked if he could come in and talk and was allowed to do so after disarming himself. After a long period of time in which Nelson became more disturbed and violence-prone, Sergeant DiMaggio saw a moment when Nelson's finger was removed from the trigger of the shotgun. The Sergeant rushed him and, after an intense struggle for the weapon, succeeded in disarming the gun wielder with no loss of life.

Superintendent of Police

DISTRIBUTION:　A.　To personnel concerned. To be read at roll calls where the personnel affected are assigned.

PERSONNEL ORDER NO. 73-110

DiMaggio, unarmed, went in and negotiated with the man. Eventually, after a scuffle, he was able to disarm him. He was given his first Award of Valor for his heroism.

Chicago Police Department

CHICAGO POLICE
1091

proudly presents to

Sergeant John DiMaggio
CID AREA 6 ROBBERY SECTION
the

Superintendent's Award of Valor

In recognition of an outstanding act of bravery with no regard to self or personal safety with great individual courage and with dedicated devotion to duty.

August 14, 1972 (date of occurrence)

The Public Safety Officer Medal of Valor is the highest decoration for bravery exhibited by public safety officers in the United States, comparable to the military's Medal of Honor.

POLICE RECOVER STOLEN COPPER WIRE

A cache of stolen copper wire, valued at $24,000, has been recovered by police. Checking the coils, in short supply due to extended copper strike, are policemen (l. to r.) Frank Pernice, Ken Arens, John DiMaggio and Richard Riccio. The wire is in garage at 856 W. Erie. It was stolen Thursday from the Lenz Electric Co., 1751 N. Western. (Sun-Times Photo)

John DiMaggio and Richard Riccio (*third and fourth from the left*).

274

THIS

Department **Commendation**

IS AWARDED TO

Sergeant John Dimaggio 1091
Intelligence Division

FOR

an outstanding act or achievement which brings credit
to the Department and which involves performance above
and beyond that required by the member's assignment.

RICHARD J. DALEY, Mayor
JAMES M. ROCHFORD, Superintendent

More arrests means more paperwork for Detective DiMaggio.

Weeping rapist of five offers apology, shakes judge's hand

By Lee Strobel

A MAN WHO had pleaded guilty to five rapes made a tearful apology to his victims Wednesday, then shook hands with the woman who prosecuted his case and the judge who sentenced him to 5 to 20 years in jail.

John M. Moran, 31, formerly of 2021 N. Clifton Av., was sentenced by Judge Philip J. Romiti of Criminal Court after the prosecutor, Patricia C. Bobb, an assistant state's attorney, argued for more than the minimum four-year penalty.

"Six women will never feel safe or secure again, even in their own homes, because of John Moran," she said.

Calling Moran an "educated, intelligent man," Bobb said, "that makes him even more dangerous and makes the acts he committed even more frightening."

IN ADDITION to the five rapes, Moran had pleaded guilty March 18 to an attempted rape and eight counts of deviate sexual assault.

He had admitted telephoning potential victims and posing as a survey taker to get personal information about them.

At that time, Bobb had told Romiti that Moran got women's names from newspaper listings of apartments to sublet and later talked his way into their homes where, brandishing a knife, he would tie them up and assault them.

Standing before Romiti again Wednesday for sentencing, Moran said: "It's very difficult to admit having done a rotten thing. I only wish the girls were here today so I could apologize to them....I only hope they can recover."

THE ATTACKS OCCURRED between September, 1973, and October, 1974, at a time when Moran was separated from his wife. They were later divorced. "I had a beautiful wife, a beautiful home, and beautiful sisters," he told Romiti. "The best thing the country could give to us, and I let it get away."

After Romiti sentenced him, Moran shook the judge's hand and said, "Thank you, your honor."

Romiti replied, "Good luck to you."

Moran then extended his hand to Bobb, who shook it. None of the six North Side women were in court Wednesday, but Bobb told Romiti: "They should not be forgotten. They have rights, too."

ILLINOIS DEPARTMENT OF CORRECTIONS
INTERNET INMATE STATUS

AS OF: Friday, November 18, 2011Friday, November 18, 2011

 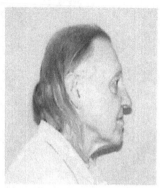

C71009 - DOMINIQUE, ROBERT S.

Parent Institution: BIG MUDDY CORRECTIONAL CENTER
Offender Status: IN CUSTODY
Location: BIG MUDDY RIVER

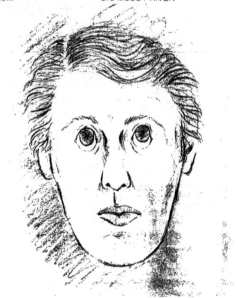

Police artist rendering of suspect Robert Dominique in 1975.

Attacker of Loyola coed found guilty

A MAN ACCUSED of repeatedly stabbing a Loyola University coed who refused to submit to his advances was found guilty Tuesday of attempted murder, aggravated battery, and deviate sexual assault.

A Criminal Court jury deliberated about four hours before returning the guilty verdict against Robert Dominique, 31, of 12 W. Van Buren St.

Dominique was charged with attacking a 21-year-old Loyola student in a North Side alley on Nov. 13, 1975, according to William Hedrick and Gregory Ginex, assistant state's attorneys.

The woman testified during the month-long trial that Dominique demanded she perform a sex act with him. When she refused, he stabbed her five times with a nine-inch hunting knife, puncturing both of her lungs. Dominique was arrested a week later in a flophouse hotel, prosecutors said.

DOMINIQUE'S attorney, T. Lee Boyd, contended his client was insane at the time of the attack and suffers from organic brain damage. Prosecutors countered with experts who testified that Dominique is legally sane.

Dominique is charged with three similar knife or hatchet attacks on women on the North Side. The attacks were committed within two weeks of the assault of the Loyola student. Those charges are pending.

Arrest suspect in 4 'impulse' hatchet attacks

By Barry S. Felcher

A suspect in four "impulse" hatchet and knife attacks on women was arrested Friday in his downtown hotel room.

Robert Dominique, 30, was taken into custody at the New Stadium Hotel, 12 W. Van Buren, and later identified as their attacker by three of the four women. Homicide Lt. Julien Gallet said.

All of the attacks occurred on the North and Northwest sides during the last 2½ weeks. Three of the women remain hospitalized.

DOMINIQUE, who gave police a written statement admitting the attacks, blamed the attacks on "an impulse he had" Gallet said. Gallet refused to identify the victims, saying they "are scared to death."

Gallet described the attacks, in the order of their occurrence, as follows:

● A woman in New Town was stabbed several times as she entered the hallway of her home. Her purse was taken.

● A week later, during the early morning hours, a woman in Rogers Park was grabbed in the hallway of her home and struck several time on the head with a hatchet. The attacker ran away after taking several articles of her clothing.

● Another Rogers Park woman was stabbed with a hunting knife near her home. Both of her lungs were punctured.

● The fourth woman was whacked repeatedly with a hatchet in front of her home in the Lawrence-Kimball area.

INVESTIGATORS said Dominique believed he had left all of the women dead.

"He thought he had killed them," Lt. Gallet said.

Dominique, a short-order cook, was charged with attempted murder and aggravated battery in one of the attacks.

The Rogers Park woman who had been stabbed with a knife was allowed to leave her hospital room to view a lineup containing Dominique. She identified him as her attacker, Gallet said.

Two of the remaining hospitalized women were shown a videotape of the lineup. They also identified Dominique, Gallet said.

THE FOURTH woman was unable to make a positive identification. Dominique, however, spotted her at the lineup and said, "I'm sorry for what I did to you," investigators reported.

The women are between the ages of 20 and 40. One of them is retired, one is a student and two are office workers.

Lt. Gallet praised a team of Damen Av. and Shakespeare Av. homicide investigators for developing leads that led to Dominique's capture. A break in the case occurred when one investigator recalled the name of a man who had been arrested several years ago for attacking a woman.

A check of police records showed that the man, later identified as Dominique, had been paroled from prison last month after serving time for burglary. The investigators then tracked Dominique to his downtown address.

Gallet credited Sgt. John Maggio and investigators Andy Pontoriero, Paul Roppel, James Nolan and James Phelan with developing the leads that led to Dominique.

278

(from left to right) John DiMaggio with Jimmy Digrisc, and Walter Murphy *(second from the right)*.

Chicago Tribune

Thursday, June 22, 1978

5 Star Final
★★★★★

9 Sections   15¢

Rush St. raiders seize 30

Mob ties sought in sex raids

By Philip Wattley

RECORDS SEIZED in a series of simultaneous prostitution raids on what police termed "supermarkets of sex" in the Rush Street area and on the city's North Side were being examined Thursday by police.

Twenty-five men and women were arrested Wednesday night on charges of soliciting undercover investigators for acts of prostitution, or being keepers of houses of prostitution.

"We are looking for links between these places, and in particular for ties with organized crime," said Walter Murphy, deputy superintendent in charge of the Bureau of Inspectional Services, which oversees vice control.

HE SAID INVESTIGATORS were attempting to establish how much money these places were taking in, so the Internal Revenue Service could determine whether reported incomes coincided with financial records kept by the taverns and go-go joints.

Police also were attempting to learn how many of the lounges were able to determine the identity of vice officers.

Records found in some of the establishments listed names, ages, descriptions, and home addresses of undercover detectives.

Investigators said in most places, when a customer would present his identification, a girl would take it to a back room where a phone call was made to a suspected "clearing house" where authorities believe someone had access to a list of police officers.

BECAUSE THE IDENTITIES of so many vice detectives is known, Murphy assembled a special team of homicide and robbery investigators to pose as visiting conventioneers at night spots to obtain evidence.

"Our men went in there with name tags and phony identification," explained Sgt. John DiMaggio, a vice officer who led the investigation. "To make it convincing, we even had them come from O'Hare Airport by cab with luggage and check into a hotel. Then they'd have the cabdrivers wait and take them to places where they could find some action."

Wednesday night's raids were carried out by 75 plainclothes and uniformed policemen who swept through the Rush Street entertainment strip at 10 p.m.

HUNDREDS OF PERSONS in the night life area watched in astonishment as lawmen moved in and closed down five bustling taverns featuring nude and seminude dancers. Five taverns in other areas also were raided and closed down.

"This is the first time a series of simultaneous raids have been carried out with search warrants," Murphy said. "We will be watching this closely in court."

Night spots raided included:

Big Daddy's 848 N. Clark St.; the Bombay Club, 2974 N. Lincoln Av.; Bur-lesque A Go-Go, 1447 N. Wells St.; the Cabaret, 930 N. Rush St.; the Candy Store, 874 N. Wabash Av.; the Chestnut Lounge, 7 E. Chestnut St.; Ebb Tide, 4910 N. Sheridan Rd.; Hour Glass, 1069 W. Argyle Av; Moulin Rouge, 1007 N. Rush St., and Nite Life, 933 N. State St.

_280_

10 nightclubs hit
by special team

By Philip Wattley

POLICE DESCENDED on the "red light" district around Rush Street Wednesday night in simultaneous prostitution raids, and also raided five other "go-go" parlors elsewhere on the North Side believed to be havens for prostitution.

Hundreds of persons who happened to be along the Rush Street entertainment strip at 10 p.m. watched in astonishment as lawmen swept in and closed down five bustling taverns featuring nude and seminude dancers. The five taverns raided elsewhere were also closed down.

At least 30 pe̲ ̲ ̲ ̲ ̲were arrested in the raids, which ̲ ̲ ̲ ̲ ̲ ̲ ̲ ̲filtration of the taverns ̲ ̲ ̲ ̲ ̲ ̲ special investi ̲ ̲ ̲ ̲ ̲ ̲ James E. O'(̲ ̲ ̲ ̲ some of the ̲ ̲ ̲ ̲ the raids, c ̲ ̲ formed and ̲ ̲ O'Grady ̲ ̲ out prost̲ ̲ tionally f ̲ ̲ neers, c ̲ ̲ bled af̲ ̲ lar vi̲ ̲ tavern ̲ ̲

DE ̲ ̲ on t'̲ ̲ and ̲ ̲ itir ̲ ̲ m(

"To make it convincing, we even had them come from O'Hare Airport by cab with luggage and check into a hotel. Then they'd have the cab drivers wait and take them 'where they could find some action'."

DIMAGGIO said such painstaking detail paid off, for the undercover agents found themselves questioned closely once inside the taverns about their hotels. In some cases, women called the hotel at which the investigators were registered to check their stories.

The questions the undercover "conventioneers" were asked were virtually identical at every tavern, DiMaggio said, as was the procedure by which the officers were solicited.

Customers were asked to buy drinks ̲ ̲ ̲en in the taverns, and the wom-̲ ̲ ̲ ̲ ̲sk the customer to buy ̲ ̲ buy

Women arrested on prostitution charges at the Candy Store, 874 N. Wabash Av., cover their faces while waiting for the police patrol wagon Wednesday night. Ten North Side cabarets were raided.

Tribune Photo by Val Mazzenga

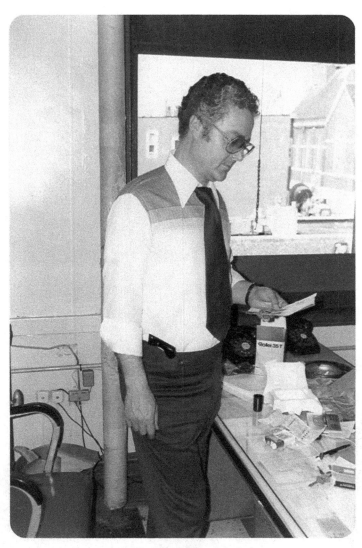

Sarge at his desk with his trusty Snubnose.

White cop testifies in reverse-bias suit

By K. O. Dawes

A white, highly decorated Chicago policeman who is suing the city, charging reverse discrimination, yesterday testified he was "flabbergasted" when he was summarily transferred out of an elite unit by a new boss.

Sgt. John A. DiMaggio and 12 other white male officers have charged in federal court they were shifted from the Office of Municipal Investigations to lesser posts by the Washington administration for racial and political reasons. One of the officers in the suit has died.

DiMaggio said that when Raleigh Mathis took over as director of OMI in April, 1984, one of his first actions was to order a special roll call to "compliment" the staff.

"He said there would be absolutely no changes—maybe a few down the road, but if we did our job we would stay," DiMaggio said in the second day of the jury trial before U.S. District Judge Milton I. Shadur.

DiMaggio, a 29-year veteran of the force and the only holder of two awards for valor, among many others, said he was given "absolutely no reason" for his transfer.

"I was called in [by Mathis] and told, 'You are leaving. I'm bringing in my own personnel,' " he said.

No one at OMI told him where he was going, he said. He was transferred to a detective job.

Earlier yesterday, Mathis's second-in-command on OMI in 1984 testified that he and Mathis knew the unit did not reflect the racial and gender makeup of the city.

Arthur E. Lindsay, then director of operations for OMI, also said all their actions had the approval of the mayor's office.

The police complement in the unit was 28 white males, one Hispanic woman and four black men, according to the plaintiffs.

The woman, blacks and one white male were retained by Mathis. The white officer was an irreplaceable computer programmer who "fixes everything that nobody else knows how it works," according to testimony by Lt. Paul Lewis, current OMI director of operations.

Lindsay said the new personnel included some white male officers as well as blacks, Hispanics and women.

284

Frank O'Driscoll, Frank Riggio, Attorney John Gubbins, John DiMaggio,
Wojnar and Tom Flanagan celebrating the Reverse-Bias sι

(*above*) John DiMaggio with his wife, Rosemary. (*below*) John at home with his wife and three kids.

CHICAGO POLICE DEPARTMENT

JOHN DiMAGGIO
SERGEANT
BUREAU OF INSPECTIONAL SERVICES
INTELLIGENCE DIVISION

744-6285

(left) Detective DiMaggio on the landline before the time of fax machines, cell phones, computers and scanners.

JOHN A. DI MAGGIO

RETIREMENT PARTY

HONORING

SERGEANT
JOHN DIMAGGIO
1091

**AREA FOUR DETECTIVE DIVISION
ADMINISTRATION UNIT**

FRIDAY, 22 MARCH 1991

CHATEAU RITZ
9100 NORTH MILWAUKEE AVENUE
NILES, ILLINOIS

Sarge's former boss, James Maurer, from Area 4 – Violent Crimes Unit.

(*above, from left to right*) Dennis Farina and John DiMaggio. (*below, from left to right*) John DiMaggio, Dennis Farina, Nick Nickeas, Andy Martorano and Mike Chasen.

Ask Sarge. . .

John DiMaggio, *a retired highly-decorated Chicago police officer and author of the forthcoming book "Sarge! Cases of a Chicago Police Detective Sergeant," will answer selected questions about police procedure each month in Clues. Submit your questions directly to Sarge at* DIMAGG26@AOL..COM *Please note that while he will do his best to respond, Sarge cannot answer all submissions.*

Question from AJR: Sarge, I've been reading and hearing a lot about identity theft. Has it become a big problem lately in comparison to other thefts, and what suggestions can you offer to prevent it?

Sarge's Answer: Identity theft has become the most prevalent crime in the U.S. It's a Part One felony because forgery is used in most of the reported cases, and it's the most accurately reported crime because of the use of lost, stolen, or fraudulently duplicated credit cards.

The crime can be curtailed with the help of people and cooperation by credit card companies. Pre-approved cards are mailed to the public by many companies and banks, and thieves break into mail boxes and search through garbage for discarded cards and other forms of identification. Photos on credit cards and other forms of ID should be mandatory; presently, only a few do it and only if the user requests it.

Here are my suggestions:

Make copies of credit cards and all forms of ID, including driver's license. Keep updated and in a safe place.

Call local police if someone has used your ID to fraudulently establish credit, and report to credit reporting agencies to request a fraud alert in your file:
Experian: 888-397-3742.
Equifax: 800-525-6285.
TransUnion: 800-680-7289.

Contact SSA's Fraud Hotline at 800-269-0271. Also state DMV. Also file complaint with FTC's identity theft hotline at 202-326-2502.

CLUES   PAGE 4

Remove SS number as an ID code on everything, and don't carry a SS card.

Guard mail from theft by taking bill payments to post office. Consider mailing items from work instead of home.

When mailing payments, consider not writing account number in memo portion of check. If stolen, thief could use the number, address, and bank number for a variety of crimes.

Don't download personal information on your computer, especially credit cards and expiration dates, bank records, or any ID with SS number that hackers are constantly seeking.

If you're writing a book about ID theft, bear in mind that for many years gangs of thieves invaded cities throughout the country, usually for a one-week period. They sent advance people to establish bank accounts, rent stores, and install banks of phone lines. The crews then come in and have five to ten specialists cash fraudulent checks, usually counterfeit payroll checks for large amounts, flood the city, and move on.

We can't stop them, but we can minimize their illegal activity. Through excellent investigative techniques and cooperation with police agencies throughout the country, many of these gangs have been caught.

One further suggestion: buy a shredder and use it. They are low-priced and very useful.

See you next month. Keep the questions coming.

Clues Needs News. . .

Clues is a true crime newsletter, not a work of fiction. My true, we mean a newsletter containing real news about members involved in writing about crime. Thus, we need news of members, bookstores, writer's groups, news of anything pertinent in a mystery vein. Send to editor Bruce Clorfene at   or to 2620 Central St., Evanston IL 60201.

John DiMaggio's daughter, Debra, pictured reunited with Sarge's retired cop buddies. (*top row, from left to right*) Richard Stevens, Sherwin Ruer, Jack Kennedy, Debra, James Maurer, and Frank Riggio. (*bottom row, middle and far right*) Tom Minisola and Mike Conforti.

18

FREDDIE

This story covers several years, so let me go back to when I was a newly promoted detective sergeant in the Robbery Unit.

Even at home, an officer never knows what is going to happen when he picks up a phone. One day I grabbed the receiver and said, "Hello?"

"Sergeant DiMaggio?" asked an unfamiliar woman's voice. "I'm *Marge, *Freddie Lewis' wife. He's spoken of you so often, I feel I know you. Sergeant, I think you're the only one that can help him." Despite her words, she spoke calmly, "I know that I won't be able to call you back, so please listen and try to help us. Freddie beat me and the kids up and he's smashing up the house—"

"He's doing that now?"

"Yes, but I don't know what set him off. He's a good guy, sergeant, but he's prancing around with a gun, threatening to kill himself. I don't want to call the police because I know that they'll kill him, or he might kill them."

She hung up abruptly before I could ask any more questions. I threw on some clothes and gave my wife just enough of an explanation to get her worried all over again, but I wanted her to know that I was going to Lewis' house. Marge didn't give me her address, but after one of her husband's arrests I had recorded it in my notebook, thinking that someday I might have to make a visit there.

The house was just about ten minutes away. During my

drive, I thought about Freddie. He was the kind of person you can't get out of your mind. He was insistent, annoying, eager to please, sincere, and irrational, and I firmly believed that I knew him better than anyone.

We had met one night at the Panther Lounge, a police hangout partly owned by a friend of mine, Jimmy Jack, a former police detective and boxer who also served as the bouncer.

Officers went to police hangouts to bring themselves down from the pressures, emotions, and highs of their work so that they could mingle with the real world and talk to normal people again until the next shift. However, these bars saw some of the same riffraff that show up around the police stations. The hangers-on offered unneeded shoe shines or asked for handouts, if only for carfare to get away from the police. Like most officers, I usually dug into my pockets and gave them something.

This time the man asking for a handout was about five-feet-eight, a hundred and eighty pounds, and had long arms and a drawn-out leathery face. His eyes were so big you usually saw them half-lidded, and his voice was like a sixteen-wheeler skidding on cinders. With his olive skin and deep black hair, he looked Greek. He wore old clothes that might have come from some relative in the Old Country, because they seemed a little out of place in mid-America. There was also something else about him, a kind of foreboding expression—he seemed to be living in one world and looking at another, and not a better one. As I soon learned, no one ever understood Freddie because no one else looked into that troubled other world.

"John," Jimmy Jack said to me, "I want you to meet Freddie Lewis. Be careful, he's dangerous." Jimmy Jack was smiling, and I thought he was joking. He wasn't.

Freddie lowered his beer and talked to me more than I wanted to hear. In his monotone, he mentioned that he owned a gas station on the far Northwest Side but that Sinclair Oil was trying to put him out of business because he'd missed a couple of lease payments. He spoke like someone who would want to put the giant company out of business single-handed. I knew the area well; a few weeks earlier my partner and I had conducted a stakeout at Touhy and Harlem for information about stolen property this same Lewis supposedly was receiving. Of all places, we set up an observation post in a nearby monastery. The brother superior provided us with breakfast and lunch, and he made dinner for our relief detectives. After one week, the detail was called off because we had been unable to verify the report.

It was odd to see Freddie close up rather than through binoculars, and without his grease monkey outfit and brimless cap. I might have stayed at the Panther Lounge longer but didn't want to keep hearing what life was doing to him. Before I got off the stool, Freddie glanced at me with a forlorn face and asked if I could lend him ten dollars. He said he needed the money to buy milk for the kids.

Assuming I was being suckered, I went ahead and gave him a ten dollar bill, visualizing that it had wings. However, that was probably the best investment I ever made. Freddie seemed surprised that I gave him so much. Actually, it surprised us both since I never expected to see that money again.

Three months later, Freddie returned to the bar, shook my hand, and gave me my ten dollars back.

"Have a seat and I'll buy you a drink," he said.

It was one of the few times I ever saw him grin. He was better dressed and was wearing a narrow-brimmed black hat that made him appear moderately successful. However, during the conversation, Freddie said he was going to lose everything because Sinclair Oil was refusing to renew his lease.

"I'm in hock for everything," from his stock to all the tools he bought, he explained. He used me as a sounding board, and I nodded a few times to show that I was listening.

I left him at the bar and had a little talk off to the side with Jimmy Jack about him. Jimmy remembered Freddie from the time he served in the old 33rd, now called the Jefferson Park District. Freddie had been suspected of petty offenses, including receiving stolen merchandise, but no charges were ever filed because police could never prove the items were stolen.

"He's a street-smart guy with a little larceny in his heart," Jimmy Jack said, "but for the past few years he's been working his ass off in that gas station. He started out as a fairly decent mechanic, without tools, and somehow he amassed a great deal of them and they're worth a good buck. He's a good guy in his way. He comes in here two, three nights a week and has a few beers that take him three to four hours to drink. He thinks he's repaying me for treating him nice when I was in the district."

"You really think he's dangerous?" I asked.

"I can't put my finger on it, but yeah."

I turned and looked at Freddie again. I had the same feeling. Just like Jimmy Jack, though, I couldn't put my finger on why.

By then I was permanently assigned to the four p.m. to 12:30 a.m. shift, which gave me more time with my young children during the daylight hours, but our wives thought of it as the "four to four" watch because we usually had to stay late or had a few drinks at a police hangout. Occasionally at work, I'd think of Freddie's large, sad eyes.

The next time I saw him, it was in a newspaper. Freddie had called reporters and told them he was going to destroy the Sinclair Oil Building downtown at high noon. When all the news photographers arrived there, he climbed into his tow truck and drove straight into the front entrance on North Wacker Drive, and then he went to a nearby restaurant to wait for his arrest. Although the damage was in the thousands of dollars, and he had used a company-owned tow truck he had snatched from a repossession, corporate leaders decided not to press the case. Freddie was given traffic tickets and allowed to go his way. This was not the last time he would make headlines.

He had become Chicago's Don Quixote. The city had not seen the likes of Lewis the Destroyer since Cap'n George Streeter, a shotgun-toting squatter who battled millionaires owning the lakefront.

There were other attacks—many more. Lewis shot out two panels of a revolving door in the Sinclair Oil Building, and another time he set fire to the gas station he used to own. He rammed his truck into the station a couple of times, and five more times plowed into the corporate headquarters. Once, he ripped out the gas tanks at his former station, hauled them across the city, and dropped them off at Sinclair's door. He even threatened to bomb the U.S. Attorney's Office for not prosecuting the company for violations that evidently were only in his mind. There were so many attacks that the papers finally stopped covering them.

In another time, Lewis might have been thought of as a folk hero, but Freddie was more like the corporate symbol of Sinclair Oil—a dinosaur.

The Freddie Lewis I came to know was completely different. It began with a call two months after he first rammed the downtown building, and I was still just a detective.

"Hi, John, how you doing?" he started out. "I don't want you to think I'm a stool pigeon, but I have some information on a rat that should be caught. The guy's raped three or four girls in my neighborhood. Do you think you can handle it?"

"I can handle it if you give me enough information to work with."

"Well, the guy drives a red car and his license plate number starts with one-one-five. He lives around Pulaski and Irving. That's all I know. See what you can do." Then he hung up.

The detectives in Homicide/Sex told me and my partner, Steve Pizzello, that they were about to prepare a crime pattern for the attacks, but it was not known if the man drove a vehicle. This meant Freddie had given us a solid lead—if it was reliable. I might have turned the tip over to the detectives assigned to the case, but I wanted to make sure it was bona fide first. At least that's what I told myself. The main reason probably was that I wanted to get in on the action. So Pizzello and I finished our paperwork on other cases to avoid wasting time driving in the evening rush hour crawl, and then we hit the streets.

The first time I met Pizzello, I didn't like him. He was tall and had possibly the biggest hands in the police department. He seemed like a cold, stand-offish sort of guy, and I had the impression he was being teamed up with me because my last two partners had been quickly promoted and someone had hopes for him. My opinion about his personality changed just a few hours later.

We rushed to an apartment where a man was firing at the police. From my position behind a car parked across from the building, I saw him poke a rifle out the front window and fire off a few shots. Suddenly, Pizzello's hand reach down like a mechanical claw, grabbed my shirt and the collar of my suit jacket, and yanked me entirely away from the car.

"What the fuck is wrong with you?" he boomed, "don't you think the bullets can go through glass?"

I was sure I'd been safe at a good vantage point to return the man's fire, and I was ready to yell back at Steve. But just then reality in the form of a spinning bullet crashed through one window and then the other. It came out with plenty of force just where my head had been a split second earlier. The sniper must have seen me behind the car but missed Steve pulling me away.

I looked at Pizzello with an expression that must have shown my gratitude, and he smiled as if to say, "You'll learn." The seemingly cold and aloof Steve Pizzello remained my friend ever since.

We joined the officers firing back at the sniper, wounding him, and then taking him into custody.

Pizzello was able to nurture invaluable contacts in the burglary world. So it was throughout the department. All officers were *trained* alike, but they *acted* in their own way on the streets.

I had six partners in my career. All had different personalities and work habits, and each of them brought to the job a different grasp of situations and ways of solving problems. Throughout my career, I found myself carrying a little of each of my former partners with me in the way I sized up a case and jumped in, or in the decision not to jump in.

On the night of Freddie's tip about the rapist, Pizzello and I drove around side streets looking for license plates beginning with 115. One hour later we found them on a red Ford parked outside an apartment building. We could have checked the plate and gone looking for the owner of the car, but we decided to sit and wait a little while. About half an hour later, *Norm Boettinger came out and opened the driver's door. He fit the description of the rapist. We grabbed him, brought him to headquarters, and turned him over to the homicide detectives. Homicide detectives never became upset when you did some of their work for them because their case loads were so heavy.

When they asked us how we caught him, I said—not entirely truthfully—that we had received an anonymous tip. Boettinger was later identified by all three victims, and it was probably the easiest arrest of my career.

I called Freddie and thanked him, and I invited him to have lunch with me and Pizzello when we were through for the day. After we ate and said goodbye to Freddie, I asked my partner, who was ten years my senior, what he thought of my informant.

"I think he's a fruitcake," Pizzello told me straight out.

"Aw come on, Steve," I said. "He's okay. The guy just likes me because I lent him ten dollars."

"Be careful of him," my partner warned.

Freddie called several more times, always beginning with, "I'm not a stool pigeon but ..." His information was always accurate, unlike the dope addict informants who hung around police stations. Over those two years, he somehow rubbed elbows with the crime syndicate. Freddie even testified in the defense of loan shark Sam DeStefano and was charged with perjury, but nothing came of it. Within a year, DeStefano was assassinated, presumably by fellow mob figures.

One of the last cases Freddie informed on was his own—someone had stolen his mechanic tools, and he gave me information on the fence who was handling them. Once he got back his $2000 worth of vice grips, lug wrenches, and calipers, he said, "John, I could have taken care of it myself, but I wanted you to get the credit." What a guy—and I believed him.

We were not exactly friends. We had a few lunches together, and I sometimes saw him at the Panther Lounge, but I kept him at a distance. He sensed my unwillingness to be close to him. He was becoming harder to figure out, as if that other world he sometimes seemed to be staring into was at last coming to claim him.

Then I received the call from his wife that he was threatening to kill himself. I wasn't thinking about how dangerous he might be—I just rushed there to repay old debts. Maybe then we'd be even.

I stopped on a dime in front of the shingled bungalow and ran up the steps, only then telling myself that I should have called for backup. Marge opened the door for me. She wasn't bad looking, but she was thin, had stringy hair and a sunken, sad expression. Her eyes were swollen and bruised.

"You're John? He knows I made the call, that's why I had to hang up. He made me tell him who I was talking to. He's waiting for you in the bathroom. He still has the gun."

Sometimes a person's personality comes through even though he or she is terrified. Marge seemed like a soft-spoken, friendly, homey woman, but then what other kind of wife would stay with a husband who was disintegrating so dangerously?

As I walked quickly through the house, my mind was on Freddie and the gun. I hardly noticed the frightened faces of his two adolescent children.

"Freddie?" I called out at the door. "This is John. Come out, I want to talk to you."

"John ..." His rough voice was lower than usual. "I ... need help."

I slowly opened the door. There he was, sitting on the floor, his head almost touching the bathtub. He gripped a powerful .45 caliber automatic gun. His legs were folded and his arms were wrapped around his knees. His large eyes glared at me as if trying to pop out.

This wasn't the Freddie Lewis I had known for the past couple of years—this was someone bent on suicide or murder. This was the person Jimmy Jack and Steve Pizzello had been warning me about.

"I knew you had the balls," he said, "but I didn't think you'd come here tonight."

I had to concentrate on every gesture and word, even his breathing, to judge how far I could go in bringing him out of his black mood. He didn't budge as I reached for his elbow—not as a friend, but as someone who understood. He let me bring him to his feet, but her jerked his gun hand behind his back so I wouldn't try to grab the .45.

"Let's go somewhere and talk," I suggested, meaning somewhere like a restaurant, but Freddie pushed past me and went into the living room. Instead of taking a chair, he sat on the floor and resumed the fetal position. The floor was strewn with books and loose leaf papers that appeared to be official documents. We didn't speak. I didn't know what to say, and even if I did, I didn't want to say it at the wrong time. Instead of talking, Freddie groped around the mess and started handing me pages of the documents, still holding the automatic.

At first I had no idea what he was giving me. They were in no order, he was just handing the papers to me without looking at them. Then they all started to make sense. They were reports from a military psychiatrist detailing Freddie's case history. I wished I could have gone through the clutter, put the pages in order, and started at the beginning, but this was Freddie's game now. Even so, some words leaped out from the documents, such as "afflicted with psychosis."

One sheet said the possibility existed that "Marine Officer Freddie Lewis is a psychopathic killer," apparently referring to overzealousness in the war, and that he was unfit for further military duty due to his "unstable mental condition."

"Do you think I need help?" Freddie asked as he slouched with his head lowered.

I got off my chair and sat on the floor next to him, my right arm consolingly around his shoulders. My left hand reached for the gun in his limp hand and placed it on the floor out of his reach. I wasn't exactly taking the gun away from him, I just didn't want to seem threatening.

"You know you need help, and that's why I'm here," I said. "Let me take you out of here and get you some help. We'll take my car, and we can talk along the way."

"Okay, John, let's go." His wife and children in the adjoining room cried with relief.

As I got up, I discreetly covered his automatic with the pages that were on the floor and left it there. I led Freddie away, making sure I stood between him and that gun, and I was determined he would never have it in his hand again.

"Get me a pack of cigarettes," he said to his wife, "and a few dollars I might need." He knew where he was going, the sprawling mental institution four or five miles away. He hugged his wife, the woman he might have shot a few minutes ago, and then faced me.

"All right," he said to me, "I'm ready."

As I led him outside, I pointed so Marge would know where the gun was hidden under the papers. I didn't want Freddie to come back and use it on his wife and children.

I drove past the gates of the Read Zone Center and the guard waved me through. Many of the doctors and nurses at Read remembered me from when I brought in patients during my days at the 33rd District when the institution was called Dunning. Freddie was at home with the check-in procedures ever since his Marine days, I suspected.

"Take good care of Freddie," I told an attendant in front of Lewis. "He's a friend of mine."

"Come visit me," he said as I was leaving. "And, John—I like bananas."

I returned to his home and removed all the guns I could find. I unloaded the three weapons and Marge put them in a paper bag. I took them to work the next day and inventoried them, listing Lewis' name as the person from whom they were confiscated. Then from time to time I visited Freddie at the asylum and brought him bananas.

I wish I could say that this was the end of the story, but a year later I got a call from Lewis, who was back home and angry because I'd removed his guns.

The .45 was one he'd "taken" when he was discharged from the Marines. He made a few inquiries and learned they had all been destroyed, either stoked in the blast furnaces in Gary or "deep-sixed" in Lake Michigan, as was department policy when weapons were not claimed within a reasonable time.

"Are you through now?" I asked, weary of his tirade.

"Yeah, I'm through, for the time being—but it's not over yet." I knew that was a threat, but we never spoke or saw each other again.

Freddie apparently drifted into selling stolen goods and was friends with Hugh Ruttenberg, a fairly young antiques dealer.

In October 1979, Marge went to Ruttenberg's shop on Addison Street and found her estranged husband and Ruttenberg shot to death, fully clothed on a bed in the loft. All around were presumably stolen stereos and other electronics equipment.

The autopsies failed to show who shot whom. Freddie's family believes both men were murdered by a professional killer.

I was not involved in the investigation. I was long gone from my homicide assignments then, but police officers who talked to reporters assumed that Lewis had killed Ruttenberg and then himself, guessing this only because of his unstable mental history bordering on violence. I never understood the killings, and I think I'm one of the few people who ever came close to Freddie Lewis. I probably could have made a few calls and learned about what happened, but for some reason I didn't concern myself with his demise. Maybe it was because of that last phone conversation.

"It's not over yet."

19

MAY THE ROAD RISE UP TO MEET YOU

A little after roll call one Tuesday afternoon, I looked around and noticed that Jimmy Nolan was the only detective remaining in the office, typing away with his legs crossed. Typing was not Jimmy's idea of police work.

"Where's Roppel?" I asked.

"Personal errand," Jimmy answered, knowing that he didn't have to cover up with me. The two of them had put in plenty of time on their own, and I didn't care if they occasionally took a little time off if things were quiet.

The phone rang. At the other end of the line was Sam Lavacarre, one of the few policemen who never called me "Sarge." Sam was one of the biggest officers on the job, standing at least six feet five and weighing about 350 pounds of muscle. Sam was a wagon man out of the East Chicago Avenue District. Usually he called me in a clear, calm no-nonsense way. But not this time.

"It happened at St. Clements," he yelled into the phone. "It's a bad one, John. Two nuns and a priest. When we got there we found them in the rectory, blood all over. My God, all three of them were slashed pretty bad, but they were still breathing. We had to put 'em in the back of the wagon and rush 'em to Henrotin (a North Side hospital). John, I don't think any of them are going to make it."

"Thanks, Sam," I said and hung up. I turned to Nolan and told him what I'd just heard, and my mind started up. I couldn't call headquarters to make the notification, it was five-fifteen and all the bosses had gone home. I yelled out to a detective sergeant from Robbery who was making coffee, "Tommy, you're going to have to answer the phones, we're going to Henrotin—two nuns and a priest have been slashed."

Nolan and I ran down three flights of stairs and jumped into a squad car. Nolan was in his element—with the siren blasting and the front emergency lights flashing, he treated the rush hour congestion as an obstacle course. If he never became a cop, he probably would have been a race car driver.

Thoughts scampered through my mind. Should I try to reach the homicide commander on the police radio and have him meet us at Henrotin? *Absolutely not*, I thought. Our messages were constantly monitored by reporters in the large press room of police headquarters. Besides, the savage attack had not been verified. I still had a few minutes before I reached panic time.

"Shut down the siren for a minute, Jimmy," I said.

As it droned down, I picked up the mic from the glove compartment. "This is Eighty-Six-Ten, call Eighty-Six-Oh-Five and Eighty-Six-Oh-Six for a meet with me," I told the squad operator. The eighty-six number meant Homicide Unit, Area Six.

I was told 8605 and 8606 just went down on separate investigations. "Then try Eighty-Six-Oh-Seven for me," I said, sounding calmer than I really was. I knew the bosses were listening.

The response was that 8607 was on the way to motor maintenance with a bad radiator.

There was an unsettling silence. Nolan zipped into every opening in traffic he could find with just blinking lights to warn other motorists that we were coming through.

"Squad," I said, "get hold of a Burglary car and send a team to interview the pastor at St. Clements." I had to weigh my words and make it seem that nothing of major consequence was being broadcast on the police airwaves. I put down the mic and told Nolan to put the siren on again. When we were about six blocks from the hospital, I told him to cut it. No use disturbing the patients.

Henrotin was a busy place. The neighborhood had

millionaires and bums, the cardinal's mansion, and public housing. The Secret Service had the hospital on its list of trauma centers in the event that the president or vice president got shot while visiting the city. We parked on a side street and suspected the worst as we ran toward the emergency entrance. The driveway was filled with three patrol wagons, two ambulances, and at least five squad cars. The emergency room was unusually crowded even by Henrotin standards.

As Nolan made inquiries on his own, I scanned all the faces for someone who might know about the attack. Seeing two priests standing near the curtained service area, I went over to one and said, "Father, what can you tell me?"

"I can only tell you, my son, that I am here to give the last rites," he answered in a somber monotone.

Then I saw two uniformed policemen and asked, "Where do they have the priest and the two nuns?"

"A priest and two nuns? For what?"

I didn't answer them. Looking around, I saw that the emergency room lacked the hurly burly you would expect from a brutal assault at a church. I felt as if the world had just turned and I hadn't. Something was wrong, but I couldn't imagine what.

Nolan returned from a similar experience and grabbed my arm in concern. Leading me to the exit, he asked, "Are you sure Lavacarre told you Henrotin Hospital?"

"Yes, absolutely, Jimmy, I'm positive."

"Then it's got to be a joke, Sarge. Nobody knows anything about it. We've been duped. Oh, they really got us good this time. Two nuns and a priest! Who do you think did it?"

We walked out of the hospital not knowing what to think. All the cars I had called for were facing in our direction with their flashing emergency lights blinking. There stood John Toenings and the nearly always serious Paul Roppel leaning on a squad. Both of them were smiling and slowly waving at us. It was a scene from *The French Connection.*

Then it hit me. This was payback time. Nolan and I had played only one trick on the two of them together, the mock fight in the barroom four months before at the end of the

Dominique case. This, however, was not a practical joke, it was a masterpiece of planning. They had picked a slow day. They recruited the most conscientious patrolman possible, Lavacarre, to call in the phony report. They had called me at precisely the right time, knowing I wouldn't attempt to contact the homicide commander on the air. They also had two of the cars go "down" with the squad operator on investigations, knowing that I would immediately attempt to contact assist units, especially to cover the crime scene. They also deviously had the other car go down with the alleged broken radiator so that I wouldn't become suspicious that more than two cars were on cases.

Nolan and I didn't say much when we returned to headquarters, which was now filled with men and activity. Passing through each unit was like walking a gauntlet.

"How was the case, Sarge? Pretty bad, I hear," came the chant from Burglary.

"A priest and two nuns, must have been awful," was the comment from Auto Theft.

"Back so soon?" Sergeant Kelly in Robbery asked. "You guys must work fast."

We reached our office annoyed, but a little amused. "Well, Jimmy, I can't really blame you for falling for it." I sat behind my desk, and with a pretend growl, I said, "Now go back to your fucking typewriter and finish your reports."

Things went back to normal.

As I said, I joined the team of Nolan and Roppel only when I could get away from my normal duties. One time I wished I could have gone with them was when they grabbed their coats and hats to investigate a smoking gun homicide. It was given that name because it was a simple case. At the same time we learned that a woman was found dead in the prestigious Astor Street neighborhood near the cardinal's mansion. I made a snap decision that the killing near the mansion might draw the most heat and decided to accompany the detectives assigned to the case.

"Aw shit, Sarge, come with us," Nolan said, "we always have more fun, don't we?" Indeed, the Musketeers always seemed to wind up with the strangest cases, and the interplay of our personalities took the work out of the job.

"Jimmy, I have to go to the one on Astor Street. Just drive Roppel to Winthrop Street and do your usual bad job," I kidded.

By the way, "smoking gun" had nothing to do with the murder weapon. It could have been a gun, a knife, or a frying pan. The phrase just meant that when police arrived on the scene, it was obvious who the killer was—usually a spouse, relative, or friend.

While Nolan and Roppel went to the Winthrop killing, I went with detectives John Philbin and John Toenings to the Astor Street case in which a woman was found brutally stabbed for no known reason, and there were no witnesses. It was called a "starter case"—start with nothing and then develop leads.

When Toenings and Philbin dropped me back some hours later, the Musketeers were typing away. As soon as they saw me they jumped from their chairs in excitement.

"Sarge," Nolan said, his eyes as wide as saucers, "you should have seen it. Holy Christ, we never saw anything like it. You said it was a smoking gun case—it was a smoking *body* homicide!"

"Jesus, Sarge," said Roppel, the least excitable of the team. "When we got there, we walked into this filthy apartment and the patrol officers were talking to the wife. She was sitting at a small kitchen table and one of the officers told us to take a look in the bedroom. She looked like she was battered pretty bad. We got about ten feet from the opened door and saw a naked body on the bed. It was smoking from his head to his genitals."

"You should have seen it," Nolan continued. "The body was opened up like a can of tuna and the guts were sprouting out. The face was gone—there were no eyes, just holes, and smoke was coming out of the sockets."

"The crime lab guys came about five minutes after we got there," Roppel said. "We went into the kitchen and questioned the woman while they processed the body. She was pretty calm. She was holding a bloody towel to her cheek, and every once in a while when she dabbed her face you could see a gaping hole that would require at least ten stitches. Her arms had a lot of scars, old ones. The patrol officers said, 'Wait until you hear this story,' and they were shaking their heads as they filled out reports."

Roppel read from his copious notes and the whole scene played before me.

Nolan had told the wife, "Just tell us what happened and we'll take you to the hospital and get you fixed up."

The woman looked up at the detectives and said, "I just couldn't take it anymore. It's been going on for about five years, ever since we came from the south. He couldn't find any work and we had starved stomachs for many nights, and then he'd go to a tavern and get drunk and come home and beat me. It wasn't so bad at first, but the beatings got worse. I just couldn't take it anymore."

She continued by saying, "He's been working for a guy cleaning pools for two or three days a week, and he's been afraid to leave the chemicals in the truck for fear someone would steal them. Just to be mean, every once in a while, he'd throw a glassful of those chemicals on me and my whole body would blister up and I'd suffer for a week. You all have been looking at my arms, but my whole body is scarred. Here, let me show you."

Nolan and Roppel had to stop her from undressing.

"I just couldn't take it tonight," she said, not afraid to look into their eyes. "he came home drunk and he just started punching me for no reason at all. I had his dinner ready, but he just started shouting and swearing and punching. He went to bed and I was just sitting here at the table thinking and my eyes were staring at those chemicals under the sink, and then it was like a dream and I was smiling all the time. I took a big pail and then I poured those cans into the pail and stirred it with my pasta spoon, and all that shit started smoking and smelling real bad. I brought the full pail into the bedroom and heard him snoring and then I turned on the light. I started on his head, slopping the liquid out like filling a hog trough. I knew I would hurt him, and he gave out one big scream. Then I started to pour out the liquid on his chest and then his stomach and then his genitals.

"I knew I was enjoying it because his hands started

flopping up and down. At first he grabbed for his face when he was screaming, but his hands went for his stomach and he was pulling his innards and then everything started smoking. There was just a little more in the bucket, and I threw it on his face and it seemed like his head come up and he was trying to get at me. I went down the hall and called the police from Jenny's apartment, and then I came back here and went into the bedroom and just watched him die away. I left the door open so they could get in. I just couldn't take it tonight."

The chemicals were sulfuric acid, calcium lime oxide, and sulfonic acid.

"I'm surprised she didn't blow up the whole building," Nolan remarked.

The killing occurred at a time before wife abuse became a common concern and there was no such thing as a protection order. During the woman's trial, Nolan pointed out mitigating factors, contending that she had been driven past her breaking point. During a recess, the prosecutor asked Lieutenant Gallet and me, "Whose side is Detective Nolan on?"

Largely because of Jimmy's support, the judge found the woman guilty of manslaughter instead of murder, with a minimum sentence of "time considered served," meaning the time she had spent in jail awaiting trial.

The team of the Three Musketeers was so successful that we thought it would last forever. Our unit handled every kind of homicide imaginable, including what we called the Tropicana Turkey Case. For me it began with a call at headquarters.

"Sarge," the beat officer said, "we're at the Tropicana Motel and we got a bad one. I think you better get right over here."

I hopped into a car with Gallet and two detectives, and we rushed to the motel on Sheridan Road, just off Lake Michigan. Employees and half a dozen uniformed policemen were waiting for us on the cool, sunny April day, some of them pointing the way to the second floor balcony.

We knew the case was really bad because the uniformed officers chose to stay outside rather than be with the body. Detectives preferred crime scenes that way, since it meant the well meaning officers would not be stepping on and contaminating evidence.

We entered the room not knowing what had happened or even where the body was. We looked all around, darting our eyes as soon as we opened the door, and found an ordinary motel room. The two beds were made, nothing had been disrupted, and there was no litter on the dresser. A fast look under the beds showed nothing. We glanced at the bathroom, and it was exceptionally clean ...except for the headless body in the tub.

The corpse of a black man floated in the blood-red water, and the tub was about to overflow with a few more drips from the faucet. The victim had been dead for maybe twelve hours. His shoulders butted against the bathtub, the left arm down and the right arm protruding. The hand was missing.

Without touching anything, we backed up and discussed what our follow up procedures should be. I called the mobile crime lab and posted district officers at the door to preserve the crime scene, which was now defined as the entire motel room. Lieutenant Gallet, showing no strain from his usual twelve and fourteen hour days, went into a vacant adjoining room to call the homicide squad rather than disturb anything. He requested that additional detectives be sent to the motel and told the desk officer to make the downtown notifications.

Gallet and I then joined the arriving crime lab technicians about ten minutes later and assisted in processing the scene and searching for possible evidence. You would think that in a beheading, there would be plenty of blood on the floor or walls, but there was nothing. We assumed the killer had used a cleaver rather than a knife or saw, or a combination of all of them. Since the head and hand were not in the apartment, they apparently were carried away in some type of container or plastic bag. The killer then washed his hands in the sink and used the bloody towels left behind. Someone, possibly not the killer himself, then cleaned up that room until it could pass inspection by a hospital accrediting board or a Marine sergeant inspecting the barracks of recruits.

No one went near the body until the technicians took photos from every possible angle.

Someone had to move the floating body aside and open the drain, so I handed my suit jacket to Gallet, rolled up my shirt sleeve, and fingered my way to the drain. The water didn't go down. I moved my hand past the headless corpse and through the bloody water to find what was blocking the flow. I hauled out a few fingertips-full of sinew, bone fragments, and cartilage, and put the mess on the tub ledge. As the water began gurgling down the drain, I noticed a leg emerging as a bloody stump. When the tub emptied more, I called out to Gallet, who was standing behind the washroom door, "No head, no hands, and no feet. He looks like a turkey!"

A team of detectives and up to a dozen patrol officers were assigned to search all the dumpsters and garbage cans within a radius of several blocks from the motel for body parts or weapons. All they found was ordinary trash. Later, officers searched Park District trash barrels and the shallow water along the lake shore. Detectives also interviewed motel workers about whoever rented the room and learned that a black couple had checked in and used names that, not surprisingly, turned out to be fictitious.

Just when we thought the victim might keep his "John Doe" tag in the morgue, detectives found a car that had been ticketed for parking in violation of the seven a.m. to nine a.m. ban. A registration check showed that it belonged to *Morris Williams of suburban Evanston. Roppel and Nolan, who had been called at home to come in and help work on the case, interviewed Morris' live-in girlfriend, and she said he didn't come home that night. They took her to the morgue to view the abbreviated remains. Nowadays, relatives and friends look at a closed-circuit TV screen in a dark, private room. In those days, attendants just wheeled out a body and moved back a green cloth. As I worked in the Area squad room, I hoped the detectives had carefully briefed the girlfriend on what she would—and would not—see. Not all officers took that precaution, and it ended up with a hysterical witness who never fully recovered from the shock.

An hour later, Roppel called in to the lieutenant, "The witness made a positive identification," he said in his formal way.

"There's no head, how can she be positive?" Gallet asked.

"She is absolutely sure. She identified marks on his body and warts on his penis. She called it his 'Jones'."

Gallet turned to me and whispered, "Warts on his penis." I laughed and stopped my work to hear more.

"Did you prepare her prior to viewing the body that he was missing some parts?" Gallet asked.

"We didn't have to. The lady was calm, cool, and collected. She didn't get upset, and she took her time examining the body, searching for all the various warts and marks. We recorded them in a notebook, and she signed it."

"Good work," Gallet said and hung up.

On the drive back to Evanston, the woman told Roppel and Nolan about Williams' drug involvement and an auto accident he had been in a few years before. This allowed the two day shift detectives who had been assigned to the case to identify the body positively by matching the fracture lines shown in the hospital X-rays with those they had requested from the morgue.

They were also able to fan out their questioning from names listed on his arrest records. From this, they learned that Williams had made a living by selling drugs to a gang leader by the name of *Ricky Pogsy. Pogsy was in Cook County Jail awaiting trial for murder, and Williams was expected to testify against him. The plot, as they used to say, thickened.

A short time before Williams was murdered, two men who owed Pogsy a favor walked away from custody in the courthouse across from the jail. One of them was *Black Marble McBlain, whose attractive common law wife had sex with a guard after he promised to switch bond slips so that McBlain and another man could be released when they appeared in court for a routine bond hearing.

Black Marble was still at large, but his wife was located and thrown in jail for the escape conspiracy. While there, she bragged to a cellmate that she had persuaded Williams to take her to a motel so she could buy some narcotics and they could have sex. Black Marble was already there, waiting for them to rent the room. The wife left the door unlocked and he slipped in. Black Marble surprised Williams and knocked him unconscious, and then the two of them cut off his head, feet, and hands, and she cleaned up afterward. The wife told her cellmate that she was upset because the police were able to identify the body "after all the work we went through." She even remarked that they had cut his feet off because they believed he could have been identified by his foot prints taken when he was born, but no mention was ever made of how or where they disposed of the body parts.

We were certain Black Marble would be asking around where his wife was.

Although the detectives were unable to secure a warrant on a secondhand jailhouse confession, a judge authorized phone taps on her friends and relatives. Before long, the phone company was able to trace a call to an apartment at 63rd and Wentworth. That was well known to South Side police officers as the home of dope dealer J. D. McChristian, a founding member of the city's notorious El Rukn drug, robbery, and extortion gang.

Roppel, Nolan, Philbin, and four other Area Six detectives sped to the location, called in uniformed officers, and surrounded the building.

The structure was heavily fortified with iron bars on all of the doors and windows and a pit bull guarded the fenced-in backyard. Everyone kept in communication by radio, and a sergeant's car was called in to neutralize the dog with tranquilizer darts.

The detectives approached the building, rang the doorbell, and knocked, but no one answered. They were armed with an escape warrant, and when they started to batter down the door a man reluctantly opened it, let them in, and stood back. The officers saw a maze of doorways. After about fifteen minutes of searching, Roppel, Nolan, another detective and two uniformed men noticed a slight movement under a stairwell.

There was Black Marble McBlain, wearing a mask, and he had a .45 caliber automatic pistol in his hand. They resisted the temptation to fire at the first sight of the gun.

"Put the gun down," one of the detectives ordered.

Black Marble let the gun go and came out with his hands held up at shoulder level. He gave them a phony name, but as the officers led him out, neighbors angrily pointed and said, "He's him, he's the Marble!" They had been deathly afraid of McBlain for the horrendous tortures he had inflicted on the community, and now they looked as if they wanted to stone him.

Although the Marble didn't exactly confess, he made a partial admission and was charged with murder.

A judge found that his admission and the testimony of his wife's cellmate were inadmissible. The murder charge was dropped, but McBlain stood trial for escape along with a previous home invasion and rape and he received a long prison term.

Prosecutors said they were happy. To them, the case was closed because they got a conviction on *something* and they knew who had committed the "turkey killing."

McBlain's wife was sentenced to five years for her involvement in the escape.

It was a reminder that one of the few constants in police work was that you win some and you lose some ... and shit happens.

One grueling night we were on the midnight shift handling one homicide after another, each seemingly bloodier than the last. By then, we had moved into a new Area Six building at Belmont and Western Avenues. We didn't finish our reports until 8:30 in the morning. Most people outside were just bustling to start work or reach school, but we were exhausted and hungry. Roppel and I were also feeling a little down.

"Let's go across the street for a drink," Nolan said. "Come on, I have a good reason."

The bar was called the Slammer—the most famous police hangout in the city, maybe even in the country. It was run by two former cops who named the place after the nickname of a police lockup, and they personally know most of the officers who came in.

The Slammer had pinball machines, a new jukebox, a pool table in the back room, and something we were unaccustomed to—clean glasses. The carpet was getting that friendly feel of spilled liquor and dirty shoe prints.

Jimmy Nolan got his highs not so much from drinking as from pulling pranks. He had just bought a can of Dinty Moore stew to put one over on one of the owners, Frank Notaro. The Kid let out just enough hints for us to be in a fog over what he had in mind.

At the threshold of the bar, Nolan became limp and fell into our arms. We walked him into the tavern and down the aisle as he pretended to be dead drunk. Speaking with a slur from the corner of his mouth, with his head sunk between his shoulders, Nolan said, "Givushalldrinks."

Frank took our order and then turned his back to get the right bottles. Nolan stood up on his own and readied his opened can of beef stew and then pretended to be drunk again. Frank set up our drink, and then Nolan made a gaseous bilious sound, and the stew seemed to spill from his mouth. Then his head plunked sideways into the mess.

"Hey, that looks good," Philbin said, and he scooped up a little on his finger and tasted it. Nolan fought every muscle in his body to keep from laughing. Then Philbin, Roppel, and I lifted Nolan's head and began to eat the cold stew with our bare hands. I remember plucking up a large piece of cold potato and it didn't taste as good as I mimed. Frank the bartender went pale and stared at us as the drink he'd been pouring slipped out of one hand and a bottle in his other crashed to the floor.

Suddenly, Nolan dropped the act, held up the empty can, and said, "Hey, Frank, want to join us?"

Frank was so angry that he probably wanted to throw a punch. He was upset at first but then thought the joke over and laughed uncontrollably as he wiped up the bar.

A few years later a similar scene appeared in the movie *The Great Santini*, but Nolan did it first. He never copied anyone— that would have spoiled the fun. He did not pull pranks recklessly, he usually did them to cheer up his partners or friends. He always wanted to be around happy people.

Jimmy managed to avoid the serious injuries and wounds a lot of detectives suffer after a few years, but he did develop a digestive problem. He got a burning sensation after eating or having a couple of beers. Doctors told him it was nothing serious, just a hiatal hernia.

In July 1979, he went to the hospital for a simple operation. He was able to receive visitors the next day.

I was back in uniform at the time, but for some odd reason I took a break and traveled halfway across the city to see him. As I walked into his room his eyes widened and he shouted, "John, they're killing me!"

I laughed, thinking it might be one of his pranks, but when I saw that he was serious, I chided him. "Pain? You should have the problems I had with my back. Hey, remember the stories I told you? We're tough guys, remember?"

"John, I mean it. It's real bad."

"You can handle a little post-operative pain. With my back operation, I thought I couldn't take it anymore, but I did. Give it a day or two and you'll be all right. Just tell the doctor when he comes around and they'll give you something. I'll buy you lunch when you get out."

"Thanks, John. You're a good guy."

"Yeah. Well, I got to go. Goodbye, Jimmy," I said, and I walked out. I had kept my visit brief because the hospital was some distance from the district I was working in, and I really wasn't authorized to make the visit.

The next day I received a call from Paul Roppel. "John," he said calmly, "Nolan is dead." Straight out and to the point. "The doctors say he had some kind of unexpected complication."

"*No!*" I shouted, not believing what I heard.

"John, I'm right here in the hospital and that is what they're telling me."

Damn you, Paul, I thought, *you're always so formal.*

I stopped asking questions and hung up. Jimmy was dead. *Dead.* It took me a while to grasp what that meant.

So that was the end of the Chicago Police Department's Three Musketeers, two partners and a supervising sergeant who often went along with them.

Nolan was thirty-three years old. His funeral card contained the Irish blessing:

May the road rise up to meet you, may the wind always be at your back, may the sun shine warm upon your face, and the rains fall soft upon your fields. And until we meet again, may God hold you in the palm of His hand."

The funeral service at St. Cornelius Church was crowded with patrol officers, detectives, supervisors, and his loving family. Officers who were shot without warning received bigger funerals, but there was more heroism in the day-to-day police work of dedicated officers like Nolan than in being the victim of unexpected violence.

The evening of the burial, TV newscaster Peter Nolan, who was of no relation to Jimmy, ended his report by mentioning that he had run into Jimmy a few times.

"In my years as a newsman, I have come into contact with all kinds of police officers all over the country," he said and paused. *"Chicago cops are a special breed. There are few that you feel lukewarm about. You either love them or hate them. I'm sure that after twelve years as a policeman, Jimmy received the normal amount of cynicism that goes along with the job of cleaning up after society's mistakes. But the hardening of the heart that sometimes afflicts veteran policemen never set in with Jimmy. He was a compassionate cop with that rare understanding of the basic frailty of the human beings he dealt with."*

20

THE INSANE FISH

There were a lot of transfers in the department after combative Jane Byrne was elected mayor, and her top command wanted to bring up officers they favored. I didn't think the changes would affect me because I had never played politics. Besides, at the time I was one of the few sergeants chosen to be assigned to investigations in the license unit after my work in homicide and a temporary special detail in the Prostitution Unit. One Friday, though, I received a call from a former partner who told me I was being put back into uniform and assigned to the Shakespeare District station, on the first floor of the former Chicago Boys Club.

"Somebody is really sticking it to you," he remarked.

I drove down to have a word with my lieutenant at the Maxwell Street station on the West Side. He may have been a nice guy off duty, but he never liked me because I wouldn't play on his team—you'll just have to read what you will into that statement. I caught him after he had a five martini lunch. His words were slurred but he made himself clear pretty well.

"Yeah," he said, "I had to eat you (inherit you from the previous administration), but now you're gone, you're history," and truthfully, although I didn't deserve the dump, I understood the reasoning behind it.

I returned to my office and cleaned out my desk, expecting a telephone call or the formal transfer order to come out. I had not worn my uniforms for nineteen years except for yearly inspections, special details, and riot duty, but they still fit when I tried them on.

So I was being dumped, and trying to make it sink in. I was back in uniform and assigned to a district that in some ways was the worst in the city. It was nothing personal I assumed; it was happening to dozens of officers, some of whom were very good. I found challenges in every assignment, but I didn't like the sneaky, vengeful way the supervisors were trying to gain authority by eliminating anyone who might question their wisdom or be a threat to them.

As it turned out, maybe my leaving the License Unit wasn't so bad after all. Several members who remained because they *were* players on the lieutenant's team were scrutinized by a federal grand jury on suspicion of corruption. That might have explained why he had wanted to get rid of me, but who knew?

I reported in uniform for the midnight shift on Monday and was surprised to see that the captain in charge of the first watch was my old friend Thomas Flavin. He introduced me to all the new officers at roll call and tried to impress them with my experience—it wasn't often a detective appeared in blue— but they held back their yawns.

I had bad feelings about this district because there was something tense about it. The problems started with the commander, whose idea of leadership was histrionics. I knew him when he was a detective and was violating every rule in the book because he always thought he knew a better way and that usually turned sour. He was disliked by most officers who attributed his rapid promotions to his being the protégé of a well-known Congressman.

On this first evening, I went to the station washroom and noticed the words "Insane Fish" crudely printed in a couple of places and assumed it was the name of a street gang. The words, and sometimes just "I/F," were in common areas all over the district station. I had also seen the initials in different parts of the city but never more obvious than here. I didn't think much about it but wondered why no one tried to remove the graffiti.

The Shakespeare District wasn't like the lazy old 33rd, which was several miles away. This was a diverse neighborhood with something going on all the time. There were relatively few major crimes in the district, but we were kept busy with tavern brawls, family squabbles, and street fighting between gangs. The neighborhood formerly was largely Polish, but many Hispanics were moving in. For them, defending one's gang became a macho point of honor. We were so busy on my first tour of duty that there wasn't time to finish a paper cup of coffee between assignments, yet the officers told me that Mondays were the slowest night of the week.

There were two ways an experienced officer might respond to being dumped. He could decide he didn't give a damn anymore, or he could try even harder in hopes that someone would say, "Hey, we made a mistake, let's take this guy out of the district and put him back where he could do more good."

I was looking forward to patrol and jumping once more into the scenes of crimes as soon as they happened, but I didn't want to spend the entire rest of my career in uniform. That, I thought conceitedly, would waste all my experience in investigative strategy.

When I reported for the second night, Captain Flavin had a little talk with me.

"John, let me tell you a story." He often began like that. "This is one of the busiest districts in the city. The officers go through hell on all three shifts and they get hurt a lot. They encounter everything imaginable—you'll find that out very soon—and most of them do a great job. But their accomplishments are ignored. We have a district commander who, you know, is nuts about the inspection division because he was there before this assignment. You might not want to be here, but it's nice to have you aboard. You spent a heck of a lot of years in the detective division, so maybe you can help things out."

As it turned out, I couldn't—no matter how hard I tried. A unit or station took on the character of its commander, and sometimes newcomers put in the middle only made things worse.

Around this time, there was an arsonist running around in the area of North and Western Avenues, so fire calls were common. Just after the 4:30 p.m. roll call one day, Lieutenant Milton Rosenstein asked if I would have coffee with him. We were to meet in a restaurant on busy North Avenue. While I was driving there, I saw smoke pouring from an apartment above a store. I notified the squad operator, and then pulled up near the building. I made sure I left room for the fire engines that would soon arrive.

I jumped out of the car just as a frail old woman came to the window, waving her hands and shouting, "Help me!"

Without giving a thought to what I was doing, I ran through the opened apartment doorway, bounded up the stairs, and saw that the entire kitchen was ablaze. I groped through the dense black smoke and grabbed the old woman around the waist. My running up the stairs had made me gulp in enough smoke to make me feel as if my lungs were filled, and I could barely tell when I reached the doorway.

Then, from the flames burning through the smoke, I saw a young boy near the fiery kitchen. Still clutching the woman, I forced myself to go ten more steps, seized the boy with my other arm, and then, flames lapping at my back, found my way back to the hallway. For some reason the two of them only seemed to weight about ten pounds each.

I almost blacked out before I reached the stairwell, but the shouting of firefighters rushing up the stairs shocked me back to my senses. I was disoriented, but I carried the woman and boy to the sidewalk. I had no more strength—my eyes were tearing, everything was a blur, and my lungs seemed shut. I drifted toward my squad car in a daze, sat down on the curb, and started choking. My coughing brought out spit as I cleared my breathing in spasms from the inside out.

A hand gripped me on the shoulder. I looked up and saw the lieutenant.

"You're crazy," Rosenstein said, "you're absolutely batty. What do you think we got a whole Fire Department for?"

The paramedics arrived and rushed toward me after I'd been coughing for five minutes. They put an oxygen mask over my face and at last I was able to take a few breaths that didn't taste like smoke.

"Thanks," I told them. "I feel fine now." Well, almost. Turning to Rosenstein, I said, "Let's go for that coffee, you're buying."

The lieutenant wanted to write me up for an award, but I made him promise not to. I had reached a point in my career where, especially after being dumped, I just wanted to get on with my work. *Let the new guys get the awards,* I thought. I felt like the canvas of a sailboat when the wind suddenly stopped.

Each day I reported for work, I had the strange feeling that the other uniformed officers were giving me the cold shoulder. I couldn't figure out why. When I asked two patrolmen what the problem was, they let me know flat out. They and the other officers thought I was checking up on their response times when I was going out on calls with them.

"Let's keep this private chat under out hats, and don't tell the other men," I said, "but I want you two to know that I'm out here to work with you if you need help. I'll never try to get another policeman in trouble for what I consider to be minor infractions. I don't like inspectors or bad supervisors any more than you do, and if you see me here or there it's because I really like responding to calls. It makes the time go by. But the only one I'm watching over is me."

The ice melted and good friendships began, and I was catching up on some of the action I had missed when I was a driver for Superintendent Wilson.

Then, when someone mentioned the latest attack by the Insane Fish, I saw actual fear on the faces of the supervisors. It didn't take a genius to figure out what was going on. The I/F wasn't a gang, it was a group of uniformed policemen determined to harass each and every worthless supervisor. They struck like Zorro. Sometimes a sergeant or lieutenant found that his car had been pelted with rocks or set on fire— even when it was parked across from the station. This was not hatred of authority. The revenge was directed only against supervisors who were unfair and irrational. There seemed to be a leadership among the Insane Fish in that they knew precisely when to strike and were never caught, but I never heard who among the men I worked with was involved.

I sympathized with their anger, but not with the way they were expressing it. I feared that they would be caught and dealt with harshly.

We had a brand new sergeant whose father was one of the top police officials in the city. The sergeant wanted to advance himself by being a strict disciplinarian and, needless to say, he got along well with our commander. Several times, I saw this new sergeant writing up officers for the slightest reasons.

"Look," I said to him, believing that he could be a good cop if he loosened up a bit, "if you do everything exactly by the book, the officers won't go out of their way for you. You have to give them a little leeway."

"I want to be like my father," he told me, and from then on we had a strained relationship while working on the same watch.

His personal car was damaged twice by the Insane Fish and he was forced to take public transportation to work, which meant that he sometimes arrived an hour early. Three months passed before he thought it might be safe to drive in again. This time, however, he was careful and parked his auto three blocks away. When he returned after his shift was over, he found that all the windows were broken, the tires had been slashed, and the car was battered with iron bars or baseball bats. Someone must have taken a real dislike to him! The new sergeant couldn't take it anymore, and a short time later his connections got him transferred to the detective division.

As Captain Flavin had warned me, much of the good work in the district went unrecognized. Even when there was praise, there was something false about it. In November 1981, the tantrum-throwing commander gave me an Honorable Mention, which was no more than a piece of paper congratulating an officer for a job well done.

Telling the story backward, let me quote what he put on paper:

On 14 November 1981 at approximately 0215 hours you were on routine patrol in the area of Medill and California Ave. You heard several gunshots and observed two subjects in a vehicle at that location. One of the subjects was seen firing a pistol wildly out of the window of the car. Disregarding your own personal safety, you approached the subjects and disarmed them. The subject was found to have been firing a 9mm semi-automatic pistol. The subjects were placed under arrest, advised of their Constitutional rights, and subsequently charged with weapons violations.

Due to your efforts and expertise, two armed subjects were apprehended without injury to yourself or others, and an unregistered handgun was confiscated.

Congratulations on a job well done.

Much to his credit, the commander could have ignored the incident, but why did he and his staff intentionally minimize what happened?

The true story: I was driving by and heard gunfire coming from a car parked in front of the post office just down the street from the Shakespeare station.

Parked directly behind was an unmarked police car with its emergency headlights blinking for trouble. The gunman was shooting at a man in a suit and tie who, in that blue collar neighborhood, must have been a police detective. He was crouched beside the concrete steps of the post office. The 9mm pistol kept going *ba-boom, ba-boom* …

Well, let's not make this a shooting circus, I thought as I decided against using my Mars light and siren. I positioned my car alongside the gunman's, leaving me enough room to open by driver's side door.

The driver of the other car turned toward me and found himself staring into the barrel of my .38 caliber revolver. I put my gun to his head and yelled to his passenger, "Stop firing and drop it!" If the passenger had tried to twist around and shoot me, I'd have got him first by firing around or through his friend's head. The shooting stopped and I heard the gun clatter to the street.

The man in the suit came over, picked up the automatic, announced that he was a detective, and ordered the gunman out of the car. I did the same with the driver. Patting him down, I found a second 9mm pistol tucked in the man's waistband. We simultaneously handcuffed the men, and I called for a squadrol.

"Thanks, Sarge," the detective said, "and I *really* mean thanks!"

He then explained that the men had been driving suspiciously. He checked the hot sheet and found the license plate number listed. Because the detective's partner was off that night, he decided to pull them over and question them alone. Once he got out, he saw the passenger pull a gun, and that's when the shooting began.

The detective was so pleased that I had helped capture the men that he made a trip to the commander's office and personally gave him all the details of the incident. This apparently prompted the commander to write up the Honorable Mention for me, but why did he state that I had arrested someone who was merely "firing wildly," and why omit the facts that the men were also charged with auto theft, two counts of armed robbery, the possession of *two* guns, and the attempted murder of a police officer?

Well, as we used to say, the commander was a realllly niiiiice guy.

At the 14th District were dozens of eager young officers who were trying to do their best, but their supervisors always looked over their shoulders and wore out their ballpoint pens in making petty reports. Officers were written up if they were just a little late responding to a call because they were still tied up with a previous assignment. Even though officers now had their radios attached by Velcro to their shoulders, near their ears, that didn't mean they could drop everything. A radio red-line violation resulted in an automatic one day suspension, and no excuses were accepted. So I gathered the officers together and told them a plan I had worked out, violating all procedures.

Supervisors, including myself, were exempt from red-lining, and that to me seemed to be a double standard. If we weren't available at any particular moment, the dispatcher called someone else. Why not do something like that for the beat officers?

"If it appears that Beat Fourteen-Thirty-One is not going to answer a call within the three minute limitation," I said, "then I would like Fourteen-Thirty-Two to answer, using Fourteen-Thirty-One's call number. Then if Fourteen-Thirty-Two is tied up at the same time, then I will answer up for it, all the way up to writing the report. Now, if you guys agree to it, remember that we all could be disciplined. But we can say we just made a mistake and answered the wrong call."

"Won't work," one of the men said. "The dispatchers see us all the time, they know our voices."

"That's the beauty of it. The dispatchers are like us and they understand. Besides, why complain if it gets the job done?"

The system would work only in districts where the officers were especially dedicated, and it went off like clockwork at the 14th. Response times held at three minutes or less, and red-lining virtually stopped even though Shakespeare led the other districts in nearly every category of police statistics. Was our district commander happy? Absolutely not!

"The number of infractions has dropped drastically," he told me with disappointment on his face.

"That's amazing," I said with mockery intended to go over his head. "It's probably the example of your leadership."

"No," he barked, "it's because you and the other supervisors don't know how to catch those people dirty. Now, I want to see more reports on men not doing their job. Is that understood?"

"Not really, commander, I thought it was our job to catch the bad guys dirty." He walked away from me.

What was understood was that, by nature, he would misconstrue facts just to maintain a mild current of paranoia. One night when he was working late he called me into his office and accused me of stealing the three by ten inch sign reading "DISTRICT COMMANDER" from his door. Yeah, like there was a big black market for them.

I think the morale went up a little after the commander started fuming over the pilfering. I can honestly say that the Insane Fish were not responsible for all the misdeeds in the 14th District. If I stood accused of stealing that damn sign, so be it! I told the commander to register a complaint with Internal Affairs if he wanted to pursue it.

One day a rookie was assigned to investigate "the well-being of a citizen" in a basement apartment on North Central Park Avenue on a hot July day. I drove to the two flat and saw the young officer sweating profusely and shaking.

"What's going on?" I asked.

He couldn't speak and appeared to be in shock, but he pointed to the partly opened rear basement door. I unstrapped my holster and kept a hand on the butt of my gun as a precaution. I found the body of a young man, wearing only black pants, who had killed himself with a high powered rifle. Even with all my years behind me and my experience in the Homicide Unit, I had never seen a body like that. His brains were splashed on the wall. His eyes had popped out from the concussion, and his eyeballs—looking impossibly huge by their detachment—dangled at twisted angles on his cheeks. The inner skull was empty like a bowl scraped clean and yet his scalp was intact. I could see that his hair had been recently combed.

I went out and talked to the rookie. I didn't tell him so, but I knew he'd soon learn that all the formalities of notifying the dispatcher, requesting a supervisor, calling the morgue, and securing the scene would in time take away the horror—until his next similar assignment.

A couple of days afterward, two burly young officers and I answered a call of a violent quarrel in a home about a mile from the station. I arrived at a second floor landing with the wagon men and the rookies right behind me, followed by Lieutenants Rosenstein and Bernie Crotty. We saw a woman lying wounded on the floor, blood soaking her blue nightgown. She must have been stabbed forty times all over her body, and it was a miracle she was still alive.

"Who did this to you?" I asked.

She pointed to a door.

I told the wagon men to take her to the squadrol without going down and bringing the stretcher up. That was to save time in rushing her to the hospital. Just a minute could save a life.

We were left with the problem of the attacker behind the door. "Break it down," I ordered, and the two big rookies kicked it open. We saw a naked man dashing into a washroom. As the officers ran to him with their guns drawn, I saw a baby with a bloody nightshirt lying still on a couch. I picked up the lifeless infant girl and saw what turned out to be seven stab wounds. As

I held her with my fingers across her back, I could feel that the blade had repeatedly gone completely through her small body. The child was no more than a few weeks old—the youngest homicide victim in the city for that year.

"God made me do it!" the man shouted. Unconcerned about the contradiction, he added, "The devil made me do it!"

The officers led the man from the washroom and helped him dress as the paramedics arrived.

The next time I saw the woman was in the courthouse witness room, waiting to testify. Even though she'd been near death when we found her, she recognized me and thanked me for what all the officers had done.

Her common law husband—a pharmacist—was found guilty of murder and sentenced to serve fifty years in prison. Everyone we talked to knew him as a kind man, a good neighbor. Something in him just snapped.

Whatever we did didn't matter and went unnoticed. The commander was a man powered by a single idea, and there was nothing I could do to reset his priorities. He saw that I would never kowtow to his paranoid ways, and eventually he used his clout to have me transferred to the 19th District, where he had already dumped Captain Flavin. That was better for both of us.

By the way, I kept his DISTRICT COMMANDER sign as a trophy.

21

STREET CRIMES

As shown by the Insane Fish of the 14th District, officers always made it known when they detested a supervisor. In the 19th District he was *Lieutenant Pat Melody. Every day he carried a can of kitchen cleanser to wipe off his name and insulting remarks from washroom walls of the station, which took up the first floor of the new Area Six building at Belmont and Western Avenues.

Fortunately the commander, Bill Moyer, was a great guy, and he kept things that were occurring in his district well balanced. Moyer called me and Captain Joseph McCarthy into his office to let us know that Melody had registered an unofficial complaint claiming I was working too closely with McCarthy, which was certainly a jaundiced view.

Captain McCarthy had taken over when Thomas Flavin retired. He selected me to be his partner as he rode the streets. I would have to agree with kitchen-cleanser Melody that this was unusual, and maybe I wasn't spending as much time in my sector anymore.

Before leaving the commander's office, Moyer told McCarthy and me to "keep up the good work." He said the two of us had made more arrests in the previous month than the entire fifteen member Tactical Unit. Then he said, "I don't think you will be having any problems with Lieutenant Melody in the future."

Well, there he was wrong. When I reported for work the very next day, Melody sneered at me and said, "You haven't heard the last from me, DiMaggio. I'll get even."

"Throw your best shot, lieutenant," I replied.

He did, or at least he tried every chance he got. He kept trying to give me low efficiency ratings while my production was high, but he was always rebuffed by Captain McCarthy and Commander Moyer.

When McCarthy headed the West Side's 13th District, he routinely rode around with his officers, and he let it be known that no one worked "for" him, they worked "with" him. He earned the respect of everyone who ever worked "with" him and they fondly called him "Patrolman Joe."

McCarthy was tall and thinner than his newspaper photos suggested, but he was solid. He was prematurely balding and had a broad forehead. His usual walk was a slow shuffle. On his second day at the 19th, McCarthy yelled out after roll call, "Hey, Sergeant DiMaggio, stick around for a little while, I'll be riding with you tonight."

Desk Sergeant Richard McKelvey came over to me just to shoot the breeze, and he had a lot of it. McKelvey weight around 300 pounds and used to wrestle under the name "the Masked Marvel" because he would enter the ring with a hood over his head. He was one of those people who are always joking, and you sometimes are not quite sure what they really mean when they say something to you.

"Be prepared for an interesting evening," McKelvey said with a smile. "Riding with McCarthy is an experience you won't forget."

McCarthy followed me out of the station and to my squad car. He didn't say much, but he told me not to bother with my daily log sheet of all the men and women assigned to my sector. He just wanted me to drive him around to familiarize himself with the district, and that made a lot of sense to me. However, no more than five minutes after we got into the squad we saw a car flying through a red light and endangering traffic and pedestrians. Usually supervisors don't chase traffic violators, but this one was dangerous.

I gave McCarthy the radio that was clipped to my belt. "Take this, captain, it looks like we've got a chase going."

It must have been like old times for him. I'd turned on my

siren and the flashing Mars light but the car ahead was not slowing down. "Squad Nineteen-Twenty," he called in.

"Go ahead," the dispatcher replied.

"We have a chase westbound on Addison. We're in the twenty-five hundred block and the car is a Nineteen-Eighty red Camaro containing two occupants. It has Illinois plates, but we're not close enough to read the number."

Well done, captain, I thought to myself. Smooth and calm.

Addison Street happened to be under construction and narrowed to two lanes in front of a high school stadium and the WGN-TV studios. Just as I was narrowing the distance between us, I saw the other car go airborne, the tires four to six feet off the street, then crash down on the pavement. Sparks flew all over. The only way we could catch up was to gun the motor and do the same with our siren howling to keep traffic moving away from us We sailed in the air for a second and slammed down with a bounce that felt as if we were being hit with baseball bats on our shoulders and the seats of our pants. The Camaro darted around oncoming cars, sometimes hitting the curb, but most of the time weaving right down the center of the street.

Captain McCarthy kept a running account of the chase as he held down the radio button and I concentrated on driving as fast as I could safely handle the squad car. The driver ahead of us finally lost control while he was attempting a right turn. The Camaro shot against a tree.

We jumped out with the dispatcher still asking us questions. We knew that this time we didn't have to approach cautiously with guns drawn. The front half of the Camaro was crushed like an accordion, and the steaming radiator spewed boiling water. McCarthy eased a young man from the driver's seat, and I unstrapped his sixteen-year-old girlfriend from beside him. The young driver should have been scared or worried, but he was grinning. I couldn't smell alcohol but his pupils were dilated and he was higher than a kite. A search of his car showed why he seemed so pleased with himself—we found a stash of marijuana. For him, that wild ride must have been quite the trip.

With district officers gathering around, McCarthy made all

the assignments for writing up the traffic report, seizing the cannabis, and taking the driver to the station. Then McCarthy went back to the radio, and on an open channel, thanked all the officers of the 19th and 17th Districts who assisted in the chase. What a difference from the 14th, where if the officers walked on water the commander would write up a report saying that they "couldn't swim."

The next day, McCarthy asked me to stick around after roll call—he wanted me to be his "partner" again. He was still looking forward to a guided tour of the 19th's hotspots. When we were barely moving in heavy traffic, the captain's attention was drawn to some young people from the Lathrop housing project. One of them started running at the sight of our car. McCarthy ordered me to make a fast U-turn, and then he scrambled out and began sprinting after him. The captain found the youth hiding behind garbage cans in the rear of a liquor store.

"Get up and keep your hands where I can see them," he commanded.

The captain frisked him and handed me identification cards from the young man's wallet.

"Run him on the radio for warrants," he told me. We soon learned the reason the young man had been running—he was wanted for burglary.

The desk sergeant, "Masked Marvel" McKelvey, saw us bring in our second prisoner in two nights and laughed out loud.

The partnership of DiMaggio and McCarthy hit the streets again, and one of our hunches led to the arrest of a man wanted on robbery warrants. McCarthy was uncanny when he plucked someone from the street because the man acted suspiciously, remarking that the guy had that "penitentiary look." He was careless about safe police procedures, though, and any one of the men he stopped could have whipped out a gun instead of an ID. He was a captain and a former deputy superintendent, but I saw that we needed a little face-to-face talk.

McCarthy climbed into my squad car after I was off for two days and he became suspicious of my silence. "You know, John," he said, "after we made that arrest Monday, I sort of got the idea I maybe did something wrong to get you mad at me. What is it?"

The straightforward talk was unlike any from a boss I've had. "You're a captain and I'm only a sergeant," I began, "so right now I should keep my mouth shut and just go along with your program and follow your instructions, but I'm not that type of policeman. I've always expressed my opinion regardless of the rank involved."

"So I heard."

"That last arrest we made has been bothering the hell out of me. We both could have been put in jeopardy. No one I worked with ever got hurt because of my mistakes. One reason is that I make it a habit of anticipating what people may do in a certain situation."

McCarthy had heard it all at the academy, just like the rest of us, but for some reason it never sank in.

"You know, John," he said, "I've worked with a lot of partners before, and none of them had the guts to tell me what you're saying now. And you're right. It's just that—when you make so many arrests and nothing happens, you get into a certain routine. Thanks."

Then he asked me what I felt like doing, and I suggested that we watch the Melrose Apartments, which had been having some seedy customers lately. McCarthy instantly recognized two bond-jumpers, Rodney Kane and Daphne Williams, when they came out of the apartment-hotel. We hauled them into the station.

"So you got 'Rodney the Puke' and 'Daffy Duck,'" huge McKelvey roared. "Those two dopers were my arrests when I was in Narcotics. They blew off their court dates and dropped out of sight." He made a grotesque face to taunt our prisoners and asked, "Remember me?"

"The laugh's on you, McKelvey," I said. "I hereby notify the officer who placed the warrants on these two citizens that they are officially in custody. That means you go to court tomorrow, early, on your day off." Then we went out again and made some more arrests.

One night we stopped a man so high on dope that he could

barely walk. Rather than bring him directly into the station we decided to put him in our squad car and, after a short talk, he agreed to lead us to a large building that had an apartment called a "shooting station," a drug crash pad. Rather than call for backup, we went directly to the building. This was in a neighboring district, the 23rd, and we actually had no authority to be there. That didn't bother us because McCarthy always reminded me that our stars said "City of Chicago."

The addict—a burglary suspect, as we later found out—led us up the stairs and turned a key in the lock, and then we moved him back for his own safety.

We opened the door just enough for a peek inside. It was later determined there were at least twenty men and women and a few runaway juveniles lying in a stupor on the floor, on couches, on chairs, and on the two beds. Hypodermic needles and spoons used to cook heroin were in plain view. You could tell the place was a shooting station from the acrid smell that's something like overcooked medication or an overdose of permanent-wave solution at a beauty shop. I stepped back and suggested that we call for backup.

"Good idea," McCarthy said, looking around, "but where the heck are we?"

There was something I learned early from Hugh Phillips in the old 33rd District—always know exactly where you are, even if you're just driving around. "We're at 1391 West Winnemac, southeast corner, second floor, building two," I answered.

McCarthy was in many ways a top cop, but he was also inexperienced because he had been promoted so fast that he'd never been a detective. I liked helping out new officers but I felt uneasy being a mentor to my boss. He really was just a gutsy patrolman at heart, and that was why he was respectfully nicknamed "Patrolman Joe."

I radioed for twenty police officers. We met in the alley, where I assigned five men to make the initial entry into the apartment. The officers, including McCarthy and me, would conduct a room-to-room search. If no one tried to flee out the back, one of us would then open the rear door and let in the seven officers waiting there. They would then call in the officers positioned around the house. It seemed like overkill at first, but we soon learned that *all* would be needed.

At first the apartment looked like a hasty, temporary morgue, but then the "bodies" stirred. They were so doped up that those who were awake didn't even try to run out. We pulled guns out of their shoulder holsters and waistbands, and we found a few other weapons stashed in the bedroom. With around forty addicts, district officers, and detectives moving around that apartment, there was little room to move. We had made a highly successful raid with very little planning, and somehow that left me a little uneasy.

Heads at the station shot up when we came in with a parade of prisoners. Teams of officers assumed specific duties in the processing, and we finished at ten the next morning. The district commander called the team of McCarthy and DiMaggio into his office. We suspected it was because we had wound up in the wrong district and happened to know just what was inside the apartment before the raid began.

"You guys did a great job and I want to congratulate you both," he said. "I can't wait to see that masterpiece report you've been typing, John. But something seems fishy." He was smiling. "I just can't seem to put my finger on it."

"Just routine police work," McCarthy bantered as a former commander to a current one.

Moyer looked at him with an even more skeptical eye, and then tossed his suspicions from his mind. "How about we all go out for brunch? It's on me."

We were given the midnight watch off because we would have to be in court the next morning. Afterward we had to work our usual shifts *and* appear in court a few hours later, for days and weeks. I was unhappy that such a chunk was being taken out of my life, simply because I'd done it so often early in my career—but McCarthy enjoyed it.

As could be expected, Lieutenant Melody threatened to report me to the commander because I was still not submitting *any* supervisor logs.

A few weeks later, we returned to the seedy Melrose Apartments in mid-December and stopped three suspicious characters as they ran toward the front entrance. As I waited for communications to report whether any of them was wanted on a warrant, I saw from the corner of my eye that the captain was dashing up the stairs. I had to decide whether to keep the three men in my control or provide backup for McCarthy. I chose to wait in the lobby unless I heard sounds of trouble, but those were very long seconds.

"The three men are all clear," communications said at last.

"Ten-four," I replied and told the men to get the hell out of there. Then I raced up the hotel stairwell, passing cockroaches, rats, and drug addicts.

As I hastily searched for my lost captain, I heard shouting from the floor above. Rushing up and kicking open the door, I found Captain McCarthy slugging it out with a man and a woman in a tiny kitchen. I pushed the woman aside to get between the two battling men. The apartment was so small and cluttered that there was hardly any room to swing.

Once the men stopped hitting each other, the resident told me, "It ain't right, damn it—he busts into my home and starts some shit with me and my old lady."

"Settle down," I said. "You shouldn't be fighting with a police *captain*."

"I just opened my door and he came running into my home!"

"John, he was a suspicious man running up the stairs and he had a bag in his hand," McCarthy humbly explained to me.

"My food was getting cold," the resident said.

"What?" I asked, knowing the answer and yet telling myself it couldn't be.

"My food was getting cold. That's why I was running. See that? It's cold!" His wife nodded.

"Nobody's hurt?" I asked. "All right, captain, let's leave these people alone to have their supper. I'm sure it's good, missus."

"You know, John, that's a good idea," McCarthy said. He shook the man's hand as we were leaving. I didn't say a word as we walked down the stairs. I was saving that for when we were back inside the car.

"Damn it, Joe, how in the hell could you go off like that without telling me!" I didn't care if I was ending our partnership or I was getting myself transferred again. "I'm supposed to know what you're doing at all times, and you're supposed to know what I'm doing. If you get yourself killed then I'm going to be very much embarrassed. I never had a partner get hurt, and I don't want to start now. You put me in a bad position. Suppose I'd gone right up after you and one of those men we had in the lobby was wanted for murder and had a gun hidden somewhere. What then? I didn't even search those guys because I didn't have a partner."

"I'm sorry, John, I screwed up. It won't happen again." And then he had to add, "But the guy had a bag and I thought ..."

I just smiled at him and shook my head. He was the type of guy you couldn't help but like.

After the usual post-election reshufflings were over, I was assigned to the prestigious Office of Municipal Investigations and reluctantly said goodbye to Captain McCarthy, Commander Moyer, and a not so reluctant farewell to Lieutenant Melody. I was out of uniform again but somehow missed the street action. One compensation was that my office on Lake Shore Drive overlooked the beach and Lake Michigan. Bankers embezzled for views like that.

"Patrolman Joe" remained on at the 19th District, and he still took the time to make street stops and raids. Occasionally I heard from him, and we reminisced about our times together.

22

THE HEART OF A COP

At the Office of Municipal Investigations I was put in charge of a talented squad of men and women police officers who gathered evidence against corrupt city workers. The assignment lasted only a few months because of the continual political reshufflings, and this mass transfer would have serious ramifications.

The transfers decimated the unit and, as a result, thirteen officers, including me, filed a political and racial discrimination suit against the city. The federal suit, heard by eight jurors and two alternates, ruled in our favor and awarded an extremely high monetary judgment in punitive and compensatory damages. Newspaper headlines blazed across the country, and the suit, *Cygnar vs. the City of Chicago*, would be considered a landmark in fighting reverse discrimination.

The deposed director of the Office of Municipal Investigations, James A. Maurer, became the commander of the Area Four detective division on the West Side and, at his request, I became his administrative sergeant. Area Four was considered by many to be the worst in the city because of drugs, gangs, violent crimes, and a general public hatred of police. The situation was so bad that police working on one crime would often encounter officers working on one or two others close by. The morale was extremely low at the time, but fortunately for the personnel, Maurer had the leadership qualities and the personality to turn it around and make it the number one area for crimes solved and arrests made. In the coming years,

Commander Maurer proved to be one of the best bosses I ever had, as well as my best friend.

In May of 1986, I was driving an undercover squad when a young man, trying to outrun an unrelated police chase, ran a red light. He hit my car at a hundred miles per hour, verified by the 480 feet of skid marks. The impact ripped off the whole right side of his car and the entire front of the squad, scattering parts all over. He kept going, sliding and laying rubber as he jammed his brakes, and finally stopped when he rammed into a light pole. Despite all this, the driver, a good-looking teenager out for a night of fun, was able to walk over to my police car and await his arrest. I wasn't so lucky.

My life was saved by my seatbelt, but my body was wrenched in an unnatural position across the center of the front seat, the seatbelt clasp poking into my back. This was the moment Dr. Kolb and all the other specialists had been warning me about. My 1971 spinal fusion had become unfused. In a faint, strained voice, I radioed for assistance. Help came immediately from the officers who had been in the chase and had lost sight of the vehicle.

While in the hospital for three weeks, I chose to suffer rather than say yes to another back operation. Soon after my discharge, when I couldn't take it any longer, I went through my second fusion in early 1987. The procedure had improved considerably. I was out of the hospital in a week, and before long I could take two mile walks. I still needed neck therapy three times a week.

At my request I was able to return promptly to work and permitted to take the therapy on my duty hours. My hospital therapist was excellent. While she was on vacation, her assistant, Bill, helped me lie on a table with a machine behind my head. Straps from the machine were placed around my chin to provide a slow, pulling motion at ten to fifteen second intervals. As soon as Bill turned on the switch, my head was contorted violently, hitting the machine.

"That *hurt!*" I said in a polite understatement.

Bill stopped the mechanism, readjusted my position, and turned a few dials. When he started up again, the same thing happened, only more jolting. I had fantasies of strangling him if I hadn't been lashed to the table. He finally turned off the machine and made this classic statement, "I think I'd better get someone who knows how to operate this thing."

Soon after I went home, my entire body went into convulsions and the pain was excruciating. I stayed awake, suffering through the night. The next morning I felt that I was having a heart attack, and my hands once more became numb.

I became an emergency patient at three hospitals within a three month period, and experts at last determined that a bone chip had become lodged in my neck near the spinal cord, and said it would be extremely dangerous to remove. So there it remained, sometimes presenting problems.

Once again I was offered full disability. Although the temptation was there, I was determined to make a full recovery and return to full time duty assignments. It took a considerable amount of work, but before long I persuaded everyone that I was fit for duty.

At Area Four I was in charge of a staff of about twelve people. My job description would have kept me in an office and at a desk all of the time, but the commander knew that I liked working the streets. He let me go out and assist the assigned detectives on major cases.

There were good officers who put their lives on the line every day, such as Eddie Jones. He was a big, black patrolman who looked tough but liked cracking jokes and felt genuine concern that all police officers should have for victims.

While I was with Commander Maurer in his office on a frigid Monday in January 1991, a Violent Crimes Unit detective put his head in and shouted, "Two police officers have been shot in their squad car in a parking lot at Western and Cermak Road!"

Eddie Jones and his partner, Dennis Dobson, had picked up a man named Alexis Green for possession of PCP, the synthetic animal tranquilizer that could make people do dangerous things. The officers frisked Green, but they didn't notice the gun under all his layers of clothing. They took him to the Marquette station for processing, which included fingerprinting, taking mug shots, and a thorough searching, but no one detected the hidden gun.

Green, an ex-con and a con man, thought he knew a way to avoid going back to jail. He offered to take Jones and Dobson to a "water house," a place where the "angel dust" was manufactured. Prisoners were always offering deals to arresting officers; you can't blame any cop for wanting to put the main source out of business.

While Green was handcuffed in the back of the squad car, he pulled out his hidden gun, leaned over almost to his knees, and shot them both at virtually point blank range. When they slumped over, he took the keys from Dobson's pocket, uncuffed himself, and fled with the wounded officer's .45 caliber gun. Dobson would miraculously recover, but Eddie Jones died instantaneously.

Maurer and I pulled on our topcoats, scarves, and gloves as we hurried out. We raced to the scene in the commander's auto and found that district officers had already cordoned off the area around the bloodied squad car. About one hundred officers soon saturated the neighborhood, using copies of mug shots that were just a few hours old. Once the bosses arrived to coordinate the search, I decided to ride along with Lieutenant Ron Kelly, one of my first partners when we started out at the old 33rd District. As the field lieutenant, he knew the streets and people well.

Kelly was in uniform, but we were using an unmarked squad in order to be less conspicuous. Not that the precaution mattered, even kids could tell a cop car coming down the street. At that very moment, relatives, friends, and dope connections of Alexis Green throughout the West Side were making decisions about whether they should protect him or not—either out of conscience or because it seemed as if the entire police force was out for him.

The search teams went in all directions, some to the far South Side areas where Green was known to frequent, and others sought out informants. Kelly and I decided to stay in the district station and work with a detail of tactical plainclothes officers who were well known to the lieutenant. Kelly put his personal instincts and contacts to good use. He suspected that we would get only stonewalling from residents in the area, so we scrambled through locations to talk to the Arabs who operated small food marts in the otherwise solidly black neighborhood. The Arabs were always happy to supply information so that one more troublemaker might be taken away.

We learned that "Lexie" Green, as he was called, usually hung out a couple miles away at Roosevelt and Kedzie. Once we got there we were pretty sure that most people who said they didn't know anything would be lying. It was time to take the shotgun out of the trunk and search him out the hard way. It was simple logic, Green would either stay in his neighborhood and try to find a hideout, meet up with some of his friends on the South Side, or try to skip town.

The cold, blindingly sunny afternoon had become a dark and bitterly freezing night. We searched boarded up buildings, a few sheds and garages, and the gutted ruins of the King assassination riot of long ago. We found homeless people huddled for warmth, some of them sitting around little fires they had started from garbage. A few of the down-and-outers recognized Green from the photo, and they suggested some places where we might look. The wind chill was below zero, but we hardly noticed.

We hit apartments where Green was known to frequent, and most of them had drug-related occupants—dealers, runners, or users. In every one of them, the people knew what he was wanted for from the news or the neighborhood grapevine, and were willing to tell us the locations of several dope dens where he could be hiding. After backup arrived, we broke down doors or crawled through windows rather than try to go through entrances that had been rigged in unusual ways. The men and women, some so high they needed help standing up, scattered as soon as they saw us, only to be stopped by the officers guarding the outside. When we assured everybody we weren't interested in arresting anyone but Green a couple of the shivering people agreed to volunteer information. One of the dealers told us to look for him on the third floor of a building at 3121 West 15th Street, an address I still remember as vividly as if it were my own.

There, Lieutenant Kelly, the tactical officers, and I found the cold-blooded killer slouched in a corner hallway. The object of the manhunt was just an ordinary-looking young man in a black and red hooded jacket. He was trembling from the cold or perhaps at the thought that we might be as merciless with him as he had been with Jones and Dobson. In a way, we had hoped that Green would try to reach for his gun, but he started moving his arms away from his sides.

"Get up," one officer ordered. Two shotguns pointed at Green's head. He slowly rose to his feet. While being thoroughly searched, his eyes darted to each of us. I've always believed he suspected he was going to hear a loud *bang*, but it was our sworn duty to serve and protect, and that meant saving the lives of citizens—even the bad guys.

As we told Green his rights, he kept showing surprise because we weren't manhandling him. Once Green was locked in a cage car, Kelly called for a meeting of all the tactical unit officers involved in the search but who had not taken part in the arrest. They met with us near a park.

"*Your* tactical team has him, it's all over," Kelly said, "but I'm sure no one wants to take individual credit for the capture by having his name in the newspapers or appearing on TV. You can do what you want, he's your prisoner, but let this be understood right now. Sergeant DiMaggio and I do not want to be mentioned as arresting officers. Treat your prisoner like a traffic violator, and when you get to the Area, don't let anybody else touch him, understood?"

Everyone nodded in agreement.

All the officers assigned to our special detail went to Area Four headquarters with our prisoner. Police communications radioed to all squad cars across the city that Alexis Green was in custody and that all officers could return to normal duty.

That was the last major arrest before I left the department in February 1991. Police life seemed natural while you were living it and you became a part of it. Then you started thinking about retirement, and it always happened too soon.

My party was at the elegant Chateau Ritz in Niles.

Commander Maurer and Lieutenant Ron Kelly were there. So were my good friends John Coughlin, Steve Pizzello, John Philbin, and Paul Roppel. One of my former partners, Kurt Bartall, came all the way from his retirement in Florida. I couldn't help feeling that officers who had died before their time were there, but we just couldn't see them.

Despite the sprinkling of white hair, the wrinkles and the added pounds, all these men from my early assignments were as familiar to me as when we were partners together—the spirit was still there. The room of laughing current and former officers and their wives became filled with memories.

I had a speech prepared to deliver to all my police friends at the party. It had taken me five years to write, but I disregarded it and just said the words that seemed to flow. There was a lot to say to a room full of memories and pieces of myself. No other profession on earth could cram as many feelings into a soul. You'd have to be a cop to know it. Not only do you put your heart and soul into your work, you're working along with other officers doing the same thing. When you wind down at slow times and off-duty, you wind down with them. They become so much a part of you that it's hard to say where memories of yourself and memories of them begin. I know I said a lot that night and profusely thanked my family for putting up with the long hours of stakeouts and details throughout my career that kept me from home. I thanked my friends and my partners, and then briefly described some of the cases we had worked on. I waved farewell and walked away from my police career.

And so now I say goodbye to you—for now—but I still have just a few things to say.

Like everyone else, I was shocked when television newscasts showed the beating of Rodney King by Los Angeles police. It has to be admitted that some officers lose control or try to impress their comrades by playing the part of a macho strongman. Such officers are not really tough. Although it would be difficult to convince the average citizen, they're in the minority and are cowards who usually beat handcuffed prisoners or destitute people under the cover of authority. They believe a star that has a number on it makes them untouchable, but believe me sometimes their crimes catch up with them and they most assuredly are despised by all the good cops.

Unfortunately people usually see police officers at the wrong time. You know, like when they say, "Get your driver's license out." Maybe the officers seem a little hard at times, but maybe that traffic officer had just finished handling a bloody accident. He also has no way of knowing whether you're just an average citizen or a killer hiding a gun. More officers are killed during routine traffic stops than when rushing into a crime in progress. The danger is something that stays with every officer each time a traffic violator needs to be curbed or a person acts suspiciously.

Some people think of us all together—as the "Police"—but each one of us is different, and many of us are different from what we seem. Such as my partner Steve Pizzello. Before he saved my life in a shooting, I took an instant dislike to him. He was from the old school, presented himself as a hard boiled cop, and he filled his sentences with coarse profanities except around women. Most of that was only because he was afraid to show people what he was really like inside.

I learned this while driving our squad car right around the holidays.

"Hey, Johnnie," he said, "stop by my car. I want to pick up a few things."

I parked close to his auto nearby, and he hauled out gift baskets of all kinds and shoved them into our trunk and back seat. At the time I didn't think much of an officer who took time out of his work to do Christmas shopping for his friends and relatives. I was wrong about Pizzello. It seems I was always wrong about him. He climbed back next to me and took out a long list of names and addresses.

"I'll tell you where to go, as long as things are slow," he said.

Those gifts were turkeys, hams, toys, and other things he gave out every year to families who had once needed his help. Some of them were having trouble paying bills— because Pizzello had put their husband or father in prison. Pizzello not only did this during the Christmas season, but he delivered such presents four or five times a year.

I offered to help pay for the gifts, but he said, "Nah, Johnnie. This is something I got to do myself. Do me a favor, don't tell anyone about it."

I never did until now.

We cops have feelings as strong as anyone. Once in a while we shed a tear. We worry about victims and sometimes about crooks if they show some redeeming trait. Unfortunately, some policemen across the city—in your city as well—are drowning their sorrows in alcohol and disguising their emotions with smiles and backslaps when they are around one another. They relate the same stories of their experiences for hours, just to hang on to others in the cop world. I was never one of those— most of these stories I'm telling here for the first time—but I could have been. As they say, only a cop can understand a cop.

This sense of an exclusive club is one reason why police everywhere resisted the first female officers. The men were afraid that the departments would be getting as diversified as the real world, and then they would wind up feeling out of place. Now women are an essential part of police work. There are a lot of male officers and other people out there whose lives they have saved.

Generations ago, the role of an officer was clearer. There was a sharp distinction between good and bad people. Then a moral plague hit communities across the country, and it's probably touching someone you know or will know, and if you read the newspaper or watch the TV news, you know it's escalating. The killers are younger and the victims are, too. This wasn't helped when the racial bigotry of Los Angeles police detective Mark Fuhrman was aired nationally during the O.J. Simpson murder trial. It showed a cop who disgraced every police officer throughout the country. It only increased public distrust. Crime festers when the public no longer trusts officers or are unwilling to go to them. Police work, after all, is a partnership of trained officers working with ordinary citizens.

Whether an officer is male or female, rookie or veteran, the person is always being pulled two ways. Police work is exciting, but it can also be boring. It is routine and it is unpredictable. Police officers often have the feeling they've seen the same burglary, robbery, or murder committed dozens of times and yet often the work can be mind boggling. If there is camaraderie, there is also loneliness. You are always second guessing someone with a different mindset—a criminal or someone temporarily insane—and that means you open yourself up for accolades or scorn from other officers and your bosses. I never considered myself to be a dissident during my career, but I most certainly spoke out when I knew I was right and the system was wrong, and a few times went against certain bosses and the Chicago Police Department.

Police officers don't ask you to love them, but just remember that they are the ones holding the seams of society together so you and your family can sleep a little easier. On the other hand, they know that they have to earn your respect even though obstacles created by the "bad apples" keep getting in the way. A concerted effort should be made to eliminate the racist, sadistic, undesirable officers from all departments by improving psychological screening and making political hiring and promotion a thing of the past.

I still have flashbacks of my life as a patrol officer, a detective, and a detective sergeant—as if my heart is still out there on the streets. You think of all the officers placing themselves in danger and sacrificing their personal lives for "the good of the service." There is no other profession where you can be surrounded by people like Jimmy Nolan, who really care about serving and protecting the public. Sometimes I see the faces again—dead faces, grateful faces, scared faces.

Many of the incidents and arrests in this book made headlines when I truly attempted to avoid publicity. Do I miss police work and the officers with whom I worked? Absolutely. But what I *really* miss is being called SARGE by some of the most dedicated and talented officers in the Chicago Police Department.

There are many more stories to be told.

More SARGE!
Show your support for SARGE! by leaving a review!
Scan the QR code below to go directly to Amazon reviews:

SARGE! Audiobook was named best Memoir or Biography for 2020 by the Independent Audiobook Awards.

Listen to SARGE! in the unabridged audiobook on Audible, Amazon and iTunes. Audio performance by Kevin Pierce. Use the QR Code to buy the book on Audible.

Use the QR Code below to read the Chicago Tribune article written by Pulitzer-Prize winning author Rick Kogan that describes how SARGE! was brought to life:

Curious about other Crossroad Press books?
Stop by our site:
http://store.crossroadpress.com
We offer quality writing
in digital, audio, and print formats.

Enter the code FIRSTBOOK
to get 20% off your first order from our store!
Stop by today!

CPSIA information can be obtained
at www.ICGtesting.com
Printed in the USA
LVHW081341040820
662193LV00024B/1178